The School Psychologist's Guide for the *Praxis*® Exam

Peter D. Thompson, PhD, is a licensed school psychologist and a long-time member of the National Association of School Psychologists (NASP). He has multiple advanced degrees in psychology and holds various leadership positions in the Douglas County School District, which is a district of more than 70 schools in Colorado. Dr. Thompson has extensive training in school neuropsychology, and is currently the school district's traumatic brain injury (TBI) team coordinator. He continues to lend his expertise to several organizations and agencies in the Denver metro area. In 2013, Dr. Thompson was named Colorado School Psychologist of the Year. Dr. Thompson authored the first edition of *The School Psychology Licensure Exam Guide* in 2004, which is now in its third iteration. He has also written chapters in *Brain Injury in Children and Youth: A Manual for Educators* (2016) and *Concussion Management Guidelines Manual* (2015), both published by the Colorado Department of Education.

The School Psychologist's Guide for the *Praxis*® Exam

Third Edition

Peter D. Thompson, PhD

SPRINGER PUBLISHING COMPANY
NEW YORK

Springer Publishing Company, LLC
11 West 42nd Street
New York, NY 10036
www.springerpub.com

Acquisitions Editor: Debra Riegert
Compositor: Newgen KnowledgeWorks

ISBN: 9780826164384
e-book ISBN: 9780826164391

17 18 19 20 21 / 5 4 3 2 1

The author and the publisher of this Work have made every effort to use sources believed to be reliable to provide information that is accurate and compatible with the standards generally accepted at the time of publication. The author and publisher shall not be liable for any special, consequential, or exemplary damages resulting, in whole or in part, from the readers' use of, or reliance on, the information contained in this book. The publisher has no responsibility for the persistence or accuracy of URLs for external or third-party Internet websites referred to in this publication and does not guarantee that any content on such websites is, or will remain, accurate or appropriate.

Library of Congress Cataloging-in-Publication Data
Names: Thompson, Peter D., author.
Title: The school psychologist's guide for the praxis exam / Peter D. Thompson, PhD.
Other titles: School psychology licensure exam guide
Description: Third edition. | New York, NY : Springer Publishing Company, LLC, [2017] |
    Earlier editions published under the title: The school psychology licensure exam guide. |
    Includes bibliographical references.
Identifiers: LCCN 2016055467 | ISBN 9780826164384 (paperback)
Subjects: LCSH: School psychologists—Certification—United States—Examinations—
    Study guides. | School psychology—United States—Examinations—Study guides. |
    School psychology—United States—Examinations, questions, etc.
Classification: LCC LB3013.6 .T56 2017 | DDC 371.7/13—dc23
LC record available at https://lccn.loc.gov/2016055467

Contact us to receive discount rates on bulk purchases.
We can also customize our books to meet your needs.
For more information please contact: sales@springerpub.com

Printed in the United States of America by Gasch Printing.

Contents

II. Practice Tests

Preface

What lies behind us and what lies before us are tiny matters compared to what lies within us.

—*Ralph W. Emerson*

As implied in the epigraph, I assume that you, the reader, have something within you that drives you to help others. You have chosen to answer a difficult call to complete a highly demanding program of study and to seek your license as a school psychologist. Few people have accomplished this admirable feat, and you are about to join an elite, altruistic community of professional helpers. In my opinion, there is no higher calling than to serve others, especially children. Congratulations for answering the call and honoring the greater matters that lie within you.

When preparing to tackle the licensure exam for school psychology, I diligently gathered as many resources as I could find. I queried several professors, used web-based services, and interviewed various graduate students. Although the availability of resources has slightly improved over the last few years, I am still concerned about the paucity of information available to help future school psychologists prepare for this important exam.

After talking with students over the years, I realized some test takers have very high anxiety surrounding this vital test. Graduate students may have stellar grades, but if they fail this one crucial exam, they have no license to practice in public schools. In other words, many people think this one test may hold the key to one's occupational future. However, the *Praxis*® exam's tough reputation is somewhat exaggerated. While it is prudent to be well prepared for this exam, do not be overly concerned about the hype you hear about its difficulty.

If you are just a few months away from taking the licensure exam, then your primary enemies are probably your emotions. As future psychologists, we know that fear is born out of a lack of control or understanding of unknown events. Therefore, instead of letting your emotions detract from your abilities, harness the energy provided by this emotion and use it to direct your actions to overcome the unknown (and reread the epigraph). Additionally, you must moderate your worries by keeping in mind that the majority of people will pass the licensure exam on the first try. Remember that you can always retake the test if you do not do well.

School psychology is built on the simple tenet of helping others in need. Consequently, my primary endeavor is to help future psychologists enter this worthy field. Although this guide is certainly not all-encompassing, I firmly believe that its information will assist aspiring school psychologists to prepare for the exam. This third iteration of the guide contains an all-new structure and substantially revised content to better reflect the newest version of the *Praxis* exam (2016). The two practice exams, in particular, include several new test questions as well as significantly modified exam items. Other areas have been revised to include updated information related to psychological tests, interventions, and school neuropsychology. Despite the improvements incorporated in this new edition, it is imperative to understand that no single book or source holds all of the answers. The reader must use every resource possible, and this book is just one piece of the preparation pie (a suggestion that I often emphasize).

Finally, there is a valuable concept I would like you to remember. The majority of test takers will soon be practitioners employed by large public school districts. Every year, millions of young students will also take important standardized tests that are just as stressful to them. If empathy is the hallmark trait of our profession, then let your current test preparation experience stew just a bit so you can truly understand how your future clients (i.e., students) feel when you evaluate them and ask them to take difficult tests.

I wish the reader good luck, not only in passing the *Praxis* exam but also in making a positive change in the lives of children!

Peter D. Thompson, PhD

Acknowledgments

A person's achievements are most often attained with the guidance, assistance, and support of others. The opportunity to spend months researching and writing the third edition of this guide would have not been possible without the help of important people in my life. As a consequence, it is only proper to acknowledge my family, work colleagues, and Springer Publishing Company for their supportive roles. Most important, I must thank my wife, Michele, and daughter, Brooke, for their love and patience. I cannot overstate how much they mean to me.

Introduction: Test Structure, General Suggestions, and Specific Advice

The primary benefit of this book is that it provides a useful representation of the structure and content of *The Praxis Series® School Psychologist Examination*, sometimes referred to as *The School Psychology Test* or *Praxis® exam.* This guide helps lift the veil of mystery surrounding how to pass this critical test necessary to become a licensed school psychologist. When people understand what to expect and have a defined strategy for approaching any task, not just a major test, their anxiety generally decreases and the probability of success increases. In other words, when emotions are tamed, clarity of thought emerges and more cognitive energy can be devoted to higher order reasoning.

I have found that the primary sources of stress regarding the exam are the lack of concise and objective information related to test items and not knowing how to organize an effective study strategy. Trying to prepare for a comprehensive standardized psychology test is like studying for a history test. History is an incalculably broad subject with an equally endless amount of information to examine. The range of topics is so vast it seems overwhelming to even start preparing. To address the previous concern, the focus of this guide was to pare down information and to prioritize it into manageable relevant sections. The following chapters contain key suggestions and information that have helped thousands of other students pass the *Praxis* exam.

The suggestions in this book are based on interviews, remarks, and observations from professors, practicing school psychologists, and interns who have taken the exam. Some suggestions might be more useful to some readers than others. However, all advice and examples (even obvious ones) have been provided due to the various needs of different test takers. People preparing to take the *Praxis* exam have vastly different levels of training, understanding of concepts, and professional background knowledge. Some test takers are from international programs or abbreviated training programs, and may not know about specific resources or information that is readily apparent to other people. The previous statements are provided because minor concerns were raised that some test questions or exam information was too obvious to be useful. Although some extremely prepared test takers might have a wealth of knowledge to easily pass the *Praxis* exam, some people find the exam difficult and must take it more than once to attain a passing score. Despite your level of training, it is prudent to prepare well in advance for the exam as much as possible. It is strongly advised that test takers *utilize multiple resources*, review previously learned material, and have a cogent strategy for passing the exam.

It is extremely important to bear in mind that any statements made in this book are founded on research, expert opinion, and professional practices. Although I sincerely offer advice and test suggestions, readers should double-check with the National Association of School Psychologists (NASP) or their professor if they have questions about this guide's information. The test taker is ultimately responsible for confirming the validity of exam-related content. Remember, psychology is a dynamic and evolving field of study. Therefore, theories, best practices, and professional positions can change with time. What was considered best practice several years ago might not be considered the same today, so it is appropriate to further examine discussion points if necessary. Finally, it is important to note that the items and ideas contained in this book are not identical to the actual test questions or the NASP study guides, but they are very similar in content and format.

How to Use This Guide

This guide was purposely written in a format that facilitates efficient studying, much like you would organize test notes in an outline structure. Previous test takers stated that information presented in a traditional book format with long explanations was too cumbersome. As a consequence of the concerns voiced by other students, I determined that the best means to present information to study for the *Praxis* exam was through bulleted key concepts and lists, and by being as *concise* as possible without sacrificing relevant information needed to prepare for the exam.

To make effective use of your time, it is *not* necessary to memorize all theories and ideas in the realm of school psychology, which would be nearly impossible. Instead, the presented format is designed to help you know which concepts to emphasize and be highly familiar with during your preparation. In general, you should focus on the ideas that are listed with numbers or letters. Also, any term or statement in boldface should be underscored for extra studying. For other concepts that are bulleted, the reader does not necessarily need to commit them to long-term memory, but the ideas should become familiar to you. With the previous comments in mind, always use your judgment when studying and know your areas of strength and areas where you need to allocate more effort.

Finally, make good use of your time by reviewing the summary sections every night about 2 weeks before the exam.

Study and Test-Taking Strategies

Many people studying for the licensure exam start by defining their approach into two primary areas. The first area encompasses a *broad* understanding of the NASP's philosophy. Exam takers are encouraged to understand NASP's current philosophical orientations and position statements. The gist of NASP's positions is currently steeped in **inclusion** for students, **cultural fairness** concerns, and **social justice** issues. Once you know the broad attitudes that NASP has on a host of topics, then answers to many exam items can be logically deduced. The next approach is to develop a *narrow focus*. A narrow focus entails collecting key information that is specific and factual. Specific information will be organized along the lines of the *NASP Practice Model* (four categories and 10 subdomains), which are detailed in subsequent chapters of this guide.

General Information and Test Format

To be employed as a *licensed* school psychologist in a public school, you must complete a school psychology degree program and pass the *Praxis National School Psychology Test* (test code 5402 as of 2016) with a score of 142. The licensure exam is administered by the *Educational Testing Service* (ETS), which is the same organization that provides public school teacher credentialing exams. Typically, a passing score of 142 is required for certification as a Nationally Certified School Psychologist (NCSP), but a different score may be necessary for state licensure. Note that a school psychologist does not need to be an NCSP or a member of NASP to take this exam or practice psychology. However, the criteria for being an NCSP are typically higher than those without such a credential. Check with your state regulatory agency for current information on required test scores at **www.ets.org/praxis/nasp**. You can also check the ETS website for official information on outlines, sample test items with rationales for the best answers, and additional test-taking strategies.

The school psychology exam consists of 140 multiple-choice, computer-based questions and lasts roughly 2 hours and 20 minutes within a tightly controlled setting. It has been reported that not all exam items will be scored or counted toward the overall passing score. Normally, each question has four response choices. (Answer choices typically use an A, B, C, D format.) Your chance of merely guessing correctly is 25%; not bad, but an educated guess significantly increases the odds of a correct answer. With the previous statistic in mind, the point is not to worry excessively about passing the exam if you can provide an educated response on most items. *You can respond incorrectly to several items and still pass the exam.* Also, remember that you can always take the exam a second time if you do not do well on the first attempt.

Although specific details about test construction and scoring are difficult to ascertain, it appears there are multiple versions, or alternate forms, of the *Praxis* exam. Most likely, a large pool of questions and test items are used to construct different tests. In other words, the test changes with every administration. Although you might have a few identical items on your test as a person from a previous administration, it is unlikely you will get the exact test used in a prior session.

The content areas of the test are generally broken down into four categories (sometimes referred to as *Test Sections*). As the actual ETS test varies with each administration, it is likely that the number of questions associated with each category also vary. On your exam, you might have more or fewer questions asked from each content area. Also, be aware that some domains overlap in content with other domains; therefore, specific test items could be associated with more than one domain. For example, a test question could ask about how to utilize progress monitoring information for an effective intervention. This particular question has a link to two domains (i.e., *Professional Practices* and *Direct Services for Children*).

Insider Tip

Graduate students who have taken the test stated that, despite what the ETS website asserts, the percentage of items from each domain seems different from test to test. For example, some test takers felt that they had substantially fewer items from the *Foundations of School Psychological Service Delivery* content area, but many more items from the *Direct Services* domain than fellow classmates who took the exam a few weeks later. Because you do not know which domain might be emphasized on your exam, it is best to study all major sections of the exam, but focus on areas that you know you are weakest in as indicated on those items (areas) missed on the practice tests supplied by this guide.

General Categories of the School Psychology *Praxis* Exam Format

The *Praxis* exam's format has been modified over the past few years. Although terms used to describe major content areas (domains) have been renamed, it is important to note that information from older study guides may still be useful and found on the current exam. For example, information that was associated with the older test domain of *Research-Based Behavioral and Mental Health Practices* is now reorganized under the new test domain heading of *Direct and Indirect Services for Children, Families, and Schools*. The following table, provided by ETS, illustrates the previous structure (approximately 2008–2014) of the *Praxis* exam. The percentages are only estimates for the previous multiple-choice items.

1. Data-Based Decision Making   35%   (42 items)
2. Research-Based Behavioral and Mental Health Practices   16%   (19 items)
3. Applied Psychological Principles   13%   (16 items)
4. Research-Based Academic Practices   12%   (14 items)
5. Consultation and Collaboration   12%   (14 items)
6. Ethical, Legal, and Professional Foundations   12%   (14 items)

The following table illustrates the current (2016) content categories. As mentioned previously, the category headings are subject to modification, but a significant portion of information from previous domains is still relevant. Each of the following content areas may not be precise percentages of your actual exam, but they are provided as useful estimates. **Figure I.1** depicts the estimated percentages and range of items for each category covered by the current *Praxis* exam.

1. Professional Practices, Practices That Permeate All Aspects of Service Delivery   30%   (40–44 items)
2. Direct and Indirect Services for Children, Families, and Schools   24%   (30–34 items)
3. Systems-Level Services   15%   (20–24 items)
4. Foundations of School Psychological Service Delivery   31%   (40–44 items)

Note: It is important to consider that the categories and the subdomains under each category are referred to by the NASP as the *Practice Model*. The *Praxis* exam categories mirror the *Practice Model* and provide an essential broad format to organize your notes and information to focus your study efforts for the test.

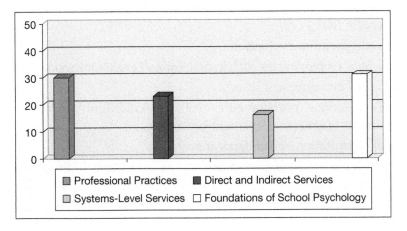

FIGURE I.1   Estimated percentage of test items per category.

Description of Exam Categories (NASP Practice Model)

I. Professional Practices, Practices That Permeate All Aspects of Service Delivery

A. Data-Based Decision Making and Accountability

1. Methods for problem identification
2. Evaluation, assessment, testing, and problem analysis
3. Measurement theory, principles, and psychometrics
4. Assessment of special populations

B. Consultation and Collaboration

1. Models of consultation
2. Collaboration for all stakeholders

Study and Test-Taking Strategies: Professional Practices, Practices That Permeate All Aspects of Service Delivery

Although consultation models are important to know, the *professional practices* content category has a heavy emphasis on *assessment, testing,* and *evaluation.* Key areas to focus your study strategy should include the following major areas:

- Principles of data-based decision making

  Data collection, assessment measures and tests, best practices in assessment, working with diverse and special populations, theories of intelligence

- Best practices of data-based decision making

  Best practices in psychoeducational services; display of data; analysis of progress monitoring; progress monitoring in reading, writing, and mathematics (response to intervention [RTI])

- Research and program evaluation

  Critiquing tests, employing research in practice, and evaluating models and methods

- Knowledge of measurement theory

  Types of evaluations, psychometrics (e.g., reliability and validity), test scores, test bias and test fairness, assessment procedures

- Models of consultation and collaboration

  Know primary consultation models such as direct and indirect models. Also know key terms associated with consultation, such as *client* and *consultee.* Also note that the major consultation models include behavioral, consultee-centered, instructional, and multicultural.

(continued)

(*continued*)

- Working with interpreters

  Effective consultation is predicated on effective rapport. Know the different ways to establish effective relationships. Once rapport is established, practitioners need to know the various models of consultation and when to employ specific consultation techniques with different specialists or personnel (e.g., medical staff and interpreters).

- **Example test question:** A large portion of questions that center on data-based decisions involve cognitive assessments, standardized measures, and informal data collection. These questions are typically straightforward and factual. For example, you might be asked, "Which subtest on the WISC-V is not appropriate for visually impaired students?"

II. Direct and Indirect Services for Children, Families, and Schools

A. Intervention and Instructional Support to Develop Academic Skills

1. Instructional/academic strategies
2. Factors related to academic success and failure

B. Interventions and Mental Health Services

1. Interventions for different levels (individual, group, systems)
2. School-based interventions
3. Psychopathology

Study and Test-Taking Strategies: Direct and Indirect Services for Children, Families, and Schools

The *Direct and Indirect Services for Children* content area focuses primarily on mental health counseling, how to address psychopathology, and instructional techniques to develop academic skills. It is important to know the strategies to intervene at both individual and classroom levels. Key areas to focus your preparation are the following:

- Prevention interventions for primary, secondary, and tertiary levels

  Promoting social, emotional, and academic success; classroom organization and management growth; service learning (*Note*: Academic interventions should focus on *reading interventions*.)

- School-based interventions, skills, and techniques

  Types of individual and group counseling techniques, applied behavioral analysis, psychoeducational support, social skills development, restorative practices

- General principles/theories

  Theories of cognitive development, theories of child development, child psychopathology, substance abuse, pharmacology

(*continued*)

(*continued*)

- **Example test questions:** The questions nested under this domain are related to research-based behavioral and mental health practices. Previous test takers have mentioned that items are typically related to counseling techniques, theories, and crisis intervention mostly at the *individual level* and for special education populations.

  - **Example 1:** Which strategies are used to help a student with assertiveness issues? (Answer: Modeling, role-playing, and rehearsal)

  - **Example 2:** Which stage of Erik Erikson's psychosocial developmental theory addresses the middle childhood years (6–12 years old)? (Answer: Stage 4: Industry vs. inferiority)

  - **Example 3:** Research-based academic questions tend to focus on teaching practices, classroom-management techniques, and how to properly monitor a student's progress. People who have little teaching experience might find this area challenging. An example question might be, "What is an effective method to teach and build comprehension skills?" (Answer: Have students ask themselves relevant questions [self-talk] while reading a passage and predict the outcome.) It is important to remember that this domain may be related to items in the other content areas as well.

III. Systems-Level Services

A. Schoolwide Interventions and Practices

1. Organizational and systems theory
2. System resource mapping
3. Educational practices and policies
4. Evaluating school-based interventions
5. Developing effective school improvement plans

B. Prevention and Responsive Interventions

1. Know various prevention programs
2. Understand various student protective and risk factors
3. Crisis prevention and intervention strategies
4. Crisis management and postcrisis supports

C. Family–School Collaboration

1. Family advocacy
2. Interagency issues related to systems intervention policies

Study and Test-Taking Strategies: Systems-Level Services

As the title of this content area illustrates, most of the information in this category is broader in scope than other areas. Many people have remarked that this area is heavy with crisis intervention and management questions, especially because crisis management is an expanding role for school psychologists. When studying broad policy and program issues related to school systems, it is helpful to know policies and practices that could negatively impact students (e.g., zero tolerance, corporal punishment). The following bullet points are key areas to consider studying:

- Crisis intervention, prevention, and response

  General prevention through planning; schoolwide planning and prevention; specific crisis prevention, intervention, and response (bullying, suicide, death, and grief)

- Effective schoolwide instruction practices

  Instruction strategies, issues related to academic successes and problems, education policies and practices, retention, high-stakes testing

- Collaboration with professional agencies and personnel

  Medical experts and other agents who do not work specifically in schools can present special challenges. Understand how to communicate effectively with outside agencies and their special sets of issues.

- **Example test questions**:
  - **Example 1:** Name an effective research-backed intervention that a school mental health team might develop for a school that has constant discord among various groups of students? (Answer: Restorative practices)
  - **Example 2**: Name a risk factor that increases student dropout rates? (Answer: Lack of parental involvement)

IV. Foundations of School Psychological Service Delivery

A. Diversity in Development and Learning

1. Cultural and individual differences
2. Needs of diverse learners
3. Biases in instruction, assessment, and decision making
4. Fairness and social justice in education and related services

B. Research and Program Evaluation

1. Effectively evaluate research and school programs
2. Utilize technology in research and program evaluation
3. Understand psychometrics and various research designs

C. Legal, Ethical, and Professional Practices

1. Ethical principles related to school psychology
2. Laws and legal issues related to school psychology

Study and Test-Taking Strategies: Foundations of School Psychological Service Delivery

This area is obviously heavy with legal and ethical questions, typically with just a few program evaluation items. Although some legal questions might be straightforward, the ethical questions tend to be more difficult to answer due to their hypothetical nature and the seemingly multiple correct responses offered. Cultural and diversity topics are emphasized more now than at any time in the past. Many times, tests may have a legal question that is tied to a diversity or social justice issue. The following areas are useful to emphasize:

- Ethical principles and standards of practice
  NASP principles, NASP professional standards, assessment procedures, laws, regulations, case law (specific landmark court cases)
- Professional foundations of school psychology
  Key experts in the field, historical milestones (timeline)
- **Example test question:** Legal and ethical questions are sometimes given within a brief case study or in a vignette format. Be familiar not only with specific case law (landmark rulings) but also the ramifications of the outcomes of such rulings. Here is an example test question from this domain: "What is a primary duty for a school official when a concerning threat has been made against a student?" (Answer: The school official has a "Duty to Warn" the parents of the student.)

Twenty-Five Tips for Studying and Preparing

1. Start studying early for the test. *Do not procrastinate.* Some people study a week before the test and soon realize that this was not enough time due to the vastness of the subject areas. In my opinion, it is best to study for *at least* a month or more prior to the test. Your first few days will entail collecting and organizing information and notes. If you study 2 to 3 hours a day for a month, this will provide you with an adequate foundation.

2. Know when to study. There is some research that suggests studying before going to sleep is more effective than studying during the stress of the day-time hours. It might be best to study about an hour after eating dinner. Go for a walk after dinner to increase your oxygen intake and blood circulation to the brain. Studying from 7:00 p.m. to 10:00 p.m., then going to sleep, is a good routine that some successful students follow.

3. Sleep is necessary for effective memory. Neuroscientists have valid research that links strong memory and retrieval of stored information to sound sleep. Lack of sleep causes a depletion of key neurochemicals in the limbic system that significantly hinders learning and memory. Make sure you are getting a solid 7 to 9 hours of sleep every night for several weeks before you take the test.

4. Hydration and diet play a vital role in brain health. Our brain contains a substantial amount of moisture. You must make sure your brain is properly hydrated to maintain your peak performance. Students who are dehydrated have significant difficulties with focus, memory, and learning. Some researchers recommend a steady diet of water, bananas, and fish when studying. Do not overdo this diet, but realize you might need to slightly increase your intake of healthy foods containing magnesium and omega-3 fatty acids.

5. Organize your notes and information according to the four broad categories (NASP model) listed previously. Have separate folders for each category. My own opinion is to have hard copies of your notes and outlines. Do not rely on your computer; you need backup documents. You might find it easier to have paper notes to quickly review information in the hours before the test.

6. Develop *keyword lists* and concise general-concept bulleted notes. I found this tip to be extremely helpful. Such lists make reviewing very time efficient and effective, especially a few days and hours before the actual exam.

7. Study general concepts and keywords more than specific facts. *Familiarize* more than memorize. Although you certainly have to memorize several facts (e.g., specific case laws, certain psychometric properties, psychological theories), understanding broad concepts provides a foundation that will enable you to answer most questions. For example, NASP's position on grade retention is that the practice is not a good idea in most cases. Questions on the test will usually be in the form of an example: "A parent comes to you and tells you her son has failed three classes in seventh grade and she wants to retain him. What is your response?" In such a case, your response should be to determine if something is interfering with the child's learning (e.g., social or emotional problems, learning difficulties) and to suggest various options that will allow the child to make up the failed subjects. Notice how this question does not explicitly ask about NASP's position on grade retention.

8. If you choose to study with a group, keep the group small. Generally, study groups are very effective if they are *kept small* (three to four people). With too many people, focusing the group and socializing become issues. *Do not overemphasize study groups*. Meet just a few times with the group to exchange information and quiz each other. Everyone within the small group should bring completed outlines and notes to the first meeting. Group members should have copies of their outlines to share. Although this is more work than dividing tasks among individual members, information gathered this way is more comprehensive and usually stimulates meaningful conversations about relevant test content.

Note: Trust yourself to study alone. You may not need a study group, but rather just a few consultation sessions with a few colleagues or your professor. Sometimes groups can be too demanding, so be guarded with your time and use it effectively.

9. Secure an undergraduate "Introduction to Psychology" textbook and read the summaries for each chapter. The textbook should be no more than 5 years old. Such textbooks are excellent for reviewing the newest general psychological theories and research. Although you will use your own graduate-level school psychology textbooks for review, most general/introductory psychology textbooks also have excellent chapters on psychopathology, neuropsychology, and psychometrics. Additionally, these textbooks are sometimes easier to digest than graduate-level texts, and key concepts are presented in a thorough manner.

10. It may be appropriate to study your weak content areas, but be careful how you emphasize any one area. You do not want to overstudy one area at the expense of other information that is just as important. For example, some students may have only four case law questions, but have 10 psychometric questions on an exam. If you feel you are weak in one of the domain areas, by all means spend a little more time on that material to bolster your weakness. However, do not skimp on studying an area because you think it is your strength.

11. Read all the chapter summaries from major textbooks you purchased during your program of study. Again, be very familiar with broad concepts and memorize only key facts. *Be very judicious in what you decide to memorize.* Do not spend too much time reading entire chapters unless you are very weak in that area. Although obvious to some students, it is still recommended to review Jerome Sattler's books on cognitive and behavioral assessments and Randy Kamphaus's works on similar information.

12. As apparent as this suggestion might be for most people in school psychology graduate programs, some students in international programs or psychologists in other fields who are retraining may not know about resources available from the NASP. For example, students using NASP resources to study for the exam should focus their efforts on chapter summaries and abstracts from NASP's *Best Practices in School Psychology.* Many graduate students attempt to read the entire *Best Practices* book. Although this is useful, it is highly time-consuming, and large sections of this book do not discuss the test. Colleagues who took the exam told me that reading the summaries and a few specific chapters was more effective. I found reading chapters that dealt with multicultural issues, testing, interventions (counseling), and consultation to be helpful.

13. Be familiar with key acronyms. You do not necessarily have to memorize them, but be able to recognize an acronym and be familiar with its importance.

14. Take as many *practice tests from different sources as possible* and discuss missed items with your study group. If you have an effective study group, have each member create a mini-test. Swap tests and discuss them at your next session. Taking practice tests is the best way to initially reduce test anxiety. It will also prepare your mind for taking timed tests. Prepare by taking the two practice tests located at the back of this guide.

15. When taking the exam, practice effective time management. To my knowledge, questions are scored equally. Therefore, do not spend too much time on any one particular item. As of this writing, there are 140 questions to answer in 2 hours and 20 minutes. Many students that reported they are slow test takers have said they had 15 minutes to spare at the end of the exam.

16. Never leave any question unanswered. Usually, you will be able to quickly narrow down your answer to two choices. If you have difficulty choosing an answer, make a mental note of the question and give it a good guess. If time permits when you finish your exam, go back and examine the question again. There is debate about whether a person's first guess is the most accurate. If you still have doubts after examining a difficult question, go with your initial response.

17. Allow yourself time at the end of the test to recheck your answers. If you have been taking practice tests, you should have honed your time-management skills. If you have extra time when you complete your test, you should do two things. First, review the entire test. Second, reread the questions you had difficulty answering and determine if *other test items might provide help.* During some testing situations, some students noticed that one test item contained information that helped answer another item.

18. Go to the NASP website and read about *NASP's position papers and best practices.* Some students have not read many position statements, especially statements dealing with current issues. The NASP endorses certain practices and provides guidelines for practitioners. For example, the NASP has strong opinions regarding inclusion, social justice, cultural issues, and the use of punishment to correct student behaviors.

19. If you are going to take a blind guess answering a question, some of my colleagues suggest that it is best to guess "C" or "D." However, if you can match a keyword in the choice section to anything in the question, answer accordingly.

20. Register to take the test as early as possible. You will be able to register early through the Internet. If you do not register early, you run the risk of not being able to take the test in a convenient location. Some people might have to drive a very long distance to take the test. Remember to *double-check your university's code,* which you will have to enter. If you put in the wrong code,

your school will not receive your scores. A few weeks after the test, a copy of your scores will be sent to your home, and a detailed breakdown of how you performed on each section of the test will be included.

21. Allow yourself to miss a few questions without stressing about it. Remember, you can miss several items and still pass the test. Do not be a perfectionist or think you have to know it all. For practical purposes, there is no difference between getting 70% correct and 100% correct; both scores pass and nobody asks you your scores after you graduate.

22. When studying general psychological theories and concepts, focus on those parts that are relevant only for the age group of 4- to 18-year-olds. For example, be more familiar with Erikson's psychosocial stages for children rather than for adults.

23. On the test day, relax, relax, and relax. Your emotions and anxiety will be elevated on the day you take the test. Some anxiety is helpful, but not too much. If you have sincerely prepared for the test, then do not second guess your efforts; you are prepared. Follow your normal routine the day of the test. Always remember that you can *retake* the test if you do not perform as well as you expected. In fact, some people study for the NASP test by taking it twice. Arrive about half an hour early and review keywords and concepts from your notes. After reviewing once, stop and enjoy a cup of coffee and wait for the test to begin.

24. As common sense as this sounds, it is emphasized again that the test-taker *utilize as many resources and books as possible.* Do not rely solely on one guide. Remarkably, it is estimated that 33% of people who are studying for the exam only use one resource. Although this particular guide is useful, there are a few other guides on the market that should be used in conjunction with it. Also, there are many people who may not fully understand that NASP and ETS offer resources as well. Although evident to some test takers, people have told me they simply were not aware of the NASP's *Best Practices* book or practice tests offered by NASP/ETS.

25. Finally, eat a decent dinner and get a full night's sleep before the test. The day before the exam, review your notes, but do not stress or try to learn new material. Relax and tell yourself if you do not do well, you will just take it again. As mentioned, it is important to hydrate yourself by drinking an extra glass of water. The brain needs water to think effectively.

Insider Observations

The following notes from students who took the exam are provided to give you a general idea of how some tests are structured. You may find that your test is not exactly the same as the following comments indicate. However, you may have several similar items and questions.

- One test had 15 long, scenario-type questions. Scenario questions are comprised of 7- to 12-sentence paragraphs. After reading the short paragraph, you have to choose the best answer from four to five choices.

- Of the 15 scenario questions, three or four of the scenarios had multiple questions associated with them. For example, one vignette accounted for questions numbered 65 through 68.

- Several questions on the exam were about one to three short sentences in length. These questions asked for straightforward information. For example, "Carl Rogers is best known for what?"

- For approximately 75% of the questions, you might be able to very quickly narrow down the choices to two responses. The two narrowed-down responses will each have kernels of truth in them. Take the best educated guess and look for keywords that match your answer to the question.

- Roughly 66% of the questions were short-example types that ask you to apply your knowledge. For example, "You have a new student who was referred for anxiety problems around test taking. What should you do first?" (Answer: Secure signed permission from the parents to counsel the student.)

- The majority of test takers completed the test with about 15 minutes to spare. It is estimated that about 66% of your colleagues will finish with about 20 minutes to spare.

- Two or three questions on the exam might help you to answer a few other items because of the information they contain. Sometimes keywords in the choices will remind you of concepts and other important ideas.

- Very few, if any, items have tricky or multiple answers. For example, most test takers did not have a choice that read, "A and C are true, but B is not."

Section I

Content Review

1

First Test Category: Professional Practices, Practices That Permeate All Aspects of Service Delivery

By no means does this guide contain everything you need to know about school psychology. As emphasized previously, this guide is purposely designed to be *concise and as easy to read* as possible, but without sacrificing key concepts you need to know for the exam. As school psychologists, we are busy practitioners who must keep abreast of new developments within various subfields of psychology, not just our own area. We must know concepts in psychometrics, neuropsychology, counseling psychology, social psychology, educational psychology, and other branches of our discipline. Consequently, using multiple streams of information is the best approach in your test preparation, especially in the area of data-based decision making. Most test items related to Category 1 ask you to *apply* your knowledge, rather than to repeat psychological or psychometric facts.

This chapter is organized into two primary sections that mirror the National Association of School Psychologists (NASP) model. The first section discusses concepts related to **Domain 1,** which is *Data-Based Decision Making.* The next major section concerns **Domain 2,** *Consultation and Collaboration* models. A summary of key points immediately follows the chapter.

Domain 1: Data-Based Decision Making

What Is Data-Based Decision Making? Data-based decision making involves the collection of formal and informal information to help a student. Initially, information gathered on a struggling student is linked to the school's response to intervention (RTI) process. If the student continues to struggle, despite the

3

best efforts of the RTI or Multi-Tiered System of Support (MTSS) team, a full and comprehensive evaluation is conducted. Before the revised edition of the *Praxis*® exam, data-based decision-making questions centered largely on standardized testing and assessments. You may still have several test questions regarding formal cognitive tests and behavioral assessments, but RTI/MTSS questions have significantly increased over the past few years.

Informal and formal data are required to inform professional judgments regarding an individual student at the following four levels:

1. **Background data collection, techniques, and problem identification level:** You must know various methods of data collection to help identify and *define* the problem.

2. **Screening level:** Data can be used to help identify at-risk students and make decisions about students who struggle with academic work.

3. **Progress monitoring and RTI level:** Data are used to determine effectiveness of the interventions (RTI) once a student is identified.

4. **Formal assessment level (special education evaluation):** Cognitive, social, and emotional data are derived from various sources, but especially from formal standardized measures.

In general, data are used for the following needs:
- To identify the problem and plan interventions
- To increase or decrease levels of intervention
- To help determine whether interventions are implemented with fidelity
- To decide whether interventions are related to positive student outcomes (effectiveness)
- To plan individualized instruction and strategic long-term educational planning

I. Background Data Collection, Techniques, and Problem Identification

When a struggling student has been identified already through various means, the initial data collected should help *define* the problem. Collected data are gathered with an emphasis on the referral question (e.g., What is the specific area in which the student is having difficulty?). Initial data collection *sources* include background information, student files, interviews, and observations.

A. Collection and Analysis of Vital Background Information (Informal Data)

1. Student files and records
2. Staff interviews and comments about the student
3. Medical records and reports

4. Review of previous interventions

5. Developmental history

B. Interview and Interview Techniques

Student interviewing: It is important to refer to the following resource for information on child interviewing: "**The Child Interview**" **by Jan N. Hughes** (1989, 247–259).

1. **Structured interviews** are more standardized and formal. The same questions are given to each child.

   - **Advantages**: Structured interviews have high validity and reliability. Children's responses can be directly compared with other children's responses. Structured diagnostic interviews indicate the presence or absence of a problem, not level of functioning.

   - **Limitations**: Generally, the interviewer is unable to modify questions to the needs of the interviewee. The interview must follow a strict format and administration.

2. **Unstructured interviews** are based on the assumption that conversational style helps to put the student at ease. The less you put structure on the child, the more the child will share.

   - **Advantage**: Unstructured interviews can be adapted to the needs of the interviewee.

   - **Limitations**: Child responses can be difficult to interpret. The responses cannot be compared with norms as seen within the more structured interview measures.

3. **Semi-structured interviews** combine the best features of both structured and unstructured interviews. They allow for flexibility and follow-up questions.

C. Observational Techniques

Observational techniques are used to observe and record behavior in a natural setting.

1. **Whole-interval recording**: Behavior is only recorded when it occurs during the entire *time interval*. (This is good for continuous behaviors or behaviors occurring in short duration.)

2. **Frequency or event recording**: Record the *number* of behaviors that occurred during a specific period.

3. **Duration recording** refers to the *length of time* the specific behavior lasts.

4. **Latency recording:** Time between onset of stimulus or signal that initiates a specific behavior.

5. **Time-sampling interval recording**: Select a time period for observation, divide the period into a number of equal intervals, and record whether or

not behavior occurs. Time sampling is effective when the beginning and end of behavior are difficult to determine or when only a brief period is available for observation.

6. **Partial-interval recording**: Behavior is scored if it occurs during any part of the time interval. Multiple episodes of behavior in a single time interval are counted as one score or mark. Partial-interval recording is effective when behaviors occur at a relatively low rate or for inconsistent durations.

7. **Momentary time sampling**: Behavior is scored as present or absent only during the moment that a timed interval begins. This is the least biased estimate of behavior as it actually occurs.

II. Assessment and Problem Analysis

A. Universal Screening

Universal screening is broadly implemented and it is systematic. Universal assessment of *all* children can be done within a given class, grade, school, or district on academic, behavioral, social, or emotional indicators that the school and community have agreed are critical for success.

1. **Purpose:** First, the **broad** purpose of universal screening is to help determine whether modifications are needed in the core curriculum, instruction, or general education environment. Second, the **narrow** purpose is to guide decisions about additional or intensive instruction for those specific students who may require instructional support beyond what is already provided at a broad level.

2. **Benefits and liabilities of screeners**: Universal screening tools are cost-effective, time efficient, and easy to administer. However, there is a chance of misclassifying some students when using screening tools. It is better to err on the side of false positives so as to provide additional support to a student who may not need it rather than to deny additional support to a student in need as a result of a false negative. This is referred to as the **least dangerous assumption**.

B. Universal Screening Measures

1. **Curriculum-based measures (CBM)** are typically reliable, but must be used only if they align with local norms, benchmarks, and standards. An example of CBM would be a reading fluency measure such as Dynamic Indicators of Basic Early Literacy Skills (DIBELS).

2. Fluency-based indicators of skills are common universal screeners. Such screeners include initial-sound fluency, letter-naming fluency, phoneme segmentation, nonsense-word fluency, and oral-reading fluency.

3. The **Cognitive Assessment Test (CogAT)** is a cognitive measure, but it is group administered and can be employed as a screener.

4. State educational agencies employ formal group-administered tests that are given to students every year to monitor student growth in reading, writing, and math. Some school districts use alternatives to a state-created test, such as the Iowa Test of Basic Skills.

5. Schools using the **System to Enhance Educational Performance (STEEP)** conduct CBMs several times a year in reading, math, and writing to identify students in need of additional support.

C. Progress Monitoring and RTI Level (read over)

Several effective data-tracking programs and procedures have been created to record and analyze a student's historical test results in specific academic areas such as reading, math, and spelling. The reader should be familiar with well-known RTI tracking programs such as *AimsWeb*.

In general, the RTI process is as follows. Typically, a student is identified with an academic or a behavioral concern (or both) by his or her teacher or parent. After a student has been identified, the school psychologist uses the first two steps of the information-gathering process (i.e., data collection and screening information). Once a student's problem area is known, baseline performance data are collected on the student's specific area of concern. Next, research-based interventions are employed and systematic tests are provided to measure the student's postintervention progress. The student's test data are formally documented, tracked, and analyzed. After several points of intervention, data are collected and an analysis is conducted that examines the difference between the student's initial baseline performance and the expected level of performance after interventions have been implemented. It is expected that the majority of students should respond to the new intervention in age-expected ways, meaning the student should make progress and close the gap between baseline data and age-expected data. However, if the student does not grow because of faithful implementation of the intervention in a reasonable amount of time (30–60 days), then a special education evaluation should be considered.

D. Best Practices in Deciding *What* to Assess

There are two levels of collecting progress-monitoring data:

1. **Subskill mastery measurement (SMM)**—Information on student progress is collected to determine whether the *specific* intervention for the target behavior is effective. SMM data should be collected frequently, even daily.

2. **General outcome measurement (GOM)**—Data are collected to determine whether the student is making progress toward long-range goals. GOMs are used less frequently than SMMs, such as once a week.

E. Best Practices in Deciding *How* to Assess and Present Data

1. Progress-monitoring data should be based on the *systematic and repeated* measurement of behavior over a specified time.

2. Frequency data, percentage correct, or number of opportunities to respond are the results that are typically recorded and displayed.

3. The horizontal axis on a graph typically represents real and appropriate intervals of time (e.g., days or weeks).

4. *Note:* There will be **three levels of analysis**.

   a. Analysis of the **variability** in data

   b. Analysis of **level**

   c. Analysis of **trend**

F. Best Practices in *Analyzing* Variability of Progress-Monitoring Data

- **Variability and sources of error**: Each progress-monitoring data point has important considerations and sources of variability.

  1. The first cause of data variability centers on the effectiveness of the intervention. Whether an intervention is effective or not is defined by its ability to change behavior. A change in behavior should be observed and measured in the progress-monitoring data.

  2. A second source of variability is called a *confounding* variable, which includes uncontrolled subject and environmental variables. Controlling these extraneous variables whenever possible is necessary to ensure that the effectiveness of the intervention is what is actually measured.

  3. The third source of variability is measurement error. Measurement error can occur if, for example, an observer was not looking when the target behavior occurred or if a CBM probe was not administered properly.

- **Consideration of mitigating factors:** If extraneous variables are not considered, then student performance may be attributed to the intervention when the changes might be because of the effects of uncontrolled personal or environmental variables.

  - **RTI analysis of *level*:**

    Level refers to the average performance within a condition.

    Example: A condition occurs when a student's performance changes suddenly following a change in conditions. A student's level of performance is often compared with the average level of performance of peers or to a benchmark level.

  - **RTI analysis of *trend*:**

    1. When a student's performance systematically increases or decreases across time, then analyzing the trend in the data is important. The pattern of change in a student's behavior *across time* can be described as *trend*.

    2. Multiple measurements are required to estimate a trend. Statistical methods can be used to calculate the slope or trend line. Slope is easily

calculated with most statistical and spreadsheet software (e.g., SPSS) and the resulting trend line can be plotted on a graph.

3. Visual analysis can also be used to estimate the general pattern of change across time. **Caution**: It is important to determine whether the overall pattern in the data is consistent and linear across time or whether another pattern (e.g., nonlinear, curvilinear) better explains the data.

- **Describing and analyzing baseline RTI data:**

  Progress-monitoring data are first collected during *baseline* to determine the current level, trend, and variability of behavior. Baseline is the condition *before* intervention.

  - **General RTI evaluation points:**

    1. One rule for baseline data is that there should be no new highs (spikes) or lows for *three* consecutive data points.

    2. Another rule is that **80% of the data points should fall within 15% of the mean (average) line** or, in the case of increasing or decreasing data points, within 15% of the trend line.

    3. Some researchers recommend collecting a minimum number of baseline data points, approximately three to five points.

    4. In schools, practical considerations often affect the amount of data that can be collected.

G. Best Practices for Making Decisions Based on RTI Data (read over)

The three characteristics used to describe behavior (level, trend, and variability) may change because of the introduction of an intervention. Initially, it is important to consider if a sufficient number of data points exists in each condition to obtain an accurate picture of the behavior under both the baseline and the intervention conditions. Next, determine if the change in behavior closely coincides with the change in conditions. An immediate change in the level, trend, or variability of the behavior is likely the result of the intervention.

- RTI decision rules

  Reasons to use RTI data: Students whose teachers use data-based decisions learn more than students whose teachers do not rely on such data. To make data-based decisions, you must first have a goal that is based on local norms, benchmarks, or classroom-comparison norms. The following are decision rules to use with RTI data.

  1. **Should the intervention be changed?**

     If two or three data points during the intervention condition fall below the *aim* line, the intervention needs to be changed. You should analyze the trend line over the last several data points and compare it with the aim line. If the slope of the student's trend line is less than the slope of the aim line, the intervention needs to be changed.

2. **Are there no correct responses for 3 or more days (or sessions) in a row?**

   If there are no correct responses for three to four sessions, change the intervention.

3. **Are the data highly variable?**

   Consider extraneous factors when data are too variable. Examples of extraneous factors include the difficulty of the probes, different examiners, failing to get a student's attention before presenting stimuli, student noncompliance, insufficient reinforcement for correct responding, or level of motivation.

4. **Is the percentage of correct responding below 85%?**

   To correct this problem, include modifications to the instruction by providing better prompts, additional modeling, or more effective corrective feedback.

5. **Is the student's performance accurate but slow?**

   If growth is slow, focus efforts on increasing the student's rate of correct responses. Rate increase is achieved through repeated practice and systematic contingencies to address student motivation.

III. Assessment of Special Population (Special Education Evaluation and Testing)

If a student fails to show a proper RTI, a more comprehensive evaluation is needed to help better understand the nature of the student's difficulty and to plan for more intensive support services. At this last level, scientific and standardized tests are typically employed. It is important to know that school psychologists are required to *use both qualitative and quantitative data* in their analysis for determination of special education eligibility. Although qualitative data are vital, the complex nature of formal psychological tests, procedures, and statistics makes the quantitative aspect more challenging to use. The reader should be well versed in psychometrics and ready to answer hypothetical case questions regarding test statistics and specific problems associated with formalized data. For example, on the *Praxis* exam, you may be asked, "Which specific test would be best to administer or why is a particular test not a valid choice to use?" Another question might be, "Why should a school psychologist *not* use the Differential Ability Scales-I (DAS-I)?" The answer should be: "Because standardized tests with *norms older than 10 years* should be used with caution due to regression problems associated with older normative data."

- Although the following Internet resource is designed to assist psychologists when evaluating students with brain injuries, the assessment area of this webpage provides you with a comprehensive list and description of specific formal subtests that can be used to evaluate a variety of cognitive functions such as memory, learning, attention, and reasoning. Make sure to double click on the area you are interested in assessing with a formal test. Go to the following link: **http://cokidswithbraininjury.com**

- A comprehensive special education evaluation will include formal and informal data within each of the following major domains:
  - Cognitive
  - Achievement
  - Communication (speech–language)
  - Motor skills
  - Adaptive skills
  - Social, emotional, and behavioral functioning
  - Sensory processing
- Be familiar with the following common assessment instruments and tests. The following tests are the typical ones that are administered by school psychologists. Generally speaking, the first five tests listed are the most common in each category and most likely seen on the *Praxis* exam.

A. Common Measures of Cognitive Function (In Order of Popular Use)

- Wechsler Intelligence Scale for Children, Fifth Edition (WISC-V; 6–16 years 11 months)
- Differential Ability Scales-II (DAS-II; 2.5–17 years 11 months)
- Stanford–Binet, Fifth Edition (2–85+ years)
- Wechsler Preschool and Primary Scale of Intelligence, Fourth Edition (WPPSI-IV; 2.6–7.7 years)
- Wechsler Adult Intelligence Scale, Fifth Edition (WAIS-V; 16–74 years)
- Woodcock–Johnson Test of Cognitive Ability (2–90 years)
- Bayley Scales of Infant Development (1–42 months)
- Leiter (2–20 years)
- Kaufman Assessment Battery for Children, Second Edition (KABC-II; 3–18 years)
- Kaufman Adolescent and Adult Intelligence Test (11–85+ years)
- Universal Nonverbal Intelligence Test (UNIT; 5–17 years and 11 months)
- Cognitive Assessment System (CAS-2; 5–18 years)

B. Common Measures of Educational Achievement

- Woodcock–Johnson Test of Achievement-IV (2–90 years)
- Wide Range Achievement Test 4 (WRAT-4; 5–94 years)
- Kaufman Test of Educational Achievement (K-TEA; grades 1–12)
- Wechsler Individual Achievement Test (WIAT; 4–50 years 11 months)

The following are early childhood achievement tests:

- Test of Early Reading Ability (TERA)
- Test of Early Math Ability (TEMA)
- Kaufman Survey of Early Academic and Language Skills (K-SEALS)

C. Neuropsychological Measures (Basic Neuropsychological Functions)

Note: Several basal neurological processes can be assessed by using a cross-subtest/battery approach. For example, to measure processing speed, subtests from the DAS-II can be employed. Common basal neurological processes include memory, attention, processing speed, and sensory. Higher order reasoning is generally assessed by cognitive test batteries, not neuropsychological tests.

- **Memory tests**
  - Wechsler Memory Scale
  - Test of Memory and Learning, Second Edition (TOMAL-2)
  - Working Memory scales of WISC-V, DAS-II, Woodcock–Johnson–Cognitive (WCJ-Cog), Stanford–Binet, Fourth Edition (SB-IV)
  - Wide Range Assessment of Memory and Learning, Second Edition (WRAML2)
- **Executive functioning and attention (after age 8 years)**
  - Behavior Rating Inventory of Executive Function-2 (BRIEF-2; standardized survey of questions)
  - CAS-2-Attention and Planning domains
  - Delis–Kaplan Executive Function System (D-KEFS)
  - NEPSY-II (Attention-Executive Functions Domain)
  - Behavioral Assessment of Dysexecutive Syndrome (BADS)
  - Wisconsin Card Sort Test (WCST)
  - Rey Complex Figure Test (RCFT; also taps visual–perceptual and memory)
  - Conner's Continuous Performance Test
  - Tower Tests (e.g., Tower of London)
  - Comprehensive Executive Function Inventory (CEFI)
- **Phonemic awareness tests**
  - Comprehensive Test of Phonological Processing (CTOPP)
  - Test of Phonological Awareness—Kindergarten
  - Nonword Spelling (Screening)
  - Yopp–Singer Test of Phoneme Segmentation
  - Rosner Auditory Analysis Test
  - Rapid Name and Phoneme Segmentation such as DIBELS
  - DAS-II Phonological Processing Domain

- **Language tests**
  - Peabody Picture Vocabulary Test-4 (2–90+ years)
  - Clinical Evaluation of Language Fundamentals-5 (5:0-21-11)
  - Various verbal reasoning subtests from major cognitive test batteries such as the WISC-V or DAS-II
- **Visual processes**
  - Beery–Buktenica Developmental Test of Visual–Motor Integration
  - DAS-II Recall of Designs
  - RCFT
- **Major neuropsychological test batteries (comprehensive)**
  - NEPSY-II
  - D-KEFS

D. Emotional, Behavioral, and Social Skills Measures

- **Informal measures for social and emotional problems:** Multiple data sources should be used, such as the number of office referrals, suspensions, and classroom-based disciplinary procedures. These can be used to detect preexisting levels of problem behaviors. These outcomes represent indirect measures of social skills as these outcomes are presumed to reflect corresponding levels of prosocial behavior.
  - **Internet resources for more social and emotional information:**

    Collaborative for Academic, Social, and Emotional Learning: **www.casel .org**

    Center for the Social Emotional Foundations of Early Learning: **http://csefel.vanderbilt.edu**
- **Functional behavioral assessment (FBA):** An FBA is a comprehensive and individualized method to identify the purpose or function of a student's problem behavior(s). FBAs are vital tools for school psychologists and you should be familiar with FBAs for the *Praxis* exam. FBAs are used to develop a plan to modify factors that maintain the problem behavior and to teach appropriate replacement behaviors using positive interventions. **(This is an excellent resource on FBA and behavior plans. Note the additional forms on this website: www.cde.state.co.us/ cdesped/ta_fba-bip)**
  - **Key aspects of an FBA:** Antecedents (A), behavior (B), and consequences (C)
  - **Steps to complete an FBA:**
    1. Describe problem behavior (operationally define problem).
    2. Perform the assessment. (Review records; complete systematic observations; and interview student, teacher, parents, and other needed individuals.)

3. Evaluate assessment results. (Examine patterns of behavior and determine the purpose or function of the target behaviors.)

4. Develop a hypothesis.

5. Formulate an intervention plan.

6. Start or implement the intervention.

7. Evaluate effectiveness of intervention plan.

> *Note:* Current research and practice inform psychologists to place emphasis on the *antecedents* of a behavior. Determine what is triggering the behavior in the environment. What can you change in the environment to make the target behavior less likely to occur?

- **Internet resources for more FBA information:**

  www.cde.state.co.us/cdesped/ta_fba-bip

  http://cecp.air.org/fba/problembehavior2/main2.htm

- **Common standardized measures to evaluate social and emotional development or problematic areas:**

  Note: Effective social and emotional measures include *at least two forms,* typically a parent form and a teacher form. Best practice is to have multiple raters and results should be largely congruent. *Multiple settings* should also be considered when evaluating students and observing them.

  - Behavior Assessment System for Children (BASC-3; Three Forms: Self, Teacher, Parent)

  - Child Behavior Checklist (CBCL)

  - Devereux Scales of Mental Disorders (Forms: Teacher, Parent)

  - Revised Behavior Problem Checklist (RBPC; Forms: Parent, Teacher)

  - Reynolds Adjustment Screening Inventory—Adolescent

  - Conner's Rating Scales

  - Beck Depression Inventory

  - Revised Children's Manifest Anxiety Scales, Second Edition

E. Additional Measurement and Assessment Considerations

- **Curriculum-based assessment (CBA):** CBA is a term used to describe a broad assessment program or process, which may include CBMs or structured observations.

- **CBM:** CBM refers to the specific forms of criterion-referenced assessments in which curriculum goals and objectives serve as the "criteria" for assessment items.

  - **Top characteristics of effective CBM**

    1. CBMs must be based on *systematic* procedures for the *frequent* collection and analysis of student performance data.

2. The key to CBM is the examination of student performance *across time* to evaluate intervention effectiveness.

3. CBM is a system to identify students who are *at risk.*

4. CBM provides *normative and statistically sound information* for students, classes, staff, and parents.

- **Examples of CBM in content areas:**

1. Reading: Students read aloud for 2 minutes from a passage of text. The number of words read correctly and incorrectly are counted and compared with the class average.

2. Spelling: Students complete a 2-minute spelling test with words presented at 10-second intervals. Words are randomly selected from the students' spelling curriculum. The number of correct words or letter sequences are counted and compared with the class average.

3. Math: Students complete a 3-minute grade-level computational exercise. Correct answers are counted and analyzed against other peers in class.

4. Writing: Students are asked to listen to a short passage and write for 2 minutes about the contents of the passage. The number of correct or on-topic sentences is counted and compared.

F. Authentic (Ecological) Assessments

- Ecological assessments are just as important as formal or standardized assessments. Ecological assessments help to determine the "goodness of fit" between the student and the learning environment.

- An important acronym to remember is **ICEL**. ICEL stands for instruction, curriculum, environment, and learner. During an ecological assessment, the evaluator must review key elements of the four aspects of ICEL. For example, a school psychologist analyzes work samples, prior grades, and assessments. Information from parents, teachers, and the student is collected. Finally, authentic assessments include observational data of the target student during instruction and in other environments.

G. Assessing Intellectual Disabilities (IDs)

- Assessment of children with an ID, which was known previously as mental retardation, requires *both* cognitive and adaptive measures.

- Significantly below-average *intellectual* functioning is a critical criterion. A **standard score (SS) of 70** or below on an individually administered cognitive test, such as the WISC-V or other similar test, is needed for a diagnosis.

- Origins of the disability must be before age 18 years.

- Child must demonstrate deficits or impairments in *adaptive* functioning (i.e., the person's effectiveness in meeting the standards expected for his or her age by his or her cultural group) in some of the following areas:

a. Communication

b. Self-care and home living

c. Social skills

d. Use of community resources

e. Self-direction (ability to be independent)

f. Functional academic skills

g. Employment

h. Leisure

i. Physical health issues

Note: Common adaptive-functional measures used by school psychologists are the Vineland Adaptive Behavior Scales (VABS-4) and Adaptive Behavior Assessment System (ABAS-4).

H. Assessment of Non–English-Speaking or Special Populations (English Language Learners [ELL] or English as a Second Language [ESL])

1. When evaluating language competency, you must assess the child's speaking, reading, and writing abilities while considering the following:

    a. Developmental history and all languages that are spoken and heard

    b. Language dominance (the language the student has heard the most in his or her environment)

    c. Language preference

2. Language proficiency in *both* languages must be assessed and the dominant language must be determined. Such information is crucial to the interpretation of any assessment data that are gathered.

3. Guidelines for distinguishing language *differences* from language *disorders*:

    a. The disorder must be present in the child's native language (L1) and English (L2).

    b. Testing must be conducted in the native or strongest language.

    c. Assessments must be conducted using both formal and informal measures. When possible, it is important to use formal measures that have been *normed on the appropriate cultural group* (e.g., Spanish WISC).

    d. Language must be assessed in a variety of formal and informal speaking contexts.

    e. Patterns of language usage must be described and error patterns must be determined.

    f. The child's language performance must be compared with that of other bilingual speakers who have had similar cultural and linguistic experiences. The child should be compared with members of the same cultural group who speak the dialect.

Note: Make sure to review possible factors that contribute to the interruption of language development. Such factors may include socioeconomic status (SES), poor instruction, lack of experience or exposure to language, school attendance, and so on.

4. Considerations when using standardized tests for Second-Language Learners

Note: The *first bullet is most important,* and you only need to be familiar with the rest of the points; it is not necessary to memorize them.

- Remember that the use of standardized tests with direct test translation (use of an interpreter) is not the best practice and is psychometrically weak if the test is not normed on the cultural group being assessed.

- When using standardized tests, recognize that norming samples are not stratified on the basis of bilingual ability and are rarely applicable to the majority of students being assessed, thus invalidating scores.

- The use of an interpreter can assist in collecting information and administering tests; however, score validity *remains low* even when the interpreter is highly trained and experienced.

- Use systematic methods based on established research for collecting and interpreting data in a nondiscriminatory way.

- Informal and nonstandardized alternative assessment strategies are often less discriminatory because they provide information regarding the student's current skill level that is not confounded with the difficulties associated with inappropriate standardized tests.

IV. Measurement Concepts and Theories Related to Learning and Intelligence

This section is intricately linked to the domain of Data-Based Decision Making and also to several other domain areas. Theories of learning and intelligence are hallmark features and foundations that define a major part of school psychology. Because school psychologists are specialists in the areas of cognitive development, cognitive functioning, learning, and psychometrics, the reader is urged to thoroughly examine this particular area for the test.

A. Key Terms and Concepts Related to Human Learning

1. **Premack principle**: This principle was developed by David Premack. In short, this theory posits that a lower level behavior can be shaped by a higher level (desired) behavior. For example, a student is not allowed to play outside unless he does his homework first. This theory is sometimes termed *contingency* learning because a desired behavior is contingent on first completing a lesser desired behavior.

2. **Immediacy**: This is a key behaviorism concept. Consequences (e.g., rewards) should occur immediately after the behavior in order to be an effective reinforcement.

3. **Negative reinforcement**: This is often confused with punishment. Unlike punishment, a behavior *increases* under negative reinforcement. A stimulus is removed, which causes a behavior to increase.

4. **Positive reinforcement**: A behavior occurs, a rewarding stimulus is provided, and the behavior *increases*.

5. **Fixed ratio reinforcement**: A specific number of behaviors must occur before a reinforcer is given.

6. **Variable ratio**: The number of behaviors needed in order to receive the reinforcer varies. Variable schedules of reinforcement, once a behavior is established by this method, are *resistant to change*.

7. **Frequency, duration, and intensity**: These vital aspects of behavior are measurable and are key parts in all behavior modification plans for students.

8. **Shaping**: Shaping is a technique that creates a behavior by reinforcing approximations of the desired target behavior.

9. **Extinction**: Eliminating the reinforcers or rewards for the behavior terminates the problem behavior.

10. **Punishment:** The introduction of an undesirable stimulus that *decreases* a behavior.

B. Theories of Intelligence and Measurement

Intelligence is a difficult term to be defined and there is some disagreement among experts related to its components and measurement. Despite some controversy involving the definition and the way to assess the construct of intelligence, it can be construed as one's ability to think rationally and act purposefully. Intelligence can also be conceptualized as a person's ability to learn effectively and efficiently. Generally, intelligence involves the way one comprehends information and *applies* knowledge to successful problem solving.

Intelligence shares some variance with wisdom and learned skills, but it is conceptually different. There are several factors that support intelligent behavior such as memory, attention, and processing speed. It is generally assumed that intelligence is solely a brain-based function and it directly impacts a child's ability to learn and achieve in school. School psychologists employ cognitive tests to determine whether a student has the ability to attain academic standards (e.g., set expectations) and to help to craft intervention strategies. *The current endorsement by the NASP is that cognitive test results need to be tied to interventions.*

1. **Spearman's theory of intelligence: Two-factor theory of intelligence:** Charles Spearman is a prominent figure in intelligence test theory. He is cited as creating the modern statistical foundation for intelligence tests. Spearman

primarily believed in a general intelligence factor known as "g." Spearman's "g" is seen in overall or full-scale IQ scores. Specific factors are correlated with specific abilities.

2. **Thurstone's primary mental abilities:** Louis Thurstone held a somewhat opposite view from Spearman, but he is equally influential in the field of psychometrics. He claimed there were at least 11 primary mental abilities. Spearman believed these abilities and dimensions were causal properties of behavior and he did not view intelligence as a unitary construct such as "g."

3. **Cattell–Horn–Carroll (CHC) theory of cognitive abilities:** The CHC theory of intelligence is *a highly regarded and widely adopted theory used to construct most major cognitive abilities tests* such as the WISC-V, DAS-II, SB-V, and WCJ Test of Cognitive Abilities. CHC is steeply anchored to well-established statistical techniques that have evolved over the decades. Although subcomponents of the theory are given, it may *not be necessary to memorize terms such as Gf, but do understand the implications of the parts that make up the CHC theory.*

- The following resource on CHC should be reviewed: http://onlinelibrary .wiley.com/doi/10.1002/9781118660584.ese0431/pdf

Components of CHC theory (statistically derived)

- *Gf*: Usually called *fluid intelligence* or fluid reasoning, this refers to inductive and deductive reasoning with materials and processes that are new to the person doing the reasoning.

- *Gc*: Referenced as *crystallized ability* or crystallized verbal ability, this refers to the application of acquired knowledge and learned skills to answering questions and solving problems that present broadly familiar materials and processes.

- *Gv*: This area involves a range of *visual processes*, ranging from fairly simple visual perceptual tasks to higher level visual and cognitive processes.

- *Ga*: Relates to *auditory processing*, such as recognizing similarities and differences among sounds and recognizing degraded spoken words such as words with sounds omitted or separated.

- *Gs*: Also called *processing speed*, this refers to measures of clerical speed and accuracy.

- *Gsm*: This refers to *short-term memory* or immediate memory.

- *Glr*: This involves *long-term retrieval*, memory storage and retrieval over longer periods.

4. **Das–Naglieri PASS model:** The PASS model of *brain function* divides the brain into four units and was originally proposed by A. E. Luria. This theory holds significant promise to help practitioners to conceptualize intelligence as it relates to brain function.

Four functional units of brain processes (PASS)

1. Planning

2. Attention

3. Simultaneous processing

4. Successive processing

C. Language Development

1. Key terms and concepts related to language development

- **Phonology:** System of sounds that a language uses. Note that people commonly confuse phonemic awareness with phonological processing. Phonemic awareness is a component of the broader construct phonological processing.

- **Phoneme:** The basic unit of a language's *sound* or phonetic system. It is the smallest sound units that affect meaning. Example: /s/.

- **Morpheme**: Language's smallest units of *meaning*, such as prefix, suffix, or root word. Example: "pre" in the word "preheat."

- **Semantics:** The study of *word meanings* and combinations, such as in phrases, clauses, and sentences.

- **Syntax:** Prescribes *how* words may combine into phrases, clauses, and sentences.

- **Pragmatics:** A set of rules that specify appropriate language for particular social contexts.

  Note: Acquiring two languages, simultaneously, as a child can sometimes slow language development. Some children will have difficulty with "code switching."

2. Language acquisition device (LAD)

Noam Chomsky is a key person to study as he is widely known as an expert on language development. He proposed that children are born with an innate mental structure that guides their acquisition of language and grammar. Chomsky also asserted that certain "universal features" that are common to all languages are innate (e.g., subject, verb, object). Perhaps, Chomsky is best known for the concept of a *critical period* for language and LAD.

Chomsky's views about language development center on the *interactionist view*. The interactionist perspective states that language is learned in the context of spoken language, but assumes as well that humans are in some way biologically prepared for learning to speak. Language interactions involve the interplay between a child's biology and social environment.

3. Brain areas involved in language

The left hemisphere of the cerebral cortex plays a primary role in language.

- **Broca's area:** Located in the frontal portion of the left hemisphere, this brain area supports grammatical processing and *expressive* language production.

- **Wernicke's area:** Located in the medial temporal lobe, this section of the brain supports word-meaning comprehension and *receptive language*.

D. Tests and Statistical Concepts

Note: For most measurements or statistical questions on the *Praxis* exam, you will most likely be asked how to interpret assessment results rather than calculate complex psychometrics. If you have to calculate a metric on the exam, it will probably be simple statistics such as the range, mode, mean, or median from a set of scores.

1. **Types of tests, evaluations, and assessments**

   a. **Cognitive abilities tests:** Cognitive tests are norm-referenced scientific instruments that psychologists use to measure human abilities that are strongly correlated to a host of outcomes. Examples of common cognitive abilities tests include the WISC-V, SB-V, and DAS-II. These tests are sometimes referred to as intelligence quotient (IQ) or aptitude tests; although some experts indicate there are differences between these terms, many practitioners still use the names interchangeably. Some psychologists use cognitive tests as a way to *predict future learning* success and to discern a student's profile of learning. Selection and placement decisions typically involve predictions about future learning or performance based on the present learning characteristics of an individual. Despite some controversy related to cognitive testing, these instruments remain a primary scientific resource to explain *why* students may have difficulty learning or not making progress in school.

   b. **Formative evaluations:** There are specific assessments used to determine a student's strengths and weaknesses. Formative evaluations typically evaluate the academic areas in which students are doing well and areas in which they are doing poorly. The results are used to guide and inform future instruction. Formative assessments can be low-stakes benchmarking tests that are given before a new class or learning a new concept.

   c. **Summative evaluations:** These provide a review and summary of a person's accomplishments to date. These evaluations are generally provided at the end of a grading period (after a formative evaluation) to provide a summary of student achievement.

   d. **Achievement tests:** These are a type of performance test that describes the skills a person has learned in school. Achievement tests are concerned with the mastery of a type of skill such as reading, writing, and math. These tests can be formal and norm-referenced such as cognitive tests. Well-known tests of achievement include the Woodcock–Johnson Test of Achievement and Wechsler Achievement Test.

   e. **Domain-referenced and criterion-referenced tests:** These are tests concerned with the level mastery of a defined skill set. Their purpose is solely to assess a student's standing on a defined standard (e.g., criterion) or performance of a specific skill. The test itself and the domain of content it represents provide the standard. These tests are not norm-referenced or standardized.

f. **Norm-referenced tests:** Normed tests evaluate a student's performance in relation to the performance of a general *reference* group. The quality of performance is defined by comparison with the behavior of others. Scores are described in terms of how far a student deviates from the mean (average) of a group. Scores fall on a normal curve of scores.

2. **Types of psychometric test scores and norms**

a. **Percentile ranks:** A *percentile rank* of a score is the percentage of scores (students) in its frequency distribution that are equal to or lower than it. An example is a student with a score at the 33rd percentile who has scored better than or equal to 33% of those who took the same test. Although most people understand percentile ranks, *the major problem with this metric is that it is not an equal interval measurement.*

b. **Grade norms and equivalents:** Students are matched to grade groups whose performance they equal. Average scores are obtained from individuals in a grade and compared with the grade group that their performance matches. An example is a student with a grade equivalent of 3.5, which means the student is performing as an average child in the fifth month of her third-grade year. **Caution:** Grade equivalent scores should rarely be used because they are considered poor metrics.

c. **Age norms and equivalents:** Age equivalents (AEs) are similar to grade equivalents. An individual is matched to the AE whose performance he or she equals. AE is the average score earned by individuals at a specific age. *As with other unequal interval metrics, this type of score should be used with a high degree of caution.*

d. **Standard scores (SSs):** SSs are psychometrically sound measures and are used to describe a person's position within the normal curve (bell curve) of human traits. These scores express the position of a score in relation to the average (mean) of other scores. SSs use standard deviations (SDs) in their formulas and place a student's score as below average, average, or above average. Mainstream cognitive test batteries typically use an SS with a mean of 100 and an SD of 15 (e.g., SS = 85–115 is average). *Most psychologists are encouraged to use SSs when possible and not other types of scores such as age equivalents.*

e. **Z-scores:** Z-scores have a mean of 0 and an SD of 1. They are not used much in education or in education reports.

f. **T-scores:** T-scores are *common scores* and they have a mean of 50 and an SD of 10 (T = 40–60 is average)

g. **Scaled scores (Ss):** Ss are *commonly reported* and they typically have a mean of 10 with an SD of 3 (Ss = 7–13 is average).

h. **Stanines**: A standard nine-point scale (stanine) is an SS used with a few educational tests. Stanines (also used within normal distributions such as Z- and T-scores) have a mean of 5, and each stanine unit represents one half of an SD (see Figure 1.1).

3. **Basic statistical terms used in descriptions of the normal (bell) curve (Figure 1.1)**

- **Range:** The difference between the highest and lowest scores within an entire set of scores.

- **Median:** The *middle* score in a set of scores wherein 50% of scores fall on either side of the middle score.

- **Mode:** The *most frequently* occurring score in a set of scores.

- **Mean:** The *average* score of a set of scores. The mean is found by adding all the scores in a set together and dividing by the total number of scores. This is regarded as one of the best measures of central tendency.

- **Variance:** A measure of how far a set of numbers is spread out.

- **SD:** A measure of the spread of a set of values from the mean value. The SD is the square root of the variance. It is a measure of dispersion. SD is used as a measure of the spread or scatter of a group of scores as a way to express the relative position of a single score in a distribution. As mentioned previously, most common CogAT batteries express their full-scale SS with a mean of 100 and an SD of 15 to indicate the "average range" (85–115 = average).

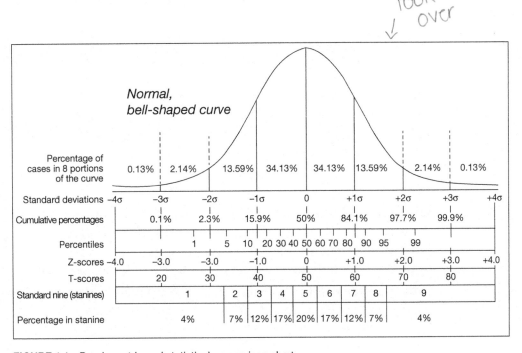

FIGURE 1.1 Psychometric and statistical comparison chart.

4. **Key test concepts: Reliability and validity of measurement (for formal standardized tests)**

   a. **Reliability:** Reliability refers to standardized test results and scores that are *consistent and stable across time*. Reliability is a crucial foundation for any test. If a test does not have adequate reliability, then the accuracy of the results is called into question. For example, assuming no intervention is provided, a test taker should score approximately the same on a test when given the same or similar test at a later time.

   - **Reliability coefficient:** This statistic illustrates the *consistency* of a score or the *stability* of a score. An appropriate reliability coefficient for standardized tests should generally be around or above $r = 0.80$. The higher the reliability coefficient, the better.

   - **Standard error of measurement (SEM):** This metric is an estimate of error used when interpreting an individual's test score. With every test, there are errors because of a host of factors. Test results rarely provide the "true score" because of error. SEM plays a pivotal role in calculating reliability.

     Note: It is doubtful you will have to actually calculate SEM or other complex psychometrics on the *Praxis* exam.

   - Methods to assess reliability:

     - **Test–retest:** Testing a person with the same test twice. The two scores are then correlated together using statistical methods. Theoretically, both scores should be highly similar if the test is reliable. A 2-week time interval between retaking the test is the minimal time frame recommended.

     - **Alternate and parallel forms:** Alternate forms of a test should be thought of as two tests built according to the same specifications, but composed of separate samples from the defined behavior domain. This method takes into account variation resulting from tasks and correlation between two test forms to provide the reliability coefficient.

     - **Split half:** Take a full test and create two tests from it, being careful to share difficult and easy items on both tests. Both tests are administered, even on the same day, and the scores on both tests are correlated.

     - **Internal consistency reliability**: An estimate of the reliability of the total test is developed from an analysis of the statistics of the individual test items. Each test item is compared with the total set of items. This statistic is expressed in terms of Cronbach's alpha.

     - **Interrater reliability:** The reliability of people administrating the test is increased by increasing the number of raters or judges. Rater's results on an assessment should be highly congruent for the test to be considered reliable.

b. **Validity:** Like reliability, validity is vital to a test's effectiveness and usefulness. Validity regards the degree to which *the test actually measures what it claims it measures*. To put it another way, validity is the degree to which evidence and theory support the interpretation of test scores. As stated with reliability coefficients, validity coefficients are acceptable if they are generally above 0.80. The higher the coefficient, the better.

- **Criterion-related validity:** Criterion validity concerns the correlation between two measures (tests) that are designed to measure human traits. If two tests measure the same trait, the correlation between the tests should obviously be higher. If one of the two tests is not designed to measure the same trait, the correlation should be lower between the two tests.

  - **Face and content validity:** This involves how rational and reasonable the test and test items look. During test construction, experts in the area being examined are asked to evaluate whether test items look logical. For example, a math test would be considered invalid if all test items asked about world history.

  - **Convergent validity:** Convergent validity is determined when a test is correlated with another test that has a similar purpose and measures the same trait. For example, if a test that measures attention deficit hyperactivity disorder (ADHD) correlates highly or "converges" with another well-known test of ADHD, then the test is said to have good validity.

  - **Divergent validity:** Divergent validity is established by correlating two tests that measure two different traits. For example, a test that measures ADHD should have a low correlation to a test that measures depression.

- **Construct-related validity:** This refers to whether a trait or construct is being measured.

  - **Predictive validity:** A valid test should have high predictive value. For example, a valid test of cognitive ability should be able to predict a student's achievement in school. A student with an SS of 75 on a cognitive test is *predicted* to struggle in school and to perform below grade level.

  - **Discriminant validity:** A valid test should be able to discriminate between students who have the trait being measured and those who do not have the trait. For example, a student scoring high on an anxiety measure could be identified with an anxiety problem from a group of students that do not have an anxiety problem.

5. **Confounding factors that may influence test reliability and validity**
   - Motivation and lack of effort when taking the test
   - Personal issues, such as lack of sleep, fatigue, or stress
   - Anxiety issues and test anxiety

- Language difficulty or not understanding directions
- Environmental factors, such as noise, lights, and distractions
- Values and beliefs of the test taker
- Racial bias
- SES of the test taker
- Family dynamics that impact the student
- Mental health issues

6. **Additional testing considerations and terms**

- If a standardized test is administered with the use of an interpreter and the test is not normed on the special population related to the student being tested, this will have a profound impact on the reliability and validity of the results. *Note:* **The NASP does not encourage the use of standardized tests with interpreters if the test is not appropriately normed.** There is a chance that a test item on the *Praxis* exam will be related to this point. Understand the difficulties when testing ESL students.

- **False positives**: A student performs well on a test, but in actuality, the student is failing in the authentic environment. For example, a student scores high on a reading comprehension test, but has difficulty reading in class.

- **False negatives**: A student performs poorly on a test, but in actuality, the student is making acceptable progress in the authentic environment with little or no problem.

Insider Tip

Although you need to be highly familiar with all points outlined in this section, the key areas to focus on should center on RTI because of the current emphasis on this practice. Possible RTI test questions involve trend and data analysis, CBM, intervention strategies, and determining when to refer students for special education after RTI. For formal assessment exam questions, remember that it is best practice to always to use *multiple sources* of information, not just standardized testing. If you clearly understand how to interpret a WISC-V or DAS-II, you should be able to answer most standardized testing questions. You may not have to study *all* cognitive tests; just be familiar with lesser used tests. Remember that any formal measure used should have been created or re-normed in the past 10 years.

Domain 2: Consultation and Collaboration

School psychologists frequently lend their expertise to students, parents, staff, and other professionals in the community. There are effective methods to employ when involved in consultation or collaboration with other people. At the heart of a successful consultation is to first establish a positive helping relationship. After a rapport is established, the people you are helping would be more receptive to the information you provide them. The most difficult aspect of consultation is to gain trust and not to convey a sense of arrogance as an expert.

There are several theories regarding consultation, but they can be largely *divided into direct and indirect approaches*. Although direct approaches might be time efficient in the short term, indirect approaches with an emphasis on building another person's skills are methods endorsed by the NASP. Indirect consultation models may save school psychologists valuable time in the long run.

Note: The term "consultant" refers to the school psychologist. The "consultee" is typically a teacher or staff member, and the "client" is the child or the student. It should be highlighted that the client can also be a larger system such as a school or an organization. In organizational consultation, the consultant attempts to make broad structural changes that might be associated with the beliefs and values of the individuals who make up the culture of the organization.

I. Foundation of Consultation and Collaboration

(Building rapport: factors that influence effective relationships)

A. Consultant Personal Characteristics

1. **Openness, approachability, and warmth**: These key traits are built on one's nonverbal body language, tone of voice, facial expressions, and gestures.

2. **Sincerity and genuineness**

3. **Trustworthiness and confidentiality**: The consultee and client believe in your competence and your ability to hold private information. You must have both genuine interest and skills to help people.

4. **Empathy**: The consultant must have the ability to accurately perceive the feelings and values of the client and communicate this understanding to the client.

5. **Self-disclosers**: Statements that reveal something personal about oneself are most effective if used sparingly and at the proper time such as to build rapport or show experience with an issue that might offset challenges.

B. Student or Client Traits and Factors Influencing Consultation

1. **Student's age and developmental stage**

2. **Coping styles:** These may be emotional, reactive, thoughtful, or logical.
   - **Externalizing coping styles:** Example of externalized coping involve acting out, behavioral problems, fighting, and disrupting class. Students

with this coping style need interventions that are focused on positive skill building.

- **Internalizing coping styles:** Students with internalized styles may develop depression, shut down, or become nonresponsive. The consultant needs to employ strategies that foster rapport and understanding and that increase self-confidence and perception of control over situations.

3. **Personality traits:** These traits represent a student's level of openness, agreeableness, conscientiousness, extroversion, and so on.

II. Models of Consultation

A. Consultee-Centered Model

1. Focus on improving and enhancing competence and skills of the consultee.
2. This *indirectly* helps the client by building the skills of the consultee.
3. The consultant is considered as a problem-solving or skill-building expert.
4. The consultee has knowledge of the problem, issue, or situation at hand, but needs skills to properly address the problem.
   - **Role of consultant**
     - Identify effective treatments for the client and teach the consultee the way to meet client needs. Focus is on the consultee rather than the client and the way the consultee deals with the client.
     - Increase knowledge base or skill level of the consultee so that the consultee can deal with similar situations in the future.
     - Consultant may have to deal with the consultee's distorted view of the client.

B. Client-Centered Model

1. This model is not as favored as the consultee-centered model.
2. The client-centered model focuses on the student.
3. The consultant *directly* helps the client.
4. Interventions provided by the consultant are directed to the child and teaches the student skills.
5. It is effective on a single-case basis, but not effective for groups.
6. It is time intensive for the consultant.

C. Behavioral Model (Applies to Consultee- and Client-Centered Models)

1. The behavioral model is solution focused and collects data to effect behavior change in a person (empirically based model).

2. The goal is to reduce frequency of undesirable behavior by altering the relationship between the student behavior and the environment that prevents the consultee from working effectively with the client.

3. This prepares the consultee to deal with similar problems in the future.

- **Basic steps of the behavioral model**
  - Identify problem (critical stage to target efforts and interventions)
  - Implement plan
  - Monitor effectiveness
  - Evaluate and make needed changes to plan
- **Conjoint behavioral consultation** is a special type of behavioral model that supports meetings with all parties (e.g., parent, student, and staff).

III. Special Considerations

A. Multicultural and Cross-Cultural Issues

A multicultural consultation is a culturally sensitive, indirect service model. The consultant adjusts the consultation services to address the needs and cultural values of the consultee, client, or both. It is critical to respect and value other cultures.

B. Interagency and School–Community Collaboration

These link the client with community resources or school-based services within the school. Examples of school–community collaboration are:

- **Child centered:** Direct service to the student such as tutoring or mentoring
- **Family centered:** Service to parents or entire families such as parenting workshops, family counseling, and family assistance
- **School centered:** Donation of money or equipment, staff development, or classroom assistance
- **Community centered:** Outreach programs, artwork and science exhibits, and after-school programs

C. Consultation With Interpreters

The use of interpreters is encouraged and necessary to build rapport with families and students who do not speak English. When using interpreters, be mindful of speech rate and use brief, simple statements so that the interpreter can relay the information efficiently.

D. Barriers to Collaboration and Consultation

- Consultee or client resists participation
- Client is unable to make a time commitment

- Funding problems for community collaboration
- Lack of leadership
- Communication difficulties
- Unclear goals or unfocused goals
- Adversarial relationships with community experts (e.g., medical doctors)

Insider Tip

Although there are many consultation models geared toward specific people, it is important to focus on the benefits and liabilities of the consultee-centered model. An essential idea to keep in mind is that the NASP seems to endorse the indirect service model, which seeks to build the consultee's skills (i.e., teacher's skills) so that the consultee can help the student. If you have questions on the *Praxis* exam regarding the most effective model, it is probably the indirect service model. Read Dr. Gerald Caplan's work on consultation models (Caplan, Caplan, & Erchul, 1994).

Concepts to Remember

1. Many concepts within this domain pertain to psychological tests and their administration. Although you may know psychometric and statistical information, be prepared to *apply* such information regarding testing and assessments. For example, know how to answer "what if" questions about standardized tests. "What if a student has an overall SS of 72 on a cognitive test battery, but also has an overall SS of 88 on adaptive/functional assessments?"

2. "Best practice" suggests that school psychologists *use multiple sources of information* to identify children with disabilities or problems. Although standardized cognitive assessments are central in the assessment process, such tests cannot be used in isolation. Both *formal* and *informal* measures should be used to support or supplement decisions.

3. Be highly familiar with *all aspects of RTI* and interpretation of RTI data. Know common RTI assessments such as CBM and RTI interventions. Know the difference between CBA and CBM.

4. Reading difficulties are the primary reason for referral to a school's RTI process. Primary interventions for reading difficulties are related to phonological processing.

5. Be familiar with the major types of behavioral observational methods used in an emotional or behavioral assessment. Some common observational methods include narrative, interval, event, and ratings recording. The narrative method provides broad and narrow information from running records.

Interval recording uses time-sampling techniques. Event recording documents the target behavior as it occurs.

6. Be familiar with the *sources of error* typically associated with behavioral assessments. For example, many behavioral surveys may have observer or rater bias. When evaluating behavioral assessments, one must study the percentage of agreement between raters (interrater reliability). Also, observers should sample behavior more than once to increase reliability.

7. Observers during an observational assessment can be influenced by the "halo effect," fatigue, and personal biases. These factors are known as *confounding factors.*

8. Know the particular characteristics of several common behavioral and emotional assessments. Some common social and emotional assessments include the BASC, Minnesota Multiphasic Personality Inventory-2 (MMPI-2), Adolescent Psychopathology Scale (APS), Conner's (for ADHD), and the Beck Depression Scales. A question on the *Praxis* exam might ask, "Which test is used to evaluate inattention in children?" The answer in this example might be the Conner's Rating Scales.

9. Know how projective measures, such as the Human Figure Drawing Test, are used. Typically, such measures are used as a supplemental part of a battery of psychological tests. Also understand the benefits and limitations of projective assessments such as low psychometric reliability.

10. Be familiar with common "adaptive/functional" assessments such as the *Vineland* and the ABAS. Most school districts suggest that SSs on adaptive assessments *and* intelligence tests should be two SDs below the mean to identify children with intellectual disabilities (SS < 70).

11. Know the steps in conducting an **FBA** (analysis). The primary steps in an FBA include determining the **antecedents** of the behavior, the target **behavior** itself, and the **consequence** of the behavior. To help remember this general outline, think of A-B-C: antecedents (A), behavior (B), and consequences (C).

12. When analyzing a behavior for intervention, a psychologist should pay particular attention to the **intensity, frequency,** and **duration** of the behavior. These three characteristics of the behavior must have a significant negative impact on the student's classroom performance and/or social development in order to qualify for special education. *Note:* A student can be formally diagnosed with a disability by a nonschool expert, but the student may not qualify for special education services because there is no educational impact and the student is making reasonable educational progress.

13. Two main functions of a behavior are either to gain something positive or to escape or avoid something negative. In addition, cognitive-behaviorists believe that *attention, power, control, affiliation, and revenge* are key motivations for behavior. During an FBA, one of your hypotheses may center on these motivations for behavior.

14. Although usually found within the "interventions" domain, you should be familiar with the way to use assessment data to write an intervention plan. Remember to include positive strategies and a replacement behavior for the negative behavior in your plan. A key concept is to always link assessment to intervention.

15. Bell curve (e.g., normal curve) data represent normative information about typical human traits. The normal curve is based on a large population of people and reflects characteristic human abilities. Sixty-eight percent of people comprise the bulk (center) of the bell curve. Most standardized cognitive assessments are predicated on the normal curve theory. You must know most common normal curve psychometrics; primarily SSs, scale scores, percentile ranks, and T-scores. Test takers should know the primary advantages and disadvantages of each norm-referenced score.

16. Fluid intelligence refers to the ability to solve problems through reasoning. Fluid problem solving is not primarily based on previously learned facts, techniques, or language. Fluid reasoning is sometimes referred to as nonverbal reasoning, immediate problem solving, or simultaneous processing. Fluid thinking involves the ability to summarize and comprehend information to solve a task.

17. Crystallized intelligence refers to the ability to solve problems by applying learned facts and language. The verbal sections of IQ tests illustrate this type of intelligence. Cattell, Horn, and Carroll (CHC) are the chief theorists behind the fluid and crystallized intelligence model. *Know the CHC theory of test construction.*

18. Part of a social and emotional evaluation may include aspects of emotional intelligence, which is the ability to be aware of one's emotional state, regulate one's emotions, and accurately read the emotions of others. Research in this area shows that students with low emotional and social intelligence have undesirable life outcomes.

19. Authentic and ecological assessments are an integral part of any comprehensive assessment. These types of dynamic assessments usually include observations, interviews, and having the student perform a typical classroom task, such as reading. These tasks take place in the actual environment in which the behavior is normally seen.

20. When interpreting the results of major cognitive tests, it is best practice to start at the broadest level and then narrow your interpretation to the subtest level. The most valid score is usually the full-scale score, followed by the major domain or cluster scores. Single test item analysis is least reliable type of interpretation, but may reveal important qualitative information.

21. Know confounding factors that can interfere with obtaining accurate test results. Some major factors include motivation, fatigue, undisclosed vision or hearing difficulties, test anxiety, and stress.

22. Know how to test special populations. For example, know what special considerations are necessary when testing visually impaired students, hard of hearing students, and ESL students. Know how special accommodations may impact standardized test results and how to interpret or report these scores with caution.

23. Most common cognitive assessments have a mean (average) of 100 and an SD of 15 points. Therefore, if a student scores 118 on a cognitive test, that student is said to be slightly *over* 1 SD above the mean (above average).

24. Watch for tricky questions regarding SDs. Remember that an SS of 100 is average, not 50. An SS of 50 is considerably far below average on mainstream test batteries. However, a score that is in the 50th percentile (not percentage) is equal to an SS of 100.

25. Some questions might ask you to compare scores, so understand how to interpret SSs based on the interpretative range in which the scores fall.

26. **Ipsative scores** examine a pattern of scores within an individual's performance range to determine relative (to self) strengths and weakness. Ipsative scores compare scores on a test to the test taker rather than to a group.

27. **Criterion measurement** is *not* based on the bell curve (normal curve) of a population or a group, but it is based on a specific criterion, skill, or content to be mastered. Criterion measurement is typically used in self-paced studies and in RTI processes.

28. Remember it is best practice to give the range of scores that a test score falls within because of the SEM. SEM is used to develop confidence brackets (intervals or bandwidths) around a score from a standardized test and the confidence interval should be clearly stated on a formal report.

29. T-scores have a mean of 50 and an SD of 10. For example, a T-score of 65 would be above average and 1.5 SD above the mean. It is important not to confuse T-scores with SS.

30. A percentile is the percentage of people who score at or below the percentile score given on a test. Percentiles use percentages but are not percentages themselves. It is very important to understand that percentiles, like some other metrics, are *not equal interval statistics*. Consequently, unequal interval statistics tend to exaggerate score differences the farther from the mean the scores get.

31. The reason professionals prefer to use SSs is that they are "equal interval" scores, whereas other types of scores are not equal in their measurements of central tendency.

32. The *effect size* is a statistic that illustrates the overall effect of an intervention based on comparing the average (mean) performance of two groups. An effect size of 0.50 or more is typically considered large, 0.30 is moderate, and 0.10 is small.

33. Standardized testing follows very strict rules for administration, scoring, and interpretation. Such tests have verifiable statistical properties associated with the test's validity and reliability. The chief benefit of standardized tests is that they compare a person with what is expected of a large population and reveal what is *normal* performance for a given trait or skill.

34. Reliability is a vital characteristic for standardized tests. Reliability is the ability of a test to produce similar results over time. Cognitive test results remain somewhat stable (reliable) across time.

35. Validity is another critical test characteristic of all standardized tests. Validity is a test's ability to measure what it purports to measure. For example, a reading test measures the ability to read, not to solve math problems.

36. Be familiar with the different types of validity such as predictive, convergent, discriminative, and divergent validity. Typically, common standardized tests use convergent validity to support their use. An example of convergent validity is when a new test is correlated with an established test. If the new test has validity, it should have a high correlation with the established test. Also, it is important to note that a test can be highly reliable, but not necessarily valid.

37. A type I error is when you state that your test results are true, but in actuality they are not true (rejecting a null hypothesis). A type II error is stating something is false, but it is really true (accepting a null hypothesis).

38. Correlation is an association or relationship among variables. For example, research has shown a high correlation between smoking and lung cancer. However, remember that a strong correlation does not mean one variable *causes* another variable to change. Correlations above 0.80 are said to be strong and desirable for test purposes. Correlations are useful in predicting events. For example, IQ tests are useful in predicting a student's future grades. This is why when a child has a high IQ but low achievement (grades), it is believed that something is interfering with that child's learning.

39. To raise the "power" of an experiment or a test, you must increase the number and/or types of participants. Raising the power makes your experiment or test more reliable and valid. Typically, the number of subjects (N) starts to approximate bell curve characteristics at 50. The higher the N, the better.

40. The client-centered or direct consultation benefits only one client (i.e., the student). For example, when a teacher has a problem with a student, the school psychologist intervenes with the student. This method can produce desired results, but it is time-consuming. Generally speaking, it is *best practice to teach staff how to help themselves (indirect model)*.

41. The consultee-centered consultation benefits the teacher by building skills that might be used to help numerous other people. In other words, the psychologist helps the teacher develop new skills to support students.

42. Know the primary benefits and liabilities of the previous two models. Be able to compare and contrast models of consultation.

43. The program-centered administrative consultation model benefits an entire program or school. For example, a school psychologist performs an in-service for a school.

44. In a consultee-centered administrative model, a school psychologist teaches skills to other key administrators to effect change at many schools or a district.

45. A common problem-solving consultation format involves the following steps:

    a. Define the problem; be specific

    b. Analyze the problem and collect data if necessary

    c. Plan an intervention monitor and modify as necessary

    d. Evaluate your outcomes, compare pre/post data, and make changes

46. Other consultation models: The ecological (systems) model examines how a person's behavior is being maintained within various settings and systems. The process consultation model uses workgroups, feedback, and coordination among groups.

47. Review the special considerations related to particular consultation cases. Some considerations include cultural issues, barriers to clear communication, barriers to effective consultation, difficulties with community experts (e.g., medical doctors), and family consultation factors.

2

Second Test Category: Direct and Indirect Services for Children, Families, and Schools

In previous years, this section of the test was termed *Intervention* and *Prevention* (before 2010). It was also called *Research-Based Behavioral and Mental Health Practices*. Although the name has changed, the content is largely similar to previous editions of this guide with the exception that academic interventions are now placed within this area. During the last decade, a significant evolution to the field of education involved concepts related to response to intervention (RTI). Although most people associate RTI with academic interventions, it is also used for behavioral issues. Currently, some school districts and experts have rolled RTI and positive behavioral interventions and supports (PBIS) practices into a broader framework called Multi-Tiered System of Support (MTSS).

To prepare for this section of the test, students should have a dual approach. First, be familiar with broad interventions designed for moderate-sized groups such as classrooms. Next, focus on intervention techniques designed for targeted (narrower scope) subjects, such as individuals and counseling group practices. For example, it is important to review individual counseling techniques such as cognitive behavioral therapy (CBT), but also study schoolwide bully prevention strategies.

Figure 2.1 provides an effective visual representation of how RTI can be constructed as the broader framework through which specific intervention techniques can be nested. A critical concept of RTI is the division of interventions into primary, secondary, and tertiary categories. On the *Praxis*® exam, there is a probability that you may be asked hypothetical questions about interventions and you must identify if the interventions are examples of a primary, secondary, or tertiary method.

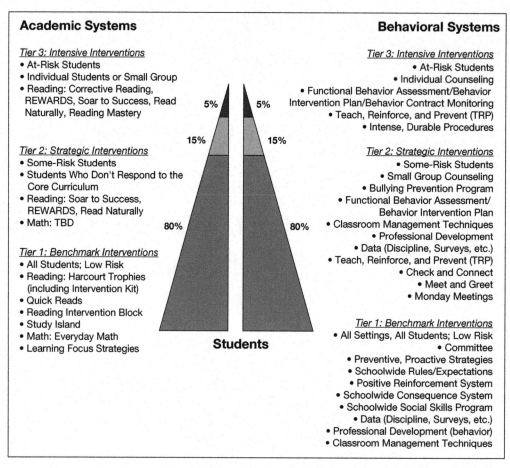

FIGURE 2.1   Response to intervention model: academic and behavioral concerns.
TBD, to be determined.

Study and Test-Taking Strategies

A helpful study suggestion is to segment your study notes to reflect major theories and practices under broad and narrow headings. You may also wish to divide your notes into mental health/behavioral interventions and also academic interventions. This division of content is illustrated in Figure 2.1.

When preparing to study mental health information, remember that students taking the *Praxis* exam must be versed in several intervention theories, not just their preferred approaches. Consequently, it is important to study the broad concepts from older venerable theories. Although there are many new techniques and intervention strategies, the majority of these ideas can trace their roots back to behavioral, cognitive, or developmental theories created several decades earlier.

Domain 1: Academic Interventions and Instructional Supports

School psychologists are expected to be experts in various types of human behaviors, especially those behaviors that pertain to learning. For the *Praxis* exam, be familiar with learning theories and current instructional practices. Learning is an intimate and personal process, and psychologists are keenly aware of the individual differences (learning styles) that influence how students acquire knowledge. Although teachers also understand the benefits of individualized instruction, in practice, teachers have great difficulty tailoring instruction for each student's learning style. There are myriad reasons why students struggle to learn, ranging from differences in cognitive abilities, to emotional problems, to family dynamics. Psychologists may be called upon by school staff for assistance with teaching students, especially those with disabilities.

I. Foundations of Effective Pedagogy and Instruction

A. Basic Principles of Effective Instruction

1. Activate a student's *prior knowledge* before teaching.

2. Make *connections* between new learning and a student's current knowledge. Make learning relevant to the student's life.

3. Do not overload students' abilities when teaching new concepts, especially their working memory. Working memory capacity is typically limited to four to seven bits of information.

4. Provide the optimum level of instruction, not too hard and not too easy. Have the student experience some success and some challenge. This concept is related to the *Zone of Proximal Development* (ZPD).

5. *Model* desired responses, have explicit expectations, and provide exemplars of completed work.

6. Allow time for practice. Provide *corrective feedback and frequent practice* of skills. Have cognitive rest periods (days) between teaching new concepts.

7. Feedback needs to be provided in an *immediate* and positive manner.

8. *Multimodal* teaching is good practice. Incorporate "learning by doing" when possible. Use visual, auditory, and kinesthetic modalities.

9. Student learning develops as target skills progress through phases: Acquisition → proficiency → generalization → adaptation.

B. Specific Instructional Strategies

Although RTI addresses some key interventions, school psychologists have to know several academic interventions and consult with teachers to support students that struggle to learn. The following are a *few examples* of common academic interventions that you should be aware of when studying for the exam.

Emphasis should be placed on the three core academic areas: reading, writing, and mathematics.

1. A good general model to follow when teaching is to have an **explicit and systematic approach** to presenting information. For example, students are told specifically *what* they are learning before their lesson starts every class period. Next, students are told *why* they need to learn the new concept(s). Third, the teacher models the new skill or concept. After new information is presented, students will practice with teacher feedback. Finally, students practice the skill over multiple trials. Explicit instruction also includes breaking down tasks or new concepts into small manageable steps. The steps to effective instruction involve the *"I do, we do, you do" approach.*

2. **Differentiated instruction** is critical when teaching groups. It requires educators to respond to the *individualized needs and abilities* of all learners within the regular education environment.

3. **Small-group instruction** allows the teacher to monitor student mastery of educational concepts, provide instant feedback, and accommodate individual learning needs.

4. **Cooperative learning**, proffered by the famous theorist Vygotsky, is a proven teaching technique. Students work collaboratively to learn new concepts. Students develop a greater understanding and respect for individual learning differences.

5. **Flexible grouping** and homogeneous grouping by skill level have been demonstrated to be effective for instruction. Changing students within groups is a good practice.

6. **Student engagement time** is a predictor of academic achievement and is defined as the amount of time that students are actively engaged in learning. Students need to be interested in the new concept or skill being taught. If students understand the reasons why learning the new concept is important and how it relates to their lives, they will be engaged. Students should have input in how they would like to be taught, and a teacher needs to create a safe classroom atmosphere that fosters free discussion (e.g., classroom management).

7. **Study skills** are critical to improving student achievement. **Metacognition** is an essential study skill that requires a high degree of self-awareness. Metacognition is thinking and reflecting about learning, what is known, and what is not known. A well-known and time-tested metacognitive technique used to build reading comprehension is *SQ3R*, which stands for survey, question, read, recite, and review.

II. RTI Model Explained: Broad to Narrow Concepts

Note: Although the concepts of RTI were introduced in Chapter 1, it is elaborated here because of its use as an intervention method, not just an assessment. It is also important to consider that school psychology training programs are moving away from isolated RTI models and into broader models that incorporate RTI into a system of comprehensive support. As of this writing, RTI questions are still found on the licensure exam and in the recommendations offered by the National Association of School Psychologists (NASP)/Educational Testing Service (ETS). The following examples illustrate the **intervention** side of the pyramid (Figure 2.1). It is important to remember that RTI can focus on both academic and behavioral issues.

A. Tier 1 (Broadest Area): Primary Prevention

This area is typically referred to as the *universal level*. This primary level involves the application of **universal interventions**.

Example of Tier 1 intervention: Positive behavior support (PBS) key ideas:

- School discipline policy is aligned with all tenets of PBS.
- Five critical features of effective PBS programs:
  1. Establish and define clear and consistent schoolwide expectations.
     - Identify three to five behavioral expectations that are specific to the needs and culture within the school. Rules should be *positively* stated.
  2. Specifically teach schoolwide expectations to all students.
  3. Acknowledge students for demonstrating the expected behaviors.
  4. Develop clear and consistent consequences to respond to infractions and violations.
     - The school should clearly identify consistent staff responses for behavioral infractions and should include a teaching and psychoeducational component.
  5. Use objective data to evaluate schoolwide efforts.

B. Tier 2: Strategic Interventions

These techniques are more targeted in scope than those at the universal level, but are less so than the intensive (targeted) level. An *example* of Tier 2 intervention is the bully prevention program.

Research indicates that approximately 20% to 30% of students are consistently involved in bullying as victims, the bully, or both. Bullying is based on the maintenance of a chronic and purposeful power imbalance within a relationship. Although some prescriptive antibully programs are effective, it is good practice to develop a system-wide structure in a school where the *culture* does not support harassment. Because of the significance of bullying in schools, more information about this topic is provided in this section.

Elements of effective bullying prevention programs (be familiar with, not necessary to memorize):

- Raise adult and student awareness about bullying issues. Staff commitment is critical.

- Address bystander behavior.
- Create a building-wide (systemic) process or culture to address bullying.
- Address student beliefs that support bullying; focus on decreasing victims of bullying, not necessarily eliminating bullies.
- Address student social–emotional skill deficits. Provide assertiveness training.
- Accurately assess bullying and victimization. Consider a survey to question types of victimization (e.g., rumors, physical harassment, teasing, sexual harassment).
- Develop a specific and clear school policy regarding bullying, especially cyberbullying.
- **Key intervention**: Increase adult monitoring on the playground, in lunch areas, hallways, and other open unstructured areas.
- Improve class climate. Staff should model the skills they want their students to use.
- Zero-tolerance policies are discouraged.
- Common effective antibullying programs are Olweus Bullying Prevention and Expect Respect.
- Build basic behavioral and cognitive social skills reinforcing prosocial attitudes and behaviors and build adaptive coping strategies for social problems.

C. Tier 3: Intensive (Targeted) Level

Typically, this level involves direct contact with the student who is having emotional or behavioral difficulties. Sometimes, small groups are identified where a student can receive a higher level of support or intervention.

Example of Tier 3 intervention: *Individual counseling* that uses CBT and role-playing of correct behavior. A *functional behavioral assessment* (FBA) may also be employed to examine the specific antecedents, actions, and consequences of the behavior.

Domain 2: Mental Health Interventions and Related Services

I. Mental Health and Behavioral Interventions (Individual and Small Group)

Interventions can take many forms. One of the most common forms of student intervention is counseling. Effective counseling is predicated upon genuine and positive rapport. The examiner needs to be well versed in most of the major theories of individual counseling, ethics, and laws. In general, before individual or small-group counseling commences, the school psychologist should adhere to the following ethical principles.

A. Ethical Principles of Counseling

1. Obtain **parental consent** if a student is to receive ongoing services. A student can be seen before consent is acquired if **safety** is an issue.

2. Students should be informed of **confidentiality** and **exceptions** to confidentiality from the beginning of counseling sessions.

   - Exceptions:

     Harm to self or others

     Safety concerns

     Student request

3. Before counseling commences, explicit **goals should be stated** and progress on goals should be monitored.

B. Major Types of Individual Counseling, Interventions, and Theoretical Approaches

1. **CBT:** CBT is based on the premise that thoughts influence feelings and ultimately control behavior. CBT is one of the most *highly effective interventions* supported by research. Practitioners typically intervene with a student's faulty beliefs (cognition) and *role-play* appropriate behaviors for given situations.

2. **Cognitive therapy:** This therapy is related to reality therapy, which was developed by William Glasser. Cognitive therapy's emphasis is on cognition and beliefs. Behavioral interventions, although important, are not the focus with this type of counseling. The psychologist tries to get the student to understand and think about the connection between behaviors and consequences.

3. **Solution-focused counseling:** This type of counseling incorporates CBT principles, but it is typically very brief and focused on stated outcomes.

4. **Behavioral and behaviorism techniques:** Behavioral interventions focus less on counseling and more on direct behavioral interventions. Behaviorism is favored by most schools because it is highly practical and forms the basis of an FBA. B. F. Skinner is regarded as the father of behaviorism and he placed an emphasis on the consequences of behavior. Skinnerian approaches believe that most behavior is shaped and maintained by the consequences that follow one's actions.

5. **Humanistic approaches:** Developed by Abraham Maslow and Carl Rogers, behavioral change cannot occur without a strong positive rapport built on unconditional positive regard and empathy. Students want to be understood by a trusted adult before they can move to change their lives.

6. **Bibliotherapy:** Bibliotherapy is a type of cognitive intervention. The therapist generally uses a student's own problem-solving skills and attempts to have the student relate to a character in a story to learn a lesson or skill that will be applicable to the student's current situation. It is important to consider a student's level of cognitive ability when implementing this type of intervention.

7. **Dialectical behavior therapy (DBT):** DBT is a type of a cognitive behavioral approach that is designed to build specific skills to help students cope with various stressors. DBT attempts to build skills related to *four primary areas*: *mindfulness, stress tolerance, interpersonal skills (assertiveness),* and *emotional regulation.*

8. **Motivational interviewing**: This is a student-centered, goal-oriented approach that is designed to *increase intrinsic motivation* of the student to accomplish positive personal outcomes.

9. Behaviorists use the **Premack Principle** to modify behavior. This principle emphasizes that a desirable task can reinforce a lower-level task. For example, a child may eat a cookie (higher level task) after he or she finishes homework (lower level task).

10. **Social learning theory** states that people learn not only through reinforcers and punishers (i.e., B. F. Skinner's behaviorism), but also through observation. Albert Bandura illustrated that children can act aggressively by merely watching the violent behavior of others. The keyword to remember for Bandura's research is "modeling."

11. **Kohlberg's stages of moral development:** (a) The preconventional stage is usually for children in whom behavior is motivated by avoidance of punishments; (b) the conventional stage is where most people are situated—it focuses on conformity to social norms and approval of others; and (c) the postconventional stage centers on high ethics and moral principles of conscience (i.e., personal principles, not just laws of society).

12. Be familiar with **Piaget's theories** because these stages are important to know when developing services and supports for children at various ages. Piaget's stages are as follows: Sensorimotor, Preoperational, Concrete, and Formal. According to Piaget, human development is the progressive adaptation to the environment through *assimilation and accommodation*. Infants are biologically predisposed to develop and acquire information by interacting with their environment. For example, a child who thinks a dime is worth less than a nickel because it is physically smaller soon learns through play or "pretend" spending that it is actually worth more.

13. Be familiar with **Erik Erikson's psychosocial stages** as they relate to school-aged children: trust versus mistrust, autonomy versus shame, initiative versus guilt, industry versus inferiority, and identity versus role confusion.

14. Freudian or psychoanalytic theory may be on some tests, but my research has not revealed that this area is the basis for more than just one or two questions. It seems Freud's contributions to school psychology are broad in nature. Instead of memorizing his stages of development, I would be familiar with the Freudian concepts that are not controversial and are practical in nature. For example, Freud was one of the first psychologists to realize the importance of "critical periods" and the significance of early experiences. Be familiar with how the id, ego, and superego interact.

C. Group Counseling

During group counseling, a therapist can employ many of the same techniques used in individual counseling. The following are important beneficial characteristics of group counseling:

- Is time efficient
- Often found within the Tier 2 intervention level
- Promotes social learning
- Promotes skill generalization

D. Service Learning

Having children help or serve others is a very effective learning tool because it teaches children in an "authentic" or real-life environment. Many times, service learning teaches students social–emotional competency and *empathy* for those they are helping.

- **Three benefits related to service learning:**
  1. Learning is effective because students are engaged and curious about issues they experience in the real world.
  2. Students remember lessons that they learn within the community context because they are real and relevant.
  3. Service learning connects students to personal relationships and promotes prosocial actions that make a difference in people's lives.

E. Applied Behavior Analysis (ABA) and Intervention

This strict behavioral intervention is typically employed with students that have autism. Sometimes ABA is referred to as a radical behaviorism approach because of the focus on overt behaviors.

- ABA uses systematic instruction and repeated trials to change behavior. ABA is usually highly structured and can use adult-directed strategies, as seen in Lovaas training or discrete trial training.
- Systematic strategies may include incidental teaching, structured teaching, pivotal response training, functional communication training, and the Picture Exchange Communication System.
- Discrete trial instruction as part of ABA is a systematic way of teaching that involves a series of repeated trials to teach and maintain cognitive, behavioral, or social skills.
- Task analysis (key component of behaviorism) involves breaking down a skill into smaller steps that are easy to teach. Prompts are used to guide learners toward correct responses when teaching tasks. In the beginning, prompts are more obvious and then gradually fade away (e.g., fading techniques). Types of prompts include physical (hand over hand), gestural (pointing), modeling, and visual.

F. Restorative Justice/Restorative Practices

Restorative justice is an approach that emphasizes repairing the harm caused by inappropriate behavior. It is best accomplished through cooperative processes that include all students involved in an incident. The focus is not on punishment, but rather restoring relationships built on mutually agreed upon responsibilities and boundaries.

G. Other Behavioral Interventions and Important Considerations

Behavioral interventions should be tailored to the student's developmental and intellectual level.

- Time-out can be an effective intervention if not used as a punishment. Time-out or sensory breaks are effective with very young children.

- As mentioned in the previous chapter, best practice in behavioral management is to conduct an FBA on a student who has behavioral problems and modify the environment as much as possible. In short, emphasize decreasing the triggering event (antecedents) and focus on a "goodness of fit" between the student and the environment.

- When using response cost, students earn tokens based on positive classroom behavior and lose them for inappropriate behavior.

- Self-management strategies are self-directed activities that require children to monitor and/or evaluate their behavior over time. This intervention is effective with older students.

- Understand differences between the behaviorist model and the cognitive model. The behaviorist model involves the structures of the environment and provides reinforcement and punishment. Generally, behaviorism takes the position that a child learns from reinforcement and punishment. In contrast, the cognitive model is based on theories of human thinking. The child is seen as an active participant who interprets information that is received, relates it to previously acquired facts, organizes it, and stores it for later use.

- Understand that there is a difference between *theoretical counseling and behavioral techniques* and *specific intervention programs*. Theoretical approaches are created from institutions of higher learning and expert research. Theoretical approaches typically take years to be developed, and they are heavily critiqued over years of publication. Do not confuse specific interventions that are programs, such as *Zones of Regulation*, with major theoretical approaches to interventions like CBT. Some programs might be *based* on theories such as CBT, but are not considered broad psychological theory. On the exam, test takers might have a few questions regarding specific intervention programs, but these items will likely include only very well-known intervention programs (e.g., Olweus Bullying Prevention program).

- **Classwide peer tutoring** is a proactive intervention to help all students. It is similar to Vygotsky's theory on collaborative learning.

  - Classwide social skills interventions should follow a modeling approach called the Tell-Show-Do-Practice-Generalize approach.

read

II. Common Disorders: Child and Adolescent Psychopathology and Learning Disabilities

The reader should review developmental disabilities and disorders typically associated with special education. Be able to _recognize_ hallmark traits, etiology, and prevalence rates for various disabilities. For example, know the traits associated with autism and pervasive developmental disorder (PDD), ~~Fragile X syndrome~~, Down syndrome, intellectual disability (ID), bipolar disorder, and attention deficit hyperactivity disorder (ADHD). Of particular consideration, know the nature and treatments associated with posttraumatic stress disorder (PTSD) as this disorder is commonly diagnosed in people after exposure to a crisis. On the _Praxis_ exam, crisis scenario questions are common, so be prepared to apply your knowledge in this area.

Important Notes: For the diagnosis of a true disorder, the problem must significantly impede general life functioning. In school systems, lower-level criteria are required to qualify a student for special education than for a diagnosis of a clinical disorder. Because of the previous reason, the term _identification_ is used in schools instead of the term _diagnosed disorder_. In the latter case, to be formally identified for an individual education plan (IEP), a student _must_ have educational impact because of his or her difficulties, or significant social impact, not just a diagnosis of a clinical disorder. It is a good idea for school psychologists to be aware of the differences between identification of a "disability" for school purposes and clinical "disorders" as outlined by the _Diagnostic and Statistical Manual of Mental Disorders_ (4th ed., text rev. [_DSM-IV-TR_], American Psychiatric Association [APA], 2000; and 5th ed. [_DSM-5_], APA, 2013).

Although the _DSM-5_ has officially supplanted the _DSM-IV-TR_, there are school psychology training programs that still focus on the _DSM-IV-TR_. A few experts assert that some information in the _DSM-5_ is controversial and may have less support from professionals than previous versions. Some controversial aspects of the _DSM-5_ include the absorption of Asperger's syndrome into autism spectrum disorder. Also, the addition of disruptive mood dysregulation disorder in the _DSM-5_ has been criticized. Although there are very few _DSM_ questions on the exam, it is important to be familiar with major categories of disorders and criticisms of the new version. The following is a good resource on the _DSM-5_: **www.isst-d.org/downloads/DSM-5website.pdf**

Common Childhood Disorders

- **ADHD:** ADHD is considered one of the most prevalent disorders seen in schools and usually co-occurs with other problems such as learning disabilities (LDs). In large schools, typically 3% to 7% of the population is diagnosed with ADHD. The disorder impacts boys more than girls, with a 3:1 ratio commonly cited. Hallmark traits of ADHD include impulsivity, inability to sustain attention, constant movement, and lack of self-regulation. ADHD may be "combined type" or "predominately hyperactivity type." ADHD may have genetic roots. Dopamine and neuroepinephrine deficiencies that cause prefrontal lobe brain dysfunction are implicated in this disorder. ADHD is largely responsive to medication treatments. Prenatal nicotine or other drug usage by the mother may be risk factors.

- **Anxiety disorder:** Anxiety is a common disorder in society, typically with 3% to 5% prevalence rate and a 2:1 ratio in favor of females. Anxiety disorder may have genetic links in some cases. Anxiety can be generalized or specific (e.g., phobias). Humans have psychological vulnerability to highly stressful or chronic stress events. PTSD is a common reaction to acute stress, trauma, and crisis.

- **PTSD:** PTSD is a subset of anxiety disorder. PTSD is a common and persistent extreme reaction to very stressful or traumatic events. People with PTSD have recurrent nightmares, hypersensitivity to environmental triggers, avoidant behaviors, and constant recounting of the stressful situation. Trauma reaction in children is a current area of attention in mainstream research. Study the effects of trauma and intervention supports for this disorder.

- **Depression:** Like anxiety, major depressive disorder has a high prevalence rate, with stated figures for males of 3% to 5% and 8% to 10% for females. Depression may have genetic links, but it also has strong situational and environmental causes. Medication is effective in many cases. Depression treatment using a combined approach of therapy and medication is most effective.

- **Bipolar disorder:** This disorder has biological underpinnings that create large mood fluctuations from depression to elation. Underactivation in the left temporal brain lobe and executive dysfunction have some research support as the cause of this disorder. It is generally responsive to a combination of counseling and medication.

- **Conduct disorder (CD) and oppositional defiant disorder (ODD):** Although some research indicates that CD may have some genetic or biological influences, school systems generally regard CD as a behavioral disorder that is mostly the result of interactions between the environment and the individual. Factors causing CD may include inadequate parenting, peer rejection, academic failure, poverty, or low cognitive abilities. A student's skill deficits related to subpar coping is also a contributing factor for CD. For the purpose of an IEP, qualification may not include CD or ODD because of the belief that this disorder has a volitional choice component.

- **Autism and PDD:** PDD spectrum disorders impact more males than females; there is a relatively low incidence of this disorder. Prevalence rates for autism spectrum disorders used to range about 1 in every 2,500 people, but now are stated to be 1 in 88. Controversy surrounds the previous figure because of changes in diagnosing the disorder and whether Asperger syndrome is counted as autism. Asperger syndrome rates are higher than the rates for autism. As mentioned, the new *DSM-5* makes the previous diagnostic categories and prevalence rates questionable.

Students studying spectrum disorders should also know key interventions. Behavior modification, "shaping," and direct hands-on teaching with pictures (visuals) are common interventions for children with autism. Also, the use of toys, increased structure, motor imitation, and family participation are useful methods. Currently, there is no cure for autism. Genetics and brain abnormalities are implicated as the cause.

- **Down syndrome (trisomy 21):** Down syndrome impacts 1 out of 700 to 800 people. The disorder is believed to be caused by an extra chromosome (chromosomal disorder). Most children with this disorder have lower cognitive abilities than the general population. Interventions associated with this disorder include hands-on learning, tight structure in the classroom, visual communication systems, and social skills training. There is no cure for Down syndrome.

- **Tourette syndrome:** Tourette syndrome is a tic disorder with a possible genetic component that can be evinced by extremely stressful events or a virus in the brain. Relaxation, social skills training, medication, and cognitive behavioral interventions are widely used with this disorder. This disorder may involve involuntary twitching and facial expression or verbal outbursts. Tics may become more apparent after the use of stimulant medication to treat a co-occurring problem like ADHD or anxiety disorder.

- **ID:** This disability is typically identified by formal cognitive and functional assessments. On cognitive tests, ID students typically have standard scores (SSs) below 70. Students with SSs ranging from 55 to 69 are considered mildly impaired, SSs from 40 to 54 are moderately impaired, and SSs below 40 are in the severe range. In addition to low cognitive test scores, a student must perform significantly low on adaptive and functional life skill measures such as the Vineland or Adaptive Behavior Assessment System (ABAS), Third Edition to receive this diagnosis.

  Note: Significant limited intellectual capacity (SLIC) is equivalent to the term intellectual disability (ID). This term changed in 2012 and now most practitioners use ID. As with ID, children who have an SLIC identification on an IEP must have standard IQ scores at least 2 standard deviations below the mean (SS = 70) *and* adaptive skills, as measured by standardized surveys, also below 70.

- **Significant identifiable emotional disability (SIED or SED):** As with LDs, schools use SIED or SED as an umbrella term that captures anxiety disorders, depression, and other mental health problems. The key to this disability is that children must be impacted in various settings, and one of these settings must be school. Emotional disturbances cannot be because of temporary situational factors, and interventions must have been attempted before qualification for special education services.

  Note: The SIED term is changing to **significant emotional disability (SED).** A school identification of SED will emphasize a child's emotional disability and will generally not be based on CD or chronic willful behaviors.

Disabilities That Impact Learning

- **Speech and language disabilities:** Children with these disabilities have difficulty with expressive and/or receptive language. Oral motor dysfunctions result in speech difficulties. Language disorders are broadly situated in the left hemisphere of the brain. Although different states use various standards to qualify for language disorders, qualifying language tests typically have scores that fall below the ninth percentile. Common speech–language assessments are the Clinical Evaluation of Language Fundamentals and Peabody tests.

- **Dyslexia:** Dyslexia is a diagnostic term for reading disorders. Schools rarely use this term on an IEP and instead use "reading difficulties," or specific learning disability (SLD). Most reading problems are linked to a phonological processing dysfunction. However, there is a minority of children whose reading problems are tied to visual processing problems. Proper assessment of dyslexia involves assessment of phonological processes (e.g., phonemic awareness, segmentation, and sound deletion). Simple word-rate reading is an effective evaluation tool.

  Note: Reading difficulties are one of the most common reasons for special education and RTI referrals. It is estimated that between 3% and 7% of the student population has a reading disorder, but this statistic may be a low estimate. Although phonological training and direct reading instruction are highly effective interventions, students with both phonological processing difficulties and fluency deficits are resistant to remediation.

- **Dyscalculia:** This is a diagnostic term for mathematical disorders. Students with mathematical or quantitative reasoning difficulties have a prevalence rate of 2% to 5% within the population, but this figure might be a low estimate. Tests frequently employed to discern dyscalculia are the Key Math Test and spatial and working memory subtests from various cognitive ability tests.

- **Dysgraphia**: Dysgraphia is a writing disability. *Dysgraphia* is sometimes referred to as a transcription disability, meaning that it is a writing disorder associated with impaired handwriting, orthographic coding, and difficulty organizing thoughts to write. Students with dysgraphia have substantial trouble writing cogent sentences, paragraphs, and/or papers. This disability is estimated to impact 5% to 27% of students, which is a large variance because of the relatively low number of research studies in this area. The higher incident rates are associated with very young children. As children age and respond to interventions, the rates of dysgraphia improve.

- **SLD:** SLD is a practical term schools use to capture various learning problems such as dyslexia, dyscalculia, or spelling disorders. In short, SLD is an umbrella term that encompasses several types of learning problems.

Other Important Terms Related to School Difficulties

- **English as a second language (ESL):** Foreign students are typically placed in ESL classes in schools because they do not fully understand the English language. It seems the NASP desires ESL students be provided education in *both* languages. Full immersion or instruction only within a child's native language is generally not supported.

- **Readiness:** This term is used to denote a student's biological and physiological maturational level to enter school (usually kindergarten).

- **Learned helplessness:** This term was coined by Martin Seligman. Learned helplessness describes a behavior that results from the belief that one cannot control the events in one's environment. People with a learned helplessness belief are prone to depression, fatalistic perspectives, low self-esteem, and low achievement. People who believe events happen to them with little control have an *external, not an internal control orientation. Students with an internal locus of control are typically more successful in school.*

- **Theory of the mind:** Theory of the mind refers to when a person begins to understand that other people have their own private thoughts, perspectives, and feelings. This theory is associated with autism.

Insider Tip

Because of the broad nature of this section's content, it will be difficult to know what to memorize. An effective approach to studying this area is to have a firm, but broad understanding of research-based approaches to social–emotional interventions and relevant theories. Know best practices for this content area and NASP position statements. A broad understanding of best intervention practices is highly useful to guide your responses on the *Praxis* exam. In general, best practice is predicated upon having a multifactored view of intervention and a realization that people will respond differently to problems and situations. If you understand CBT, you can answer several intervention questions. Behaviorism is favored by schools, so know FBA strategies. Crisis intervention in schools is based more on humanistic principles than behaviorism. Finally, study suicide and threat issues as these are a psychologist's most serious duties.

Concepts to Remember

Mental Health, Behavioral Intervention, and Related Concepts

1. Be able to compare and contrast at least two primary aspects for each of the major counseling theories. Many of these theories are presented clearly in undergraduate introductory psychology texts. Your university's library should have a few undergraduate introductory textbooks. It will be well worth your time to review these major counseling theories. Although you

might not be asked to *name* a specific theory or expert, you should know how to *apply* the principles of a venerable theory in a school setting.

2. Do not spend time studying nonmainstream or uncommon interventions, counseling strategies, or theories. Your time is best spent understanding well-known and widely adopted psychological interventions.

3. Person-centered humanistic counseling strives for congruence between the real and ideal self. Its aim is to actualize a person's full potential and increase trust in oneself. Another major tenet of this theory is the belief that people naturally seek growth toward personal and universal goals if they feel they have unconditional positive regard and relationships. See concepts related to Abraham Maslow, Alfred Adler, and Carl Rogers.

4. Existential counseling helps people find their unique meaning and purpose in the world. This type of counseling increases self-awareness and stresses the importance of "choice" in tough situations. The focus is on the present and future, not the past. See Viktor Frankl's work.

5. The primary premise of Adlerian therapy is that people are motivated by social interests and by striving toward goals. Life goals drive behavior. This method emphasizes taking a person's perspective and then altering it to yield productive results.

6. Psychoanalytic counseling is Freud's theory based on early life experiences of an individual. Unconscious motives and conflicts drive behavior. The goal of this method is to make one aware of unconscious desires through interpretations. Be familiar with different Freudian stages (covered in the next chapter), but it is most likely you do not have to memorize them. It appears that the NASP is not too concerned with Freudian techniques. Rather, emphasis is placed on Freud's general contributions to the field of psychology involving the importance of early life experiences in human development.

7. In systems therapy, or ecological theory, individuals are viewed as part of a larger living system. Treatment of the entire family and various other systems is important in the therapeutic change process. This approach to child support seems to be an NASP-endorsed perspective.

8. CBT is an intervention that is highly regarded and endorsed as best practice combined with FBA techniques. Be familiar with many of CBT's central principles. The CBT approach places an emphasis on a person's belief system as the cause of many problems. Internal dialogue plays a key role in behavior. Faulty assumptions and misconceptions must be addressed through talk therapy and then modified through role-play or other active interventions.

9. Rational-emotive counseling was founded by Albert Ellis. This approach emphasizes confrontational techniques regarding irrational beliefs. It is not used with children in school, but it is very important to consider a person's irrational beliefs within a counseling process.

10. Gestalt therapy focuses on the wholeness and integration of thoughts, feelings, and actions. Thoughts, feelings, and actions are the three aspects of the human condition and all must be considered when helping children. In this type of therapy, it is important to move a person from an external locus of control to an internal locus of control.

11. Reality therapy centers on choices people make and how those choices are working for them. (Dr. Phil seems to use this method because he always asks his clients, "How's that working for you?") The objective is to have clients take charge of their own life by examining choices. See William Glasser's work.

12. Social skills training typically involves four processes: *instruction*, *rehearsing*, *providing feedback or reinforcement*, and *reducing negative behaviors*. Modeling and role-playing are important techniques in this intervention.

13. Behaviorism is a favored intervention in schools. Positive reinforcement (rewards) is most effective in behavioristic interventions. If rewards or punishments are used, they must be given promptly after the behavior. This is called the *immediacy principle*. Additionally, rewards must be salient (valued by the person) to be effective.

14. Response cost is an effective behavioral modification method. Response cost is the removal of an earned reward that usually reduces or modifies negative behaviors. For example, a student who throws food in the cafeteria must forgo recess by cleaning up the mess. If the student is required to clean not only his or her food but also must help clean the entire area, this is called "overcorrection." Overcorrection is a key piece in another technique called restorative justice. Restorative practices are effective in many antibullying interventions.

15. Self-dialogue (self-talk) is a cognitive approach to changing behavior. It is vital to understand what a student is saying to himself or herself before, during, and after an undesirable act. Changing self-talk can modify certain behaviors.

16. Know how to perform an **FBA**. Remember the ABCs: **A**ntecedence of the behavior, the **b**ehavior itself, and the **c**onsequence (what maintains) of the behavior. Current practice states that a focus on changing the environmental factors or triggers that cause an undesirable behavior is vital to an intervention's effectiveness.

17. Several school psychologists believe that all behavior is purposeful and is initiated by its antecedent (triggering event) and maintained by its consequences. Good interventionists always ask, "What is the payoff for the behavior?" If you change the trigger and the payoff for the target behavior, then the behavior will change.

18. A general counseling format that is commonly used in schools:
    - Define the problem
    - Brainstorm ideas to address the problem

- Implement the plan or modification
- Evaluate the intervention's effectiveness

19. The key elements for effective behavioral interventions are providing sup-portive *feedback* to the student about his or her behavior, giving *choices* to the student for alternative behaviors and rewards, and finally, supplying *positive reinforcements* when expectations are met.

20. Be very familiar with how to handle general crisis issues. A thoughtful response to crisis is built on preparation and practice. Transparency of communication about facts to impacted people is important in crisis management.

21. **Debriefing** in a crisis is a technique used to relay information and a way to flag those people who may need more mental health support. Debriefing is not a therapeutic intervention per se, although it does have some therapeutic qualities.

22. Study NASP's position and practices regarding suicide. Focus on what to do and what not to do when dealing with suicide. Also, be familiar with how to prevent suicide **contagion** issues.

23. Know how to assess for suicide and the **risk factors** associated with suicide. Know resiliency factors. Finally, know best practices of **postvention** issues. This concept is also covered in the next chapter.

24. Be familiar with the symptoms and the treatment of PTSD. **PTSD** is commonly associated with a crisis. Stress symptoms may not evince themselves for days, months, or years after the trauma. Symptoms in children may be masked behind inappropriate behaviors (e.g., fighting, bedwetting, withdrawal). Psychological treatment for PTSD is similar to that of anxiety disorders. It seems that a cognitive behavioral approach is effective if it uses self-calming techniques, positive visualizations, and empathetic perspective taking.

25. Know the differences among primary, secondary, and tertiary intervention strategies. Remember **that prevention is a primary intervention**.

26. Although covered in the next chapter, threat assessments are psychological services that school practitioners provide schools. You need to be familiar with crises that are associated with violence and school shootings. There is no specific profile of school "shooters," although some general traits may exist. Bullying seems to play a central role in making some students act violently. The hallmark resource that is easy to read on school violence and school shootings is published by the U.S. Secret Service, *Threat Assessment in Schools: A Guide to Managing Threatening Situations and Creating Safe School Climates* (May 2002). This guide can be located at the following website: **www.secretservice.gov/data/protection/ntac/ssi_final_report.pdf**

Insider Tip

Psychologists are not teachers, but they will be called upon to consult with educators about how to teach students with disabilities or other students who are struggling. For the *Praxis* exam, understanding learning theories will help you to answer items related to this section. If you remember that all students benefit from individualized instruction tailored toward their specific learning style, some test items are related to the previous concept. As seen with counseling techniques, a multiple and eclectic approach to teaching (multimodal) is considered best practice. Learning by "doing" and student interest (engagement) are critical teaching aspects.

Interventions for Academic and Instructional Support

27. It is best practice to involve parents and consider the family when a student presents with a learning concern or behavior problem. Always document the time and type of parental contact.

28. The NASP endorses parental notification and involvement. Typically, teachers are encouraged to involve parents when a student is having academic or behavioral concerns. On the exam, usually any response option that involves parental contact has a high probability of being the correct answer.

29. Understand the differences between phonological instruction and whole-language instruction. Generally, the sounding of letters to form words (phonics) is a very effective instructional method for young readers.

30. The NASP endorses the use of positive reinforcement in the classroom. There is a strong movement to support and use a child's strengths as much as possible. This is called a *capacity approach* model.

31. *Token economies* (e.g., point and level systems), although using positive and effective reinforcers, are criticized as not practical because they are cumbersome to implement. Token economies or reward systems are useful if they are easy and practical to maintain. Token economies can be both academic and behavioral interventional supports.

32. A teaching method that encourages a *task analysis* and breaking a complex task into smaller tasks is a widely accepted practice when teaching new concepts.

33. Teachers should be encouraged to make *learning meaningful* to students by explicitly showing them how a lesson is beneficial to their lives or important to society. Students want to understand "why" they have to learn certain concepts. Lessons that are relevant tend to be remembered more effectively.

34. Many times, effective teachers briefly review with their students the previous day's learning and will explicitly preview the parts of a new assignment before each class. Sometimes the schedule for new learning is written on the board for all to see. (A visual component is important.)

35. Teachers are encouraged to use a *multisensory approach*. It is best practice to use auditory, visual, and tactile methods when teaching. Teachers in middle school and high school sometimes need to be reminded of the many different types of learners. It is interesting that high school lectures appeal mostly to auditory learners.

36. Know the differences between the terms *accommodation* and *modification* as they relate to special education services. Accommodations refer to changes in the environment without changing the task, such as letting a student use a quiet room to take a test. A modification is actually changing a task standard so the student can perform. For example, a student who has difficulty with writing might be allowed to complete half the number of questions than his or her peers.

37. The ultimate goal and role of special education services is to increase students' levels of independence, skills, and responsibility.

38. Review curriculum-based assessment (CBA) and curriculum-based measurement (CBM) for the *Praxis* exam. CBA is used in program evaluations. CBM is commonly used for classroom and instructional intervention planning.

39. According to cognitive behavioral theorists, learning is supported by mental representations of new concepts merging with existing mental concepts (schema) and through associations (i.e., the pairing of a skill or idea with a reinforcer).

40. Cooperative learning is an effective learning strategy. Review Vygotsky's work. Vygotsky also helped to develop the theory of the ZPD.

41. Overview of common academic interventions/areas of focus
    - Phonologically based interventions for reading problems
    - Spelling interventions
    - Math interventions, use of manipulatives and visual models
    - Differentiated instruction—excellent broad practice
    - Flexible grouping
    - Developing metacognitive skills
    - SQR3 (Survey, Question, Read, Recite, Review)—builds comprehension
    - Scaffolding
    - Cooperative learning

- Time management/engagement time
- Self-regulation skill development
- Read aloud
- Fluency interventions
- Use of visuals and visual schedules
- Chunking
- Use of assistive technology

3

Third Test Category: Systems-Level Services

The third category covers three primary domains: (a) *Schoolwide Practices to Promote Learning*; (b) *Prevention and* Responsive Services; and (c) *Family–School Collaboration Services*. Although school psychologists in the field are increasingly called on to employ their special skills to impact larger systems (e.g., school-wide, district-wide), some sources have indicated that the number of examination questions related to this section are the lowest of all the areas to study (16%–20%). It has been suggested that examination takers do not memorize too much information in this section, but rather be able to recognize key points and concepts. They should be familiar with specific policies and practices that positively and negatively impact school climate or large systems. For example, it is not enough to know about retention policies; you must also know the positive and negative aspects of such policies.

Another study consideration related to the systems-level category regards school violence. Due to the grave consequences and current societal focus related to *school violence*, it is critical that you study various crisis interventions and management strategies. Other key areas to focus your study efforts are schoolwide *bully programs*, *suicide issues*, and developing a *positive school climate*.

Domain 1: Schoolwide Practices to Promote Learning

An important legal guideline school psychologists need to be familiar with is the **Every Student Succeeds Act (ESSA).** ESSA encourages schools to employ comprehensive services that are framed within **Multi-Tiered System of Support (MTSS).** Chapters 1 and 2 describe MTSS as a robust evidence-based approach that integrates psychoeducational services and interventions throughout the school system. Because MTSS is an essential school practice, people preparing for the examination should fully understand its major points.

Answering examination questions related to the broader aspects of this category entails an understanding of best practices related to decision making and the National Association of School Psychologists' (NASP) position on the school psychologists' role in larger systems. For example, the NASP strongly encourages that school psychologists should be leaders and take on roles that transcend the individual or classroom level. *School psychologists should assume leadership roles* and lend their skills to programs and policies that impact the entire school and possibly the school district. Next, practitioners should understand *systems theory and recognize the importance of using research when making decisions* or creating organizational plans.

I. Key Broad Points of Schoolwide Policy and Practices

School systems should have:

A. *Coordinated and Effective Use of Multiple Streams of Data*

Schools must use information that informs instruction, student performance, school outcomes, and school accountability. Key concepts are **multiple sources** and **integrated information** to influence decisions and instruction.

B. *High Standards, Expectations, and Rigorous Curricula* Provided to All Students

This is a *broad NASP position* that is important to know because it influences a host of test items. It is founded on the general principle that *all students can learn* and need to be appropriately challenged.

C. *Coordinated Services* Across a School District and Within Schools

Services should center on a MTSS model. MTSS is critical to coordination of services across systems and within schools. MTSS is for *all* students (not just special education students).

D. Use Research-Backed Effective *Mental Health and Learning Supports* Found in MTSS

You should be familiar with the following **key MTSS elements and practices**.

- Progress monitoring data collection
- Evidence-based learning interventions
- Supports practices that address learning barriers (e.g., physical, social, emotional, and intellectual supports)
- Prevention supports (e.g., positive **school climate**, positive behavioral interventions and supports [PBIS], wellness programs)
- Direct school mental and behavioral health services

E. Ongoing and Meaningful *Professional Development* for Staff

F. An *Accountability System* That Offers Alternatives When Interventions Are Insufficient

II. Key Ideas for School-Based Organizational Development

A. School psychologists are trained to provide critical *"needs assessments" to organizations* and can help them develop.

B. A *needs assessment can have these primary elements*
- Details about *common barriers* to effectiveness
- Information about *ineffective practices*
- Information about *effective practices*
- Additional suggestions and *advocacy* information

C. **Create goals from needs assessment data** and link recommendations to the *NASP Practice Model*

D. Link identified needs to relevant resources (**resource mapping**)

Domain 2: Prevention and Responsive Services

This domain focuses on four critical areas that most likely will comprise many of the test items. Although it is important to familiarize yourself with various factors related to student outcomes, a special focus should be on how schools (systems) address bullying, school violence, crisis issues, and suicide. Make sure you understand those practices that are endorsed and effective as well as those practices that are not supported by the NASP (e.g., lead to poor outcomes or can be harmful).

I. Specific Factors That Impact Academic Success or Failure

A. School Climate

School climate is a *critical prevention measure* and it is created from a host of specific elements. Effective school climates are based on some of the points previously mentioned, but they are specifically defined here:

- A student's school has high expectations for learning and students believe they can learn.
- The school provides an emotionally safe and positive learning environment.
- Parents, students, and staff are involved in collaborative decision making. Parents, students, and staff are actively involved in the decisions affecting the school.
- Students come to school feeling respected and welcomed.
- Students have a trusting relationship with at least one adult in the school.
- Students explicitly know the school's academic and behavioral expectations.
- Students feel they are a valued part of their school and have a role.

B. Student Engagement and Motivation

Students who are engaged with school through extracurricular activities (e.g., sports, clubs, drama, music, art) are more likely to be successful. Schools that showcase students' work and have defined avenues to illustrate student engagement have healthy climates that support growth. Such school also develop high intrinsic motivation due to the increased school engagement and achievement.

C. Educational Practices and Policies

Students do better when schools have formal procedures in place that support evidence-based interventions, early interventions, response to intervention (RTI) process, and *data-based* decision making. The centerpiece of effective school practices is the **MTSS**.

D. Family Involvement

Families dramatically influence the degree to which children are engaged in school and how they identify themselves as learners.

E. Student Retention Practices (A Negative Practice)

Grade retention is the practice of keeping a student in the same grade due to academic or maturity concerns. A substantial amount of research *does not* support the use of grade retention. Approximately 15% of American students are held back each year with highest percentages among poor, minority, and inner-city youth.

Research indicates that *achievement declines* within 2 to 3 years postretention. Retained students are more likely to experience significant problems such as interpersonal conflicts with peers, disliking school, behavior problems, and lower self-esteem.

F. Tracking and Zero-Tolerance Policies (A Negative Practice)

- **Tracking** is a form of whole-group instruction that is characterized by a set curriculum that is delivered at the same pace for all students within the classroom. Placement into these special classes is based solely on the child's ability level and is, therefore, considered to be an unacceptable approach for the grouping of students. The NASP does *not* generally endorse this practice of tracking.
- **Zero tolerance** refers to school or district-wide policies that mandate predetermined and typically harsh consequences or punishments for a *wide degree* of rule violation (e.g., drugs, weapons, violence, smoking, school disruption). Zero-tolerance policies are generally ineffective and are not endorsed. Problems associated with zero-tolerance policies include:
  - Racial disproportionality
  - An increasing incidence of suspensions and expulsions
  - An increase of repeat suspensions
  - Elevated dropout rates

G. Bullying and Harassment

Bullying is a critical area to study for the examination. Bullying and intimidation are major reasons for student difficulties and school avoidance (low attendance). Bullying has been conceptualized as a type of *aggression* characterized by a consistent abuse of power. Bullying can take various forms such as *physical aggression, verbal aggression, relationship aggression (e.g., exclusion, social isolation and rumor spreading), and technology aggression* (e.g., text messaging and slanderous e-mailing).

Key Points About Bullying

- 20% of high school students in the United States have experienced bullying
- 28% of students in the United States grades 6 to 12 experienced bullying.
- 30% of students say they have bullied other students

II. School Violence and Threat Assessment

There is a focus from the NASP on school violence due to the extremely serious nature of this topic. The NASP *endorses an increased leadership role for school psychologists to conduct threat assessments.* It is possible that examination questions will be more numerous than in the past in regard to school violence and threat/risk assessments. Although school violence has similar content to bullying, it is a separate category to study as interventions and assessments tend to be more intense.

A. Key Risk Factors for Violence

- History of aggression, violence, and exposure to violence
- Antisocial parents
- Perceived persecution/sense of injustice
- Antisocial beliefs attitude and peer group
- Risk-taking behaviors
- Substance abuse
- Low cognitive profile
- Weak social ties and school ties
- Poverty
- Psychological conditions
- Gang affiliation
- Poor school performance
- Poor parental relationships and low supervision

B. Threat Assessment

Excellent threat assessment resources, in addition to the NASP, are provided by several government and respected research organizations. The **Virginia Model**, by Dr. Cornell, is a model for threat assessment that is widely adopted by school districts.

When studying for the examination, it is strongly recommended that you review the following information from these sites:

- **NASP: www.nasponline.org/resources-and-publications/resources/school -safety-and-crisis/threat-assessment-at-school/threat-assessment -for-school-administrators-and-crisis-teams**

- **Secret Service and Department of Education: www2.ed.gov/admins/lead/ safety/threatassessmentguide.pdf**

- **Virginia Model: www.curry.virginia.edu/research/projects/threat-assessment**

Key Concepts Related to Threat Assessment in Schools

- Best practice is to employ a team/*multidisciplinary approach* when conducting a threat assessment. School psychologists play a lead role, but should NOT conduct a threat assessment alone.

- A threat assessment is not a "test" but rather a comprehensive examination of factors and behaviors related to potential violence. Threat assessments *use multiple streams of information.* Teams should examine the student, student's family, community information, peer information, teacher information, and student records.

- There *is no profile* of a school shooter. However, there are risk *behaviors* that are examined to determine the underlying causes of aggression/violence.

- Teams should determine if a student "poses" a threat rather than making a threat.

- Assessments are moving away from "ranking systems" to a qualitative system from the *Virginia Model*. **The three qualitative labels used to categorize threats from the Virginia Model are: Transient, Substantive, and Imminent.**

- A focus of a threat assessment should be on using the information from the assessment to make **a risk mitigation plan.** Effective plans address the students' underlying needs and build coping skills through mental health support.

- Suspensions and *expulsions are not as effective* as a comprehensive risk management plan with numerous stakeholders involved in its implementation.

- Effective elements to a risk management plan for a student that has made a credible threat include increased supervision, restorative practices, restrictions on access to places and people, and mental health interventions.

- **Barriers** to effective threat assessment include:
  - Overworked staff and time constraints to conduct proper assessments
  - Lack of fidelity/implementation with the risk management plan
  - Lack of thoroughness/comprehensiveness with the assessment
  - Using trait profiling versus examining behaviors
  - Lack of a defined policy, process, and assessment to address threats

III. Suicide Prevention/Intervention

It is stated in other texts and guides that suicide is the third leading cause of death in students aged 10 to 18 years. Currently, the NASP asserts that suicide is the second leading cause of death among school-aged youth. In 2013, 17% of our nation's high school students seriously considered suicide and 8% made an attempt. Suicidal issues are the most serious tasks a psychologist must address, but suicide can be prevented. Risk factors for suicide can best be categorized as individual and environmental.

A. Individual Risk Factors

These include mental illness, depression, conduct disorders, substance abuse, psychological problems, and low coping skills related to a situational crisis, such as death of a loved one or trauma.

B. Environmental Factors

These include family stress, familial dysfunction, interpersonal conflict, and access to weapons.

- **Warning signs or risks:**
  - Prior suicidal ideation or attempts
  - Hopelessness; student does not see a future
  - Feelings of persecution/injustice
  - Sudden or increased involvement with alcohol and/or drugs
  - Suicidal threats in the form of direct and indirect statements
  - Suicide notes and plans
  - Preparations for final arrangements (e.g., making funeral arrangements, writing a will, giving away prized possessions)
  - Preoccupation with death
  - Changes in behavior, appearance, thoughts, or feelings
- **Protective and resiliency factors:**
  - Student feels connected to school and community
  - Student has future goals, looks forward to valued events
  - Family support and cohesion, including good communication
  - Peer support and close social networks
  - Cultural or religious beliefs that discourage suicide and promote healthy living
  - Adaptive coping and problem-solving skills, including conflict resolution
  - General life satisfaction, good self-esteem, sense of purpose
- **Best practice during high-risk situations:**
  - Get help and collaborate with colleagues

- Call parents or guardians and notify administration

- Supervise the student at all times. It is best to always inform the student what you are going to do every step of the way. Solicit the student's assistance where appropriate. Under no circumstances should the student be allowed to leave school or be alone (even in the restroom).

- *No-harm or suicide contracts* have little effectiveness and are not typically recommended.

- Instruct parents to make their homes suicide proof. Whether a child is in imminent danger or not, it is recommended that both the home and school be suicide proofed. Before the child returns home and thereafter, all guns, poisons, medications, and sharp objects must be removed or made inaccessible.

- Call police and get consultation. All school crisis teams should have a representative from local law enforcement.

- Document the event and provide copies to all parties. Every school district should develop a documentation form for support personnel and crisis team members to record their actions in responding to a referral of a suicidal student.

- **A Suicide Assessment and Intervention Model Assessment**
  - Determine whether the student has **thoughts about suicide**. (Thoughts or threats, whether direct or indirect, may indicate risk.)

  - Has the student **attempted** to hurt himself or herself before? (Previous attempts may indicate risk.)

  - Does the student have **a plan** to harm himself or herself now (specific details, time, method, and place)?

  - What **method** is the student planning to use and does he have access to the means? (These answers will indicate the presence of high risk.)

  - What is the support system that surrounds this child? It is critical to determine the adequacy of the student's support system.

  - Notify parents. **Parents must be notified**.

  - Provide referrals. School districts have an obligation to suggest agencies that are nonproprietary or offer a sliding scale of fees.

  - Follow-up with the student and support the family.

Suicide Postvention

Suicide postvention is the provision of crisis intervention, support, and assistance for those affected by a completed suicide. Affected individuals may include classmates, friends, teachers, coworkers, and family members. Affected individuals are often referred to as *survivors of suicide*.

According to the American Association of Suicidology (AAS), the tasks of postvention are twofold: (a) **to reduce** the chances of anyone else committing suicide by avoiding glamorization of the deceased, and (b) **to assist** staff and students with the grieving process.

It is important to be aware of cultural considerations. Attitudes toward suicidal behavior vary considerably from culture to culture.

Perhaps the greatest concern for a school psychologist after a completed suicide is **contagion**. *Contagion* is the term used to signify that one's actions might spread to others and promote more suicidal behavior, especially among teens. To avoid contagion, the school psychologist needs to advocate the following points.

- **Contagion considerations (familiarize, not memorize):**
  - Avoid sensationalism of the suicide.
  - Avoid glorification or vilification of the suicide victim.
  - Stick to facts. Do not provide excessive details.
  - The longer the delay in sharing facts, the greater the likelihood of harmful rumors.
  - Avoid sharing information about the death over a school's public address system.
  - Avoid schoolwide assemblies.
  - Provide information simultaneously in classrooms.
  - Photos of the suicide victim should *not* be used.
  - The term "suicide" should *not* be placed in the caption of a picture.
  - Provide information to family and students about school and community resources for those people who need support.
  - Staff should be provided current information regarding the death. At this time, staff needs should also be monitored and supported.
  - Provide a specific safe place for the opportunity to ask questions and express feelings.
  - Emphasize the normality of grief and stress reactions.
  - Identify students at risk for an imitative response.
  - Do not send all students from school to funerals, stop classes for a funeral, or have moments of silence for the student.
  - Do not have memorial or funeral services at school.
  - Do not establish permanent memorials such as plaques. Do not dedicate yearbooks to the memory of suicide victims or dedicate songs or sporting events to the suicide victim.

- There are several Internet resources to review on suicidal topics; however, make sure such resources are mainstream and related to schools and student-age populations:

  - www.nasponline.org/Documents/Resources%20and%20Publications/ Handouts/Families%20and%20Educators/Suicide%20Intervention%20 in%20Secondary%20Schoools%20NASSP%20Oct%202006.pdf

  - www.afsp.org/wp-content/uploads/2016/01/Model-Policy_FINAL.pdf

IV. Loss, Death, and Grief

The two primary challenges for the people faced with a death of a family member, well-known person, or a friend are (a) processing the actual death or event and (b) coping with the loss of the loved one. The range of reactions that children display in response to the death of a significant other may be highly variable. Typical reactions include emotional shock and, at times, an apparent lack of feelings that serve to help the child detach from the pain of the moment. Regressive (immature) behaviors are frequently seen in children coping with grief. Regressive behaviors include needing to be rocked or held, difficulty separating from parents or significant others, needing to sleep in the parent's bed, or an apparent difficulty completing easy tasks. Some students have acting-out behaviors that reflect the child's internal feelings of fear, frustration, anger, loss of control, and helplessness. Finally, it is not uncommon for people to repeat themselves or ask the same questions more than once when coping with a significant loss.

- **Suggestions and Considerations About Grieving Children**

  - Be mindful that children will be aware of the reactions of adults as they interpret and react to information about death.

  - Encourage children to talk about death or loss. Do not instruct children to deny thinking or talking about the situation.

  - Share important facts about the event and try to get a sense of what the children think about it and about death in general.

  - Note that grieving is a process, not a sole event. Children need adequate time to grieve in the manner that works for them. Although routines may help in the healing process, do not encourage children to resume "normal" activities without the chance to deal with their emotions.

  - People confronted with grief or crisis sometimes have a strong desire to "do something." Encourage children or others in the process to engage in positive activities such as bibliotherapy, writing, or making an item to mark the event.

- **Internet Resources on Grief and Emotional First Aid**

  - NASP: Helping Children Cope with Loss, Death, and Grief: Tips for Teachers and Parents: www.naspcenter.org/principals/nassp_death.html

  - Guidance for specific developmental levels is offered by the National Center for Child Traumatic Stress: www.nctsn.org/about-us/national-center

- **NIH**: www.ncbi.nlm.nih.gov/pubmedhealth/PMH0032576. This resource gives excellent general information, but is not specifically tailored toward children.

read over

V. Crisis: Prevention, Intervention, and Management

A. General Crisis Considerations

Crisis can take many forms, from suicide to natural disasters. Psychologists must know the principles of crisis prevention, how to assess people involved in a crisis, how to manage a situation, and finally, how to effectively follow-up postcrisis.

The most effective approach to crisis-related issues is to *prevent* them from happening in the first place. Promoting school safety is a vital component in the prevention process. In the event of a crisis, the success or failure of a response to an incident depends on whether your school has a crisis team and whether the team has adequately prepared. Crisis teams are typically comprised of the administration team and other leaders, such as the school psychologist. An effective team should have practiced various drills and reviewed key crisis processes consistently and at least annually.

The following points are important for *promoting a safe and responsive school environment climate*: (These are not necessary to memorize, but be familiar with the following.)

- Adult supervision and visibility are the most essential factors of school safety.

- Conduct a formal review of all school safety policies and procedures to ensure that emerging school safety issues are adequately covered in the current school crisis plans and emergency response procedures.

- Plan a communication system that includes both school and community responders. This should also address how and where parents will be informed in the event of an emergency.

- Provide crisis training and professional development for staff based on a needs assessment.

- Be familiar with violence prevention programs and curricula. Teach students alternatives to violence, including peaceful conflict resolution and positive interpersonal relationship skills. Cite specific examples such as Second Step Violence Prevention, bully proofing, Restorative Practices, or other positive interventions and behavioral supports.

- Join or create a crisis or safety team and identify school needs (i.e., a needs assessment).

- Target bullying and build a peer conflict-resolution process (restorative practices).

- Make apparent the presence of school resource officers, local police partnerships, or security guards.

- Monitor nonstaff and school guests in your building.

- Advocate for students to take responsibility for their part in maintaining safe school environments, including student participation in safety planning. Promote compliance with school rules, reporting potential problems to school officials, and resisting peer pressure to act irresponsibly.

- Anonymous reporting systems, such as student hot lines, "suggestion" boxes, and "tell an adult" campaigns should be part of your school's culture.

- Threat-assessment and risk-assessment procedures and teams should be clearly established.

- The presence of security systems, such as video monitoring and exit door alarm systems, is sometimes useful but cannot replace adult supervision.

B. Human Reactions to Crisis (Trauma)

A crisis can lead a person to perceive an event in a traumatic way. Trauma is when a person experiences or views an event in a severely distressing way. A crisis may be viewed in a way that completely overwhelms a person's ability to cope with life or to function normally. Traumatic events can have significant and disastrous effects on a person's physical, psychological, behavioral, and emotional functioning to the point of extreme impairment (e.g., posttraumatic stress disorder [PTSD]). School psychologists understand there are several different types of crisis and trauma-inducing events, but they are also aware that children might experience the same event, with some children impacted negatively while others are not affected adversely at all.

- **Types of traumas experienced by students:**
  - Physical abuse
  - Families with substance abuse (e.g., alcohol, drugs)
  - Emotional neglect
  - Parental separation or divorce
  - Sexual abuse
  - Family member with mental illness
  - Witness of domestic violence
  - Natural disasters
  - School violence/aggression
- **Specific reactions of youth to crisis or extreme stress**
  - **Very young children (0 to 5 years)**: Thumb sucking, bedwetting, separation anxiety, clinging to parents, sleep disturbances, loss of appetite, fear of the dark, regression in behavior, and withdrawal from friends and routines.

- **Elementary school children**: Fear and safety issues, aggressiveness, irritability, clinginess, nightmares, avoidance of routine activities, school problems, poor concentration, and withdrawal.

- **Adolescents:** Sleeping and eating disturbances, extreme emotions such as agitation, increase in interpersonal conflicts, somatic complaints, delinquent behavior, and poor attention or focus.

- Know key characteristics **of posttraumatic stress disorder** (PTSD). PTSD is a normal human response to extreme stress or disaster. People with PTSD have high anxiety and their reactions to stress are extreme. Obsessive thoughts about the crisis event, sleep problems, hyperarousal (vigilance), and externalizing behaviors such as avoidance are common symptoms of PTSD. PTSD is both a psychological and physiological reaction to trauma. Individuals with PTSD may have a dysfunction neurological system (e.g., limic system). PTSD is linked to an anxiety disorder in the *Diagnostic and Statistical Manual of Mental Disorders* (4th ed., text rev.; *DSM-IV-TR*; American Psychiatric Association, 2000).

- It is common for some people to have an irresistible compulsion to retell the story of a crisis or trauma. This behavior is normal and is associated with the mind's way of processing the event to integrate the information into the person's experience. Some experts believe that people repeat the event and recycle it in their mind in order to "make sense" of the trauma.

C. Best Practice: Crisis Response Immediately Following an Event (General)

- **Identify youth** who are high risk and provide support. Interventions may include individual counseling, small-group counseling, or family therapy. The school crisis response team can determine which students need supportive crisis intervention and counseling services.

- **Support adults**, teachers, and other school staff. Provide staff members with information on the symptoms of children's stress reactions and guidance on how to handle class discussions and answer children's question. Teachers should monitor their own needs and stress reactions.

- **Therapeutic activities** that facilitate healing postcrisis:

  - Encourage children to talk about disaster-related events. These may include a range of methods both verbal and nonverbal and incorporate varying projects (e.g., drawing, stories, and audio and video recording).

  - Reassure, validate, and normalize children's reactions and emotions.

  - Provide positive coping and problem-solving skills.

  - Strengthen children's friendships and peer support. Activities may include asking children to work cooperatively in small groups in order to enhance peer support.

- Connect people with community resources in order to provide long-term assistance. These resource relationships need to be established with the school in advance.

D. Model for Trauma Support: BASIC Ph

This model was created by Dr. Mooli. The model's focus is on six primary styles of coping that people may use to deal with a crisis or a perceived traumatic event. It is key to remember that, regardless of the coping style used, when children feel there is adult support and their reactions are normal (instilling a sense of normalcy), they are more likely to have favorable outcomes post crisis.

- BASIC Ph Model: Six Individual Coping Styles Related to Trauma
    1. **Belief**—student uses core values and religion to cope with a crisis
    2. **Affect**—student shares emotions and discusses emotional responses with adults
    3. **Social**—student uses social network, relationships, and family to help cope
    4. **Imagination**—student expresses difficulties through creative means
    5. **Cognitive**—student employs rational thought and prefers the direct approach to process
    6. **Physiological**—student uses physical activities to cope with the event

E. Additional Resources for General Crisis Intervention

- Brock, S., Lazarus, P., & Jimerson, S. (2012). *Best practices in school crisis prevention and intervention*. Bethesda, MD: National Association of School Psychologists.
- **National Institute of Mental Health (NIMH)**: www.nimh.nih.gov/health/publications/helping-children-and-adolescents-cope-with-violence-and-disasters-parents-trifold/index.shtml
- **American Counseling Association**: www.counseling.org/docs/trauma-disaster/fact-sheet-3---disaster-and-trauma-responses-of-children.pdf?sfvrsn=2
- **AAP**: www.aap.org/en-us/advocacy-and-policy/aap-health-initiatives/Children-and-Disasters/Pages/Promoting-Adjustment-and-Helping-Children-Cope.aspx?nfstatus=401&nftoken=00000000-0000-0000-0000-000000000000

Domain 3: Family–School Collaboration Services

Although this domain is relatively brief, there are a few items on the examination that are directly related to it. It is important to understand the NASP's overall orientation to collaborative services to answer relevant questions. Currently, the NASP has very strong opinions about impacted communities, fair minority access to school services, and cultural issues.

It is well understood that a home–school collaboration benefits all children. It is certainly desirable to establish a positive relationship with homes and other services. However, test takers should know that children that might have risk factors, such as *economic impoverishment, limited parental education, stressful home situations, and/or cultural barriers between home and school* are in the most need of collaborative services.

I. Practices and Key Concepts for Home–School Collaboration

- **Broad elements for effective home–school collaboration:**
  - Mutual *trust* between staff and parents
  - *Proactive* and responsive practices and services, not reactive
  - *Sensitivity* and respect for culture
  - Genuine *recognition* of teacher and parent contributions
- **Specific elements of an effective home–school collaboration:**
  - Effective *bidirectional communication*
  - *Decision making and problem solving are collaborative processes*
  - Collaboration and communication should be *consistent*
  - Services should be *coordinated*
  - Services should have continuity (long term)
- **Barriers to effective collaboration**
  - Lack of trust for large systems
  - Different cultural values about education
  - Perceived lack of acceptance of cultural values
  - School's attitudes about culture and parents (negativity)
  - Lack of qualified staff and interpreters
- **Six primary types of parental involvement (Epstein's Model)**
  1. Parenting
  2. Communicating
  3. Volunteering
  4. Learning at home
  5. Decision making
  6. Collaborating with community

II. Organizational Principles Related to Effective Home–School Collaboration

When examining organizational principles, keep in mind there are broad aspects that are relevant to a range of examination questions. Organizational theory and development within a school system is always in a state of flux and there are several models offered in the literature. The following principles are somewhat dated, but they still appear in the NASP resource archives and are still viable for you to study for the examination. Much of the information under this domain stems from the work of Linda Raffaele and Howard Knoff. Raffaele and Knoff are strong proponents of using an *ecological approach* to collaboration. The foundational work of the previous researchers is useful for you to review.

- **Helpful resource**: Raffaele, L. M., & Knoff, H. M. (1999). Improving home–school collaboration with disadvantaged families: Organizational principles, perspectives, and approaches. *School Psychology Review, 28*(3), 448–466.

A. Basic Organizational Principles for *All* Effective Schools

- Quality classroom instruction and qualified instructional personnel
- Technology and curriculum that are well chosen and adaptive to individual student needs
- The creation and maintenance of a safe school environment
- Evaluation processes and accessible databases that can monitor students' progress
- Inclusion of multidisciplinary experts and interventions for instructional and/or behavioral consultation

III. Four Organizational Principles Critical for Effective Home–School Collaboration

- An **ecological perspective** is the foundation for effective collaboration
- An understanding of parents' views on education and their children's school
- Commitment to the process
- The need to have an ongoing strategic planning process that guides all home–school collaborative efforts and adapts to change

Insider Tip

The Family–School Collaboration Services section typically has the fewest items on the test, but it is still important to study as it might be the basis for 15% to 20% of the examination. Although there are a few key elements to memorize (e.g., MTSS), it might be more effective for you to **familiarize** (enough to readily recognize information) yourself with the general positions of the NASP relevant to this section's content and know key points of the models that are effective for a systems-level service. Threat assessment and suicide issues are key areas to focus on within this category.

Concepts to Remember

1. The NASP encourages school psychologist to become leaders in their schools and school district so they can impact broader systems. Policies and practices that are in alignment with cultural sensitivity and inclusion (e.g., supports for all students) are especially emphasized.

2. Review elements of MTSS. For example, MTSS has **comprehensive supports** for behavior, instruction, and includes RTI/PBIS. **See Figure 3.1 for a visual representation of the MTSS model.**

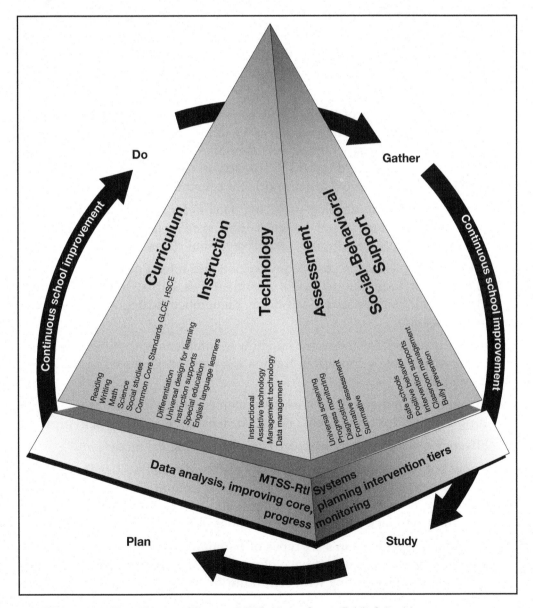

FIGURE 3.1 Multi-Tiered System of Support (MTSS; Marian County Public Schools).
GLCE, grade-level content expectations; HSCE, high school content expectations; RtI, response to intervention.
Source: Used by the permission of Marian County Public Schools.

3. Most effective systems use **multiple streams of information and multiple stakeholders** to formulate practices and policies.

4. Psychologists intervening on a systems level typically start with a **needs assessment** and address common barriers to school effectiveness. Recommendations from a needs assessment can be linked to the Practice Model for effective service delivery.

5. Review the literature on school threat assessment practices, especially the **Virginia Model.**

6. Be familiar with risk factors associated with violence, but remember there is **no profile** of a school shooter. The focus of a threat assessment is not on a profile of traits, but rather on concerning behaviors.

7. Know the impact of bullying on the school climate and on the individual, bullying interventions (e.g., restorative practices), statistics related to bullying, and well-known bully programs (e.g., Olweus Bully Prevention Program).

8. Describe the impact of ESSA. ESSA encourages schools to have high academic standards, redirects resources to improve low performing schools with achievement gaps, empowers schools to develop their own school improvements interventions (MTSS) based on research, reduces the burden of over testing, and provides supports for preschool.

9. Understand how to develop protective factors for systems to address suicide, bullying, and school violence. Key system interventions typically include a focus on developing a **positive school climate**.

10. Know best practices on suicide prevention and intervention. Key elements to review include how to assess a student's thoughts (suicidal ideation), plan, and methods related to self-harm. Remember the importance of parental notification.

11. Know details related to trauma and how to intervene with students who are traumatized. A key concept in trauma intervention is related to the BASIC Ph model.

12. Key points to remember for crisis management are to identify at-risk youth, support impacted adults, and engage students in therapeutic activities.

13. Effective collaboration models are based on **ecological** models.

14. Know both the supports for effective collaboration as well as the barriers. Some *supports* typically include trust, two-way communication, and cultural sensitivity. *Barriers* include lack of trust, different cultural values regarding education, and lack of acceptance by school staff.

15. Be familiar with Epstein's six types of parental involvement. The six types are parenting, communicating, volunteering, learning at home, decision making and collaborating with community.

4

Fourth Test Category: Foundations of School Psychological Service Delivery

In previous years, this area primarily focused on *legal* issues and how relevant educational laws impacted school practices. Although legal and ethical issues are still an area test takers need to study well, there are several test items on the other two domains related to this category. The two additional domains, *Diversity in Development and Learning* and *Research Design and Program Evaluation*, are not especially difficult areas, but there are some specific details you will need to carefully examine. For example, it will be important for you to know how different developmental levels and individual traits impact learning. Exam questions might also ask you to apply specific statistical and research design information to evaluate educational programs or intervention methods that impact broad systems.

Despite the chance that there will be only a few legal and ethical items on the exam, these items are typically the most challenging questions to answer. Do not underestimate the complexity of the ethical and legal issues school psychologists face. It will be well worth your time to have a firm grasp of the National Association of School Psychologists (NASP) guidelines that govern the ethical behavior of school psychologists. Many ethical questions on the *Praxis®* exam will not have a clear answer, but rather degrees of correctness. Some ethical response options will have components that are correct, but look for small details that spoil the answer. In other words, ethical questions are best answered by a process of elimination by considering why an answer could *not* be correct versus why it must be right. As with past recommendations, if you understand *general aspects of best practices* for school psychologists, it may help you to answer ethics-based questions. The following are examples of best practices that have ties to ethical issues.

look over again

- School psychologists should seek professional consultation when unsure about administering a new cognitive test or engaging in new practices.

- Psychologists must not practice outside their area of expertise.

- Practitioners should secure informed consent from parents when providing services to children.

A final note to consider: Over the last several years, many exams have included only a few items regarding historical events related to school psychology. Due to the broad nature of history, focus your efforts on key *landmark* historical events, not on trivial interesting events or specific dates.

Domain 1: Diversity in Development and Learning

I. Diversity, Culture, and Individual Characteristics

A general position to keep in mind is that diversity and inclusion in education are necessary for effective instructional and positive behavioral outcomes. Any exam question that is related to *diversity* in education should be answered in a way that affirms diversity as a critical consideration. The exam delineates two primary types of diversity concepts. First, there is a cultural and ethnic diversity group. The second area of diversity centers on individual characteristics of the learner that are in addition to race and culture. It is imperative to emphasize that effective pedagogy is founded on the belief that **all students can learn** regardless of the cultural barriers or special needs.

When preparing to study diversity and its influence on learning, it is key to familiarize yourself with the following points:

- Importance of culture on learning
- Importance of **individual characteristics**:
  - Gender (and gender identity)
  - Age
  - Cognitive abilities
  - Interpersonal skills
  - Developmental level (see Piaget's developmental levels in Chapter 5)
  - Race
  - Disability/disorders
  - Religion
  - Sexual orientation
  - Language
  - Socioeconomic status (SES)
  - Chronic pain/illnesses

- Effective **teaching practices for diverse learners**
  - Individualized instruction
  - Special accommodations for student disabilities
  - Use of relevant technology to support learning
  - High expectations and challenging but relevant curriculum
  - Staff are personally committed to achieving equity for all students.
  - Staff convey a genuine sense of caring and can bond with students.
  - Classes are interactive and content is meaningful.
  - Staff embrace a collaborative learning environment.
  - Content includes various cultural perspectives.
  - Staff use "scaffolding" to link content to cultural resources.
  - Staff maintain the integrity of students by acknowledging students' cultural pride.
  - Staff encourage parent and family involvement in school.
- Be aware of the concept and the impact of **disproportionality** and **bias.**
  - The NASP states that "disproportionality refers to a group's representation in a particular category that exceeds expectations for that group, or differs substantially from the representation of others in that category" (www.nasponline.org/resources-and-publications/resources/diversity/disproportionality). In other words, being part of a particular group raises the probability of being placed into another group, such as special education. It has been observed by some experts that minority groups are disproportionally placed into special programs and are likely to be identified with specific disorders or dysfunctions. The impact of disproportionality can be significant (e.g., lower self-esteem, expectations, lower wages, lower employment, higher arrest rates). Although there is no one single factor determined to cause disproportionality, a school psychologist should be aware of **biases that negatively impact children**.
- Assessment and diversity issues to consider: There are possible **biases in assessments**, especially with **English language learners (ELL)**. If psychological tests are not well normed on special or minority populations, then test results might be inaccurate. The use of **interpreters** is permitted for students who have language/cultural differences; however, test content and test construction foundations must be examined for bias (negative factors) as well.

Domain 2: Research and Program Evaluation

Psychologists must employ their expertise in statistics, test construction, and research to evaluate intervention programs or various assessments. There is an overlap of information with this domain and information from Domain 1: Data-Based Decision Making in Chapter 1. Many exam items from this area ask the test taker to *apply* his or her knowledge to answer these questions. For example, a psychologist must evaluate a new test for working memory that has a test–retest reliability coefficient of 0.60. What would this psychologist recommend to the school in this situation? Answer: Although a 0.60 reliability coefficient might be acceptable for some purposes, it is only considered moderate and not widely acceptable for use in schools. Several memory assessments are available with much stronger reliability psychometrics than 0.60.

I. Key Statistical Concepts Used in Program or Research Evaluations

Although a review of psychometric properties is provided in Chapter 1, it is critical to note that the statistical concepts of **reliability, validity**, and **power are essential to examine when evaluating programs or research**. The following is a recap of these key factors:

A. Reliability

Reliability refers to research results and/or scores that are *consistent and stable across time.*

- **Reliability coefficient:** This statistic illustrates the *consistency* of a score or the *stability* of a result. An appropriate reliability coefficient for standardized tests should generally be around or above $r = 0.80$. The higher the reliability coefficient, the better.

- **Standard error of measurement (SEM):** This metric is an estimate of error used when interpreting research results and the SEM impacts reliability. With every test, there are errors due to a host of factors, hence the higher the SEM, the lower the reliability. Tests results rarely provide the "true score" due to measurement errors.

  Note: It is doubtful you will have to actually calculate SEM or other complex psychometrics on the *Praxis* exam. However, know how SEM impacts reliability and validity.

- **Methods to assess reliability (types of reliability):**
  - **Test–retest:** Testing a person with the same test twice. The two scores are then correlated together using statistical methods. Theoretically, both scores should be highly similar if the test is reliable. A 2-week time interval between retaking the test is the minimal time frame recommended.

  - **Alternate and parallel forms:** Alternate forms of a test should be thought of as two tests built according to the same specifications but composed of separate samples from the defined behavior domain. They must take into account variation resulting from tasks and correlation between two test forms to provide the reliability coefficient.

  - **Split half**: Take a full test and create two tests from it, being careful to share difficult and easy items on both tests. Both tests are administered, even on the same day, and the scores on both tests are correlated.

- **Internal consistency reliability**: An estimate of the reliability of the total test is developed from an analysis of the statistics of the individual test items. Each test item is compared to the total set of items. This statistic is expressed in terms of Cronbach's alpha.

- **Interrater reliability:** The reliability of people administrating the test is increased by increasing the number of raters or judges.

B. Validity

Like reliability, validity is vital to evaluate a program or test's effectiveness and usefulness. Validity regards the degree to which a tool actually measures what it claims to measure, or a program does what it claims to do. To put it another way, validity is the degree to which evidence and theory support the proper interpretation of a program/tool's results. As stated with reliability coefficients, validity coefficients are acceptable if they are generally above 0.80. The higher the coefficient, the better.

- **Methods and types of validity**

  - **Criterion-related validity:** Criterion validity concerns the correlation between two measures (tests) that are designed to measure human traits. If two tests measure the same trait, the correlation between the tests should obviously be higher. If one of the two tests is not designed to measure the same trait, the correlation should be lower between the two tests.

  - **Face and content validity**: This involves how rational and reasonable the test and test items look. During test construction, experts in the area being examined are asked to evaluate whether test items look logical. For example, a math test would be considered invalid if all test items asked about cats.

  - **Convergent validity**: Convergent validity is determined when a test is correlated with another test that has a similar purpose and measures the same trait. For example, if a test that measures attention deficit hyperactivity disorder (ADHD) correlates highly or "converges" with another well-known test of ADHD, then the test is said to have good validity.

  - **Divergent validity**: Divergent validity is established by correlating two tests that measure two different traits. For example, a test that measures ADHD should have a low correlation with a test that measures depression.

  - **Construct-related validity**: This refers to whether a trait or construct is being measured.

  - **Predictive validity**: A valid test should have a high predictive value. For example, a valid test of cognitive ability should be able to predict a student's achievement in school. A student with a standard score of 75 on a cognitive test is predicted to struggle in school and to perform below grade level on complex tasks.

- **Discriminant validity**: A valid test should be able to discriminate among students who have the trait being measured and those who do not have the trait. For example, a student scoring high on an anxiety measure could be identified with an anxiety disorder and could be distinguished from those students who do not have an anxiety disorder.

C. Power

When evaluating research results, researchers examine their research hypothesis in terms of the probability of making true statements, or statements that are probably not true. Hence, power is the probability of making the correct decision if the alternative hypothesis is true. That is, the **power** of a hypothesis test is the probability of rejecting the null hypothesis H_0 when the alternative hypothesis H_A is the hypothesis that is true. A typical factor that reduces the power of a test or a program relates to the number of subjects used in the research. The lower the number of subjects used in statistical research, the lower the research study's power. **To increase research power, one needs to raise the number of subjects** used to make key inferences. When evaluating research studies, look for a subject pool greater than 50. When evaluating programs or tests, look for subjects in the hundreds (or thousands), which is more desirable and considered more powerful.

- **Errors related to research**: When making inferences about research results, experts can make two primary statistical errors, known as **type I and type II errors**. These errors are related to the power of the research design. In statistical hypothesis testing, a type I error is the incorrect rejection of a true null hypothesis (a **"false positive" is accepting a false hypothesis as correct when it is not true**), while a type II error is the failure to reject a false null hypothesis (a **"false negative" is rejecting a true hypothesis as incorrect, when it was correct**).

II. Higher Order Analysis of Research: Analysis of Variance and Effect Size

Psychological research typically concerns the relationship between an *intervention (independent variable)* and an *outcome (dependent variable)*. It is important for you to know the significance of the two previous research variables. For example, a researcher might be interested in the effect of a new medication intervention (independent variable) on a person's anxiety (dependent variable). One of the most common means to evaluating research variables has been through analysis of variance (ANOVA). ANOVA can be employed to determine if mean scores (on tests and research) on a dependent variable varies significantly across multiple time points and/or multiple groups. When evaluating research, it is important to understand the different types of ANOVA methods and if the proper method is used.

A. Types of ANOVA

- **One-way ANOVA**: One-way ANOVA is used to compare the dependent variable of three or more levels of a single independent variable at a single time point. Also, a one-way ANOVA is acceptable to use when comparing only two levels if results are equivalent to an independent sample *t*-test.

- **Multi-way ANOVA**: A multi-way ANOVA is used in complex research designs. A multi-way ANOVA might be a two-way ANOVA or a three-way ANOVA. This type of ANOVA is used to evaluate the effect of two or more independent variables, each of which has two or more levels, on a dependent variable measured at a single time point.

- **Repeated-measures ANOVA**: This type of analysis is used for research that is interested to see if results change with time. Repeated-measures ANOVA is used to evaluate the effect of an independent variable with a single level on a dependent variable measured at two or more time points.

- **Mixed factorial ANOVA**: Mixed factorial ANOVA is used to examine the effect of one or more independent variables. Each independent variable may have two or more levels on a dependent variable that is measured at two or more points in time.

- **Multivariate ANOVA**: A multivariate ANOVA (MANOVA) is used when evaluating two or more dependent variables at the *same* time. The chief benefit of the MANOVA technique is that it can use any of the ANOVAs listed earlier. MANOVA allows for the simultaneous examination of multiple independent and dependent variables.

- **Analysis of covariance**: Analysis of covariance (**ANCOVA**) is a very strong type of ANOVA and can use other types of ANOVA methods. The key benefit of ANCOVA is that it *removes bias* in the dependent variable(s). This ANOVA model **increases the accuracy of conclusions** regarding the independent variable because it accounts for covariates related to within-group variance or group error. When you account for within-group error, it enhances the ability to identify meaningful differences between groups on the dependent variable(s).

B. Effect Size

Effect size is a way of quantifying the size of the differences between two groups. Sometimes there is a large difference in scores on a research measure between two groups, but the size is not actually significant when statistical measures are used. Other times, a small difference among group performance exists, but it rises to the level of significance when certain statistical methods are used (e.g., *t-test*, meta-analysis). **Cohen** is typically cited as a resource to determine the degree of significance of a statistical result. Here are Cohen's benchmarks for significance:

- 8 = large (8/10 of a standard deviation unit)
- 0.5 = moderate (1/2 of a standard deviation)
- 0.2 = small (1/5 of a standard deviation)

For example, if a *t-test* has a 0.2 difference in scores, then the significance of the result is deemed small. Cohen's guidelines are also applied to correlation results between two or more variables. If a correlation between a working memory test and an achievement test is 0.5, then this correlation is deemed moderate. Despite the widespread use of Cohen's guidelines, there are some concerns and cautions about its use.

III. Additional Research Models/Concepts

A. Multilevel Modeling (MLM)

The concept of **MLM** is important to review because of its growing use in research. MLM is a *statistical model* of *parameters* that vary at more than one level. If there are multiple levels or variables to consider, then MLM is a useful alternative to ANOVA. When evaluating programs or research, it is important that research designs are well suited for the methodology employed.

There are several research designs associated with MLM. If there are exam questions related to MLM, such questions are probably not numerous. Therefore, the following MLM designs should be familiar to you, but not necessarily memorized in detail. For more information on MLM, refer to John Hosp's work in *NASP Communique*.

- **MLM designs:**
  - Hierarchical designs
  - Randomized block designs
  - Growth curve modeling
  - Piecewise
  - Cross-classified designs (repeated measures)

B. Correlational Studies

Correlational studies examine the strength of relationship between two or more variables. Correlational studies are *very common research designs* and result in a correlational coefficient that denotes the potency of the relationship among items. One of the most studied correlational studies related to psychology is the relationship between IQ scores on a given test to achievement scores on another test. Remember, correlational coefficients above 0.5 are considered moderate, while a 0.8 correlation is viewed as strong and at a desirable level for use.

When evaluating correlational studies, remember that a significant correlation does *not* necessarily mean **"causation."** For example, one can find that two variables have a correlation, but one cannot typically say that one variable causes an outcome.

C. Experimental Designs

Experimental designs typically involve groups of people. One group is a **control group**, while the other group is given an intervention. The results of the **experimental group** that receives an intervention is contrasted to those of the control group. Results are statistically analyzed to determine if the outcomes are significant. The gold standard in experimental designs is called the *double-blind* experiment. In double-blind experiments, both the group members and the researchers do not know which group receives the actual intervention.

D. Meta-Analysis (Meta-Analytical Studies)

Meta-analysis is a highly regarded and strong type of research method. The reason meta-analytic studies are powerful is because they are designed to examine the results of several research studies, not just one study. The ability to statistically analyze the result of several independent studies across time (sometimes decades) is extremely helpful to control the biases, confounding factors, or design flaws in any one study. Although these meta-analytic designs are robust, the same cautions apply when evaluating their results. It is cautioned to look at the bias of the researcher(s), overgeneralization of results, questionable conclusions, and statistical techniques that are not well-suited for the study.

E. General Considerations When Evaluating Research and Programs ← look over

- Examine the type of research design and determine if it is appropriate (experimental, quasi-experimental, nonexperimental, correlational, single case). *Note:* **Meta-analysis** studies are typically very strong, but can have biases and errors if improper statistical techniques are used.

- Examine the **sample size** of the study and determine if the study is sufficiently powerful.

- Analyze critical statistics related to **reliability and validity** factors.

- Determine if the **effect size** of results is significant and large.

- Are **biases** in the research held in check to the extent possible?

- Are **confounding factors** addressed so the results can be trusted?

- Be critical of the statistical analysis employed by and conclusions from the researcher.

- How was the sample collected and is it **representative** of the population (relevance)?

- Are the researcher's conclusions consistent with the results, or is there **overgeneralization**?

- **Limitations** of the research should be well reasoned, meaningful, and discussed.

- Are the **results of the study generalizable** and practical to your school's purposes?

- Are results linked to **effective interventions**?

Domain 3: Legal, Ethical, and Professional Practices

I. NASP Ethical Principles

Note: On the *Praxis* exam, all ethical questions should be answered based on the following principles. It is worth **memorizing** the following four principles. For any given legal question, determine whether each response option violates any part of these principles. If an option violates even one of the principles, it is probably not the correct answer.

A. Respect for the Dignity and Rights of All Persons

Practitioners demonstrate respect for the autonomy of persons and their right to self-determination, respect for privacy, and a commitment to just and fair treatment of all persons.

B. Professional Competence and Responsibility

School psychologists must practice within the boundaries of their competence and use scientific knowledge from psychology and education to benefit people. They should accept responsibility for the choices they make.

C. Honesty and Integrity in Relationships

Psychologists must be truthful and adhere to their professional standards. Practitioners must be honest about their qualifications, competencies, and roles. They work in cooperation with other professional disciplines to help students and families. Avoid multiple relationships that diminish professional effectiveness.

D. Responsibility to Schools, Families, Communities, the Profession, and Society

School psychologists promote positive school, family, and community environments. Psychologists must respect the law and encourage strict ethical conduct. One can advance one's professional excellence by mentoring less experienced practitioners and contribute to the school psychology knowledge base.

II. Additional Ethical Practices and Specific Guidelines

A. Test Use and Misuse

Practitioners must comprehend the technical aspects of psychometrics, testing, and measurement of human traits. Use multiple sources of information when evaluating students. Maintain assessment records and test confidentiality.

B. Confidentiality

Practitioners must adhere to strict confidentiality principles. For example, obtain written consent before sharing information, destroy documents before throwing them away, do not discuss confidential information with people who do not need to know such information, and make sure students know the limits of confidentiality (e.g., safety and harm issues). A key element of confidentiality, whether written, verbal, or electronic, is honoring the *"need to know"* *principle*. Psychologists do not share information without parental consent and only share information with those who have a "need to know." Psychologists must take active steps to protect the student and family's personal information and materials. Information between a student and psychologist is considered **"privileged"** and protected.

C. Supervision Standards

Practitioners should know the key aspects of proper supervision. Important aspects include providing at least 2 hours of supervision per week to interns, holding the proper professional license and credentials, and maintaining one supervisor for two interns ratio. It is recommended that interns are placed in schools of 500 to 700 students (1:500–700 intern-to-student ratio).

D. Private Practice Standards

Guidelines under this area involve financial issues. For example, do not charge people for the same services provided by the school district that employs you unless the client fully understands that the school's services are available for free. Do not accept money for referrals. Do not engage in private-practice work during school hours. Provide honest and complete information about yourself and your services when advertising your practice.

E. Reporting of Abuse and Safety

Know abuse laws and your mandated duties. A psychologist's duty to protect children is his or her highest responsibility. The duty to protect children outweighs confidentiality. Safety issues are critical, and you have a duty to warn others of harm. (This is a likely *Praxis* exam test item.)

F. Child Benefit Is Always the Focus

Psychologists should consult with teachers and staff, but do not counsel adults. The focus of a school psychologist's efforts is on the child and within the scope of training (0–21 years old). Provide information and resources to adults in need, but provide interventions to children.

G. Provide Balanced Information

Give research information on medications to parents, but do not pressure parents about medication. Provide balanced opinions about the benefits and liabilities of treatments or interventions that involve student issues.

H. Technology Issues

Psychologists are embedded in a culture of technology and must be keenly aware of the many ways it can enhance psychological practices, but also ways technology can harm students, **especially from the standpoint of confidentiality**. Technology issues to be considered:

- **Confidential report writing** and secure storage of electronic reports
- Confidential and **secure data storage** of student information
- E-mail transmissions that protect the identity of students
- Secured electronic communication about students
- **Secure storage** of protocols and test information (both electronic and traditional hard copies)
- Respect **copyright laws** regarding the electronic scanning and copying of data, especially test protocols and assessment information

III. Grievances → read over

Complaints about an NASP member: The following are guidelines to understand when engaged in an ethical dispute:

1. Complaints must be made by an identified person (not anonymous).
2. It is important to try to resolve concerns with the individual *before* filing a complaint. People who file a complaint do not have to be NASP members.
3. An ethics committee will decide whether to hear the case.
4. An ethics committee will examine the evidence and determine if the complaint has merit and whether the complaint is in violation of NASP ethics.
5. Notification in writing will be granted to an individual who has been filed against.
6. An ethics committee will attempt to resolve conflicts through discussion and participation of all parties in the dispute.
7. Possible actions by an ethics committee:
   - Dismiss complaint
   - Seek more information
   - Corrective measures
   - Member placed on probation
   - Require member to give compensation or provide an apology
   - Require additional training and skill development
   - Expulsion from NASP

Note: **Additional** Internet resource: NASP Ethical Conduct and Professional Practices, available at **www.nasponline.org/standards/ethics/ethical-conduct-professional-practices.aspx**

IV. Legal and Best-Practice Considerations

Issues Involving Students and Practices

A. Aversive Procedures

These are discouraged and should be considered a last resort for students (e.g., self-injurious behaviors may need temporary restraining). Informed parental consent is necessary for aversive procedures.

B. Corporal Punishment

The NASP strongly opposes the use of corporal punishment in schools. Psychologists should educate others about the harm that corporal punishment causes children.

C. General Discipline

Courts have ruled that schools should apply discipline in a fair, nondiscriminatory manner. School rules should be clearly stated and the consequences for breaking rules understood by all students.

D. Suspension and Expulsion

Schools have the authority to suspend students. Short-term suspensions are 10 days or less. *Special education students must have a special review meeting* if they are suspended 10 or more days. The Individuals with Disabilities Education Act (**IDEA**) contains *special protections for students with disabilities*. Students with disabilities who violate a school rule may be removed from school for no more than 10 cumulative days without a review meeting. For suspensions less than 10 days, schools are not required to provide educational services.

E. Change of Placement Because of Disciplinary Removals

A change of placement occurs if:

- The removal is for **more than 10 consecutive days.**
- The behavior is substantially similar in all instances that lead to the removal.
- There have been additional factors such as the length of each removal, the total number of times the student has been removed, or the proximity of the removals to each other.
- A school psychologist must also provide a functional behavioral assessment (FBA) to determine the cause of the behavior.

F. Manifestation Determination

A manifestation meeting is conducted by the individualized education program (IEP) team to determine whether or not the student's behavior that led to a suspension or an expulsion was a result of a disability. This meeting must be held within 10 days of the change of placement decision. If the behavior was a manifestation of the student's disability, the team must provide an FBA and implement a behavior plan for the student. The child may return to the original school placement or be placed in another school if it is part of the new plan and agreed on by the team.

Note: If the behavior was not determined to be a manifestation of the child's disability, disciplinary procedures may be applied to the child in the same manner as children without disabilities, except that the child still receives the same additional protections under IDEA. Additional protections to be considered in these situations are free and appropriate public education (**FAPE**) and least restrictive environment.

G. Special Suspension and Expulsion Considerations

Schools may place a child with a disability in an interim placement for 45 days, regardless of manifestation determination, if the student carried a weapon to school; inflicted serious bodily harm on another individual; or knowingly sold, used, or possessed drugs.

- Parents or schools can appeal the manifestation determination to a hearing officer.

- A child who has a disability, but has not yet received an IEP, can have the same protections under IDEA if the school or parents suspect that the student has a disability.

H. Least Restrictive Environment (LRE)

An LRE is mandated for children with disabilities. The section of IDEA that pertains to LRE reads as follows:

> To the maximum extent appropriate, children with disabilities should be educated with children who are not disabled, and special classes, separate schooling, or other removal of children with disabilities from the regular educational environment should occur only when the nature or severity of the disability is such that education in regular classes with the use of supplementary aids and services cannot be achieved satisfactorily. (http://idea.ed.gov/explore/view/p/,root,statute,I,B,612,a,5,)

V. Lawsuits for Practitioners

- **Malpractice:** Lawsuits typically occur if there is harm to a student as a result of the professional interaction. The likelihood of a school psychologist being sued for malpractice is low.

- **Supervision:** Even though interns are supervised, both supervisor and intern can be sued.

- **Negligence:** Of all legal suits, negligence is the most common offense and mostly occurs when there is a student suicide or injury that could have been reasonably prevented by the practitioner.

VI. Specific Laws and Cases Relevant to School Psychology

- **Education for All Handicapped Children Act (EAHCA), 1975**
  - The *first* special education law in the United States
  - Often referred to as Public Law 94-142
  - After various amendments, the **name was changed to IDEA** (Individuals with Disabilities Education Act)

- **Individuals with Disabilities Education Improvement Act (IDEIA), 2004**
  - Applies to students with the following disabilities: autism; deaf–blindness; deafness; hearing impairment; mental retardation; multiple disabilities; orthopedic impairments or other health impairments; emotional disturbance; specific learning disability; speech or language impairment; traumatic brain injury (TBI); visual impairment, including blindness.
  - Mandates FAPE for all children with disabilities.
  - Mandates that students receiving special education services are placed in an LRE.
  - States **must not require the use of the discrepancy model** and must **permit the use of a response to intervention (RTI) model**. IDEA may permit the use of other research-based procedures for identifying learning disabilities (LD). **(This point is a key concept of IDEA and may be asked on the *Praxis* exam.)** Note that the NASP endorses the use of RTI, but schools can actually still use other models, such as the discrepancy model, to determine eligibility for services.
  - Elaborates and further defines parental safeguards and rights presented in IDEA.
  - Provides funds for children from birth to age 3 years.

- **No Child Left Behind (NCLB), 2001**
  - Purpose is to close the achievement gap
  - Targets high-risk schools
  - Mandates statewide formal assessments for grades 3 to 8. Each state must strive for academic proficiency for students or face possible consequences by governing agencies.
  - Made public school choice available for students at schools that are low performing for 2 years.
  - Act requires highly qualified teachers for public schools.

- **Family Educational Rights and Privacy Act (FERPA), 1974**
  - Schools must adhere to strict confidential student record-keeping procedures.
  - FERPA record-keeping laws are designed to protect confidentiality and allow parents access to educational records.

- **The Rehabilitation Act: Section 504, 1973**
  - This is not a special education law; rather it is part of a civil rights law.
  - Provides a broader definition of "handicap" than "disability" under IDEA (Sped Law).
  - Section 504 prohibits discrimination against otherwise qualifying individuals on the basis of a handicapping condition in any program receiving federal funds.
  - Complaints are serviced by the Office for Civil Rights (OCR)
- **Americans with Disabilities Act (ADA)**
  - A civil rights law to prohibit discrimination solely on the basis of disability in employment, public services, and accommodations.
- **Zero Reject Principle**
  - Established *Child Find*, which requires states to locate and identify children with disabilities and provide them with full educational opportunity, regardless of the severity of the disability.
  - No **child** with a disability can be denied a free appropriate public education.
  - **Child Find Law** for children 0 to 3 years old was based on Public Law 94-457, Education of the Handicapped Act. Public Law 94-457 authorized early intervention for toddlers and families.
  - The **Perkins Act** gives rights to transition special education students into vocational programs. Provides occupational access.

  Note: Key resource to review ADA, IDEA, and Section 504 laws:

  dredf.org/advocacy/comparison.html
- **Key legal cases/case law**
  - *Brown v. Board of Education* states that educational facilities are not allowed to segregate according to race.
  - *Hobson v. Hansen* ruled that schools must provide equal educational opportunities despite a family's socioeconomic status (SES). Review laws dealing with ability tracking.
  - *Diana v. State Board of Education* states that assessments must be administered in the native language of the student in order to validate minority testing practices. This is similar to another case, *Guadalupe v. Temple School District*. In this case, it was ruled that students cannot be identified as mentally retarded unless they were properly assessed by considering the student's primary language and had scores at least two standard deviations below the mean.
  - *Larry P. v. Riles* was a landmark case in California that ruled that the percentage of minority students placed in special education classrooms could not exceed the percentage in the representative population. This ruling

was based on the fact that there was an overrepresentation of minorities classified as mentally retarded.

- *PASE v. Hannon* is a pro-special education ruling that endorsed the use of standardized tests as long as the tests are not culturally biased and are used with several other measures.
- *PARC v. Commonwealth of Pennsylvania (1972).* This is a landmark case that marks the genesis of FAPE. The court ruled in this case that intellectually disabled children should have access to public education and that due process rights shall be honored and preserved.
- *Marshall v. Georgia* is also a pro-special education ruling that stood in contrast to the *Larry P.* case. The Marshall ruling stated that the percentage of minorities placed in special education can exceed the percentage in the representative population as long as the appropriate and proper steps for placement were followed.
- *Honig v. Doe* states that special education students must have a manifestation hearing to review placement if they are suspended for more than 10 days.
- *Oberti v. Cementon (1993)* is a legal case that affirmed the rights of a special needs student to be included **(inclusion)** in regular education classes and activities. The courts also underscored that schools must adhere to the IDEA requirements especially those related to an **LRE**.
- *Rowley v. Hudson Board of Education (1982)* is an important landmark case wherein the judge stated that public schools *do not have to provide the best education, but rather an adequate education.* In other words, schools do not have to provide a Cadillac; a Ford is acceptable. (*Note:* Never repeat the previous statement to a parent.) This case defined and **provided parameters for FAPE.**
- The *Tarasoff* case is a well-known case that is an interesting story. In short, the court ruled that a school district has a **duty to warn** the parents if their child is in danger. (This is important for antibullying programs and threat assessment situations.)
- *Lau v. Nichols (1974)* ruled that schools must provide accommodations for English as a second language (ESL) students.
- *Tatro v. Irving Independent School District* was a Supreme Court case that ruled that schools must provide medical services that do not require a medical doctor to perform such medical services, even if the child needs full-time attention from a nurse.

VII. Special Education Procedural Safeguards

Know key procedural safeguards and the time frames for compliance as required by law.

- **Complaints**: Must be filed within *2 years of problem or dispute.*

- **Resolution meetings**: Within *15 days* of receiving the complaint, schools must convene a meeting.

- **Due process hearings**: Parents have the right to request a third-party hearing officer for special education disputes.

- **Consent**: Written parental consent *must be obtained before an evaluation*. Schools may proceed without consent for triennial reviews if documented reasonable efforts have been made to contact parent(s).

- **Notice**: Previous written notice must be given to parents for the initiation or change of a student's identification, evaluation, placement, change of service, or educational programming. Remember, there is a difference between a notice and consent.

- **Procedural safeguards notice:** A parents' rights booklet must be provided to parents *once per year* and at the initial evaluation if a parent requests it and if a complaint has been filed. This may be posted on the school's website.

- **IEP meetings:** Must be held within *60 days* after a parent signs consent for initial evaluation and *once a year* after that. Reevaluations are held *every 3 years*.

- **Special education team:** The team must consist of parents, at least one regular education teacher, at least one of the child's special education teachers, a representative of the school who is qualified to provide or supervise the provision of services, and someone who can interpret the evaluation results. It may also consist of other individuals who have knowledge or special expertise about the child as well as the child when appropriate.

- **Excusal from meeting**: A parent needs to submit a written note to the school that gives permission for a member of the IEP team to be excused from the meeting. However, someone must be present who can explain assessment results.

Foundations and Historical Developments

I. Timeline of Important Historical Developments

Note: It is unlikely that you will have to memorize specific dates. However, it might be beneficial if you know the time frame for the origin of psychology, when school psychology was accepted as a professional association, and important legislative acts that impacted the field (e.g., Public Law 94-142; 1975). A primary resource for historical events can be found in Fagan and Wise (2007).

The following timeline is based on Fagan and Wise's work.

- **1870 to 1909: Origin of psychology as a professional field**
  - Emergence of empirically valid psychological tests
  - Psychology gains form as a profession
  - Initial psychological practices emerge

- **1910 to 1929: Expansion and acceptance of psychology as a professional discipline**

- **1930 to 1939: First major regulations and laws for practice**
- **1940 to 1949: Accreditation bodies form**
- **1950 to 1959: School psychology subfield forms**
- **1960 to 1969: Development of professional growth and training programs, NASP founded**
- **1970 to 1979: Strict modern regulations and laws appear, association expanded, first special education laws created**
- **1980 to 1989: Evolution of NASP, first NASP exam**
- **1990 to 1999: Growth and reforms occur, new identity considered**
- **2000 to present: NASP identity and practice expanded**
- **2001: Passage of NCLB**
- **2004: Reauthorization of IDEA**
- **2008: NASP celebrates 40th anniversary**
- **2010: NASP adopts new professional standards**

Supplemental Historical Considerations and Notable Experts

- **William Wundt** is considered the **founding father of psychology** (experimental, structuralism) and started the first psychology lab in Germany in the **1870s**. He wrote the first widely regarded psychology paper on the physiology of psychology.

- The **father of** *school* **psychology** is **Lightner Witmer**. Dr. Witmer established a clinic at the University of Pennsylvania in 1896. He combined educational and psychological services to help students with learning and behavioral problems.

- The **first** *school* **psychologist** was **Arnold Gesell.** Gesell became the first school psychologist in **1915**. He believed that development in children was a parallel and orderly process. Gesell is believed to have been the first to develop tests that measured development in children.

- **B. F. Skinner** (1904–1990) was a major contributor to the field of behaviorism. Skinner believed that all behavior was shaped and maintained by consequences that followed behavior. His theories are also steeped in empirical methods. Skinnerian principles are primarily used today in school systems due to their practical and effective applications.

- **Albert Bandura** believed that cognition helped to drive behavior. Bandura added balance to the strict beliefs of the behavioristic theories of Skinner.

- Much of the work that school psychologists conduct is based on the critical premise that key human traits fall on a **normal curve** that forms the shape of a bell (**bell curve**). Several experts were involved in the initial observance of the bell curve in the 1700s, but reference **Francis Galton** for his work on the theory in 1880. **Alfred Binet** was one of the first scientists to measure the construct of intelligence and its relation to the normal curve.

- One of the most comprehensive but easy to understand resources about testing, measurement, and psychometrics is the **Web Center for Social Research Methods**: www.socialresearchmethods.net

- Factor analysis and two-factor analysis, which are key statistical methods, provide validation for the theory of intelligence tests that are based on "g." "g" correlates with other factors to varying degrees to create human thinking ability. **Spearman and Thurstone** both contributed substantially to psychometrics and cognitive testing. Spearman, especially, helped develop factor analysis.

- **Lewis Terman** studied gifted children and believed in cognitive ability testing. He also believed that bright children should have resources allocated for their special needs. Terman helped to revise the Stanford–Binet cognitive test for use with American children. In America, Terman's revised Stanford–Binet intelligence test was the first to be employed in 1916.

- The current theory on intelligence is that intelligence is based on a complex interplay of genetics (heredity) and environmental factors. Intelligence is closely associated with an ability to adapt to one's environment and apply information. A key expert to suggest this balanced view of intelligence was **Dr. Philip Vernon**. In contrast to Vernon, **Arthur Jensen** is a prominent researcher known for his work in behavioral genetics. Jensen believes that intelligence has a very strong genetic basis.

- Several widely adopted cognitive ability tests that are currently used by school psychologists are based on the **Cattell–Horn** theory of crystallized and fluid intelligence. Fluid intelligence is associated with reasoning with novel problems, whereas crystallized intelligence is related to acquired knowledge and skills. Know that the most recent theoretical basis for cognitive tests, such as the Weschler Intelligence Test for Children, Fifth Edition (WISC-V) and Differential Ability Scales-II (DAS-II), is the **Cattell–Horn–Carroll** or **CHC theory**. CHC is *statistically* derived and heavily validated. The CHC model adds several additional narrow abilities to the crystallized and fluid view of intelligence.

Insider Tip

Although it is unlikely that you will need to remember specific dates, you probably will have to know the names of landmark laws and legal cases. You might have one or two questions regarding experts in the field of school psychology, but it is probably not a good idea to memorize all experts. Study only the well-known names and their significant contributions to the field of psychology. Finally, it is critical to know what constitutes poor practices and what psychological practices are illegal. As mentioned in the Introduction, key ethical guidelines involve informed consent and practices that benefit children while safeguarding their dignity.

Concepts to Remember

1. Diversity exam questions will be easier to answer if you familiarize your-self with the NASP's general positions on the topic. Diversity is necessary in education and it entails a special sensitivity from school psychologists. A key point in this area to remember is that all children can learn, regardless of culture, special needs, and learning characteristics.

2. Familiarize yourself with the diverse set of student characteristics and the importance of individualized curriculum when teaching diverse learners.

3. Understand the negative impact of **disproportionality**.

4. Know the special considerations regarding testing English language learner (ELL) students. For example, using interpreters for tests that are not normed on a special population is not typically considered best practice due to test biases.

5. Know how to evaluate research and intervention programs for schools or systems. Effective evaluation entails that practitioners have a critical per-spective that evaluates key psychometrics and research designs.

6. School psychologists need to examine specific statistics-related concepts, such as reliability and validity. Psychologists should also know the catego-ries of effect sizes (e.g., small: 0.2, moderate: 0.5, and large: 0.8).

7. Generally know the principles of various ANOVA methods and why some methods are better suited for particular research designs. ANCOVA is typi-cally a powerful analysis method because it accounts for error variance.

8. Review statistical terms and concepts from Chapter 1; this information will help you answer test items related to research and program evaluation as detailed in this chapter. Terms such as independent variable, dependent variable, correlation, and statistical significance are helpful to know.

9. In relation to ethical practices, the NASP strongly endorses the practice of parental notification for services, informed consent, student advocacy, con-fidentiality, and community involvement. As a consequence of the NASP's endorsements, answer relevant test questions that are congruent with these concepts.

10. Especially study **IDEA Public Law 94-142** very thoroughly. Note the changes in IDEA in a more recent act called IDEIA. IDEA gives the right to a FAPE and an LRE for all students.

11. **FERPA** concepts are important to know very well. FERPA is sometimes called the **Buckley Amendment.** This Act gives families the right to review the records of their children and the files must be kept **confiden-tial**. The public and other people who do not have legal privileges cannot review a student's file. Confidentiality and a **"need to know"** is central to this law.

12. Remember that **Section 504** is a civil rights law that guarantees access to a school building and to a school's curriculum. Many people mistakenly

believe Section 504 is an educational law, but it is important to remember the Office for Civil Rights (OCR), not the Department of Education, enforces it. Section 504 is a law governing the rights of handicapped people. Students with hearing or vision problems sometimes fall under this law.

13. The NASP endorses the idea of lifelong learning and professional growth. Psychologists need to stay current, especially with ethical and professional practices in order to supervise/mentor new school psychologists.

14. Familiarize yourself with information related to supervision and mentoring. For example, there are two types of supervision: professional and administrative. Professional is the oversight and teaching of specific psychological practices, while administrative supervision centers on the logistics of service delivery and job performance.

15. Issues related to supervision and training:

- Supervisors need to be licensed and working in the field for a minimum of 3 years.

- Interns need a minimum of 2 hours of field-based supervision per week.

- Clear and effective evaluation/feedback methods for both intern and supervisor are necessary.

- Accessible supports for school psychologists are available when training.

- Provide robust training opportunities for interns/trainees.

16. Each of the landmark legal case cited in this chapter should be examined thoroughly. You should clearly understand the impact of these landmark legal cases on both students and schools.

5

Special Content Areas: School Neuropsychology, Traumatic Brain Injury, and Other Concepts

This chapter contains content and new information that do not fit neatly under the other major categories noted earlier. For example, in the first edition of this book, it was mentioned that neuropsychology would have an impact on the field of school psychology. Since that time, neuropsychology has greatly influenced school psychology and has even created a new subfield called *school neuropsychology*. Recent graduates in school psychology might have a knowledge advantage over veteran school psychologists because neuropsychological course work is now required by many graduate programs. Neuropsychological research is especially dynamic, and advances within this field are occurring frequently.

In my opinion, the largest area of influence that neuropsychology has on school psychology is within the area of pediatric brain injury. In the future, several school psychologists will serve on or lead brain injury resource teams (BIRTs) and help manage concussions at the school level. Brain injury issues are readily applicable to the practice of school psychology as practitioners routinely measure and assess brain-based functions typically associated with brain dysfunction. In fact, in more than any other profession, psychologists are the experts in the measurement of brain functioning.

Do not expect many questions on the National Association of School Psychologists' (NASP) *Praxis®* exam regarding the following areas. You might only have three or four questions that relate to this chapter. However, future NASP tests will likely have more questions related to these topics because of their recognized importance.

School Neuropsychology

Neuropsychology is the study of **brain–behavior relationships**. School neuropsychology is the study of brain–behavior relationships as they apply in a school setting and how neurological factors might impact a student's academic functioning. The term *school neuropsychologist* is still unregulated in many states, but the field and acceptance of this subspecialty is growing (see Dr. Daniel Miller's [2013] work). School neuropsychologists believe that most learning dysfunctions, behavioral disorders, and emotional disorders are brain-based issues. By understanding the neurological underpinnings of brain functioning, school neuropsychologists are better able to provide answers to parents about why their child is having difficulty in school. It is also important to remember that a traditional school psychologist may administer a mainstream cognitive assessment, such as the Wechsler Intelligence Scale for Children, Fifth Edition (WISC-V), and the results interpreted through a neuropsychological lens if the practitioner has the appropriate training.

I. Basic Neuroanatomy

At the most basic brain level are primary cells called neurons. Billions of neurons are connected to each other throughout the entire brain to create a neurological network. The network of neurons is connected to tightly bundled specialized neurons called nuclei. These neuronal bundles are found in localized areas of the brain that perform particular functions (Carter et al., 2009; Sweeney, 2009). These specific brain regions and their primary functions are illustrated in Figure 5.1. For a virtual and interactive tour of the brain, reference this website: **www.pbs.org/wnet/brain/3d.**

Scientists have various ways to organize the brain and its functions. One way to conceptualize brain processes is to organize its functioning starting from how the brain develops physiologically. The first areas of the brain to develop are the regions located at the base of the brain. Basal brain areas are generally related to basic physiological functions. For example, two important basal sections are the brain stem and the cerebellum. The brain stem and cerebellum control involuntary functions such as breathing, heart rate, gross motor movement, and arousal. Brain injuries to these basal areas are extremely serious as such injuries can be fatal (e.g., can stop heart beat, breathing, and consciousness).

The upper regions of the brain are associated with complex functions commonly associated with sensory processes, information processing, and purposeful behavior. These highly evolved brain areas influence verbal communication, fine motor movement, vision, emotions, rational thought, comprehension, and reasoning.

A. Functional Areas (Lobes)

There are four major lobes of the brain that play a major role in processing, information, thinking, memory, and regulating behavior. While sections of the

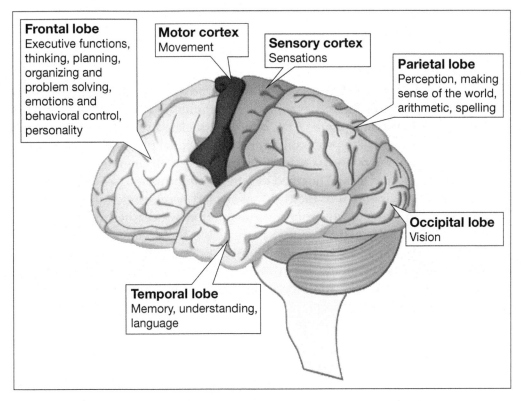

Frontal lobe
Executive functions, thinking, planning, organizing and problem solving, emotions and behavioral control, personality

Motor cortex
Movement

Sensory cortex
Sensations

Parietal lobe
Perception, making sense of the world, arithmetic, spelling

Occipital lobe
Vision

Temporal lobe
Memory, understanding, language

FIGURE 5.1   Specific functions of brain areas.

brain may play a "primary" role in specific functions, there are other areas that are typically recruited for proper functioning. In other words, one brain area is typically not 100% responsible for a specific function because the brain works as an integrated system.

1. **Frontal lobe:** This lobe is largely responsible for **executive functions**. This area does not necessarily process information as much as it controls other aspects of the brain (e.g., it is the brain manager or executive). This lobe helps in planning future actions and regulating behavior. It is also responsible for cognitive flexibility and helps people shift to different aspects of problem solving or topics.

2. **Parietal lobe:** Located roughly on the top portion of the brain, this area helps to assimilate body sensations (i.e., somatosensory). Sensory disorders are typically associated with the parietal lobe. As a secondary role, this lobe also helps with developing symbolic associations and math skills and with integrating information.

3. **Temporal lobe:** Located on the right and left sides of the brain, this lobe primarily processes auditory information and language. The temporal lobe is implicated in **reading problems** and phonological processing difficulties. Memory storage is associated with this lobe.

4. **Occipital lobe:** Located at the back of the head, this area is responsible for processing visual information.

B. Hemisphere Operations

In addition to specific brain lobe functions, another broad conceptualization of brain function relates to hemispheric operations. It is a commonly held—but simplified—belief that the **right hemisphere** of the brain is associated with creativity, holistic thinking, novel information processing, and visual–spatial processes. In contrast to the right, the **left hemisphere** of the brain is concerned with language, verbal information, sequences, and factual (learned or familiar) information (see Figure 5.2).

Currently, a refinement of the right versus left hemisphere model involves an emphasis on new versus routine information processing. Some experts believe the right half of the brain is responsible for processing novel information. Once the novel information is processed and understood, it is transferred to the left side of the brain where it becomes part of the person's knowledge base. The left side stores routine, familiar, and factual information. Previously learned information is later retrieved and used when a person engages in routines or responds to the environment (Fiorello & Hale, 2004).

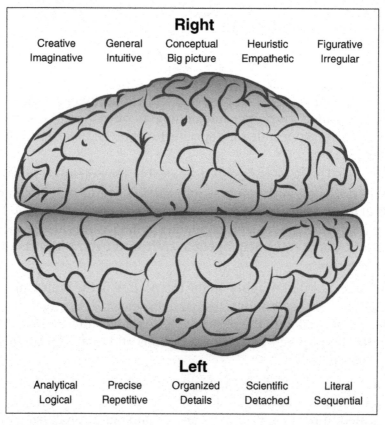

FIGURE 5.2 Left and right brain hemispheres.

C. Key Neurological Concepts

1. Although there are areas of the brain (lobes) that are primarily responsible for specific functions, the brain works as a whole unit and needs all parts working together in order to function properly.

2. It appears that no one particular area is responsible for storing all **memories,** but the medial temporal lobe plays a key role in long-term storage. A major part of the brain called the **hippocampus** is implicated in *forming* memories because of its role in associating emotions with events.

3. The **amygdala** is associated with **emotions** and emotional responses.

4. The corpus callosum is a bundle of nerves that connects both halves of the brain and allows for communication between the two hemispheres.

5. Attention deficit hyperactivity disorder (ADHD) is associated with a dysfunction and neurochemical issue within the frontal lobes. However, ADHD research is still emerging and other brain structures may be implicated with this disorder.

6. The cerebral cortex is associated with higher order reasoning.

7. Broca's area and Wernicke's area are implicated in language problems and reading difficulties. Broca's area is linked to expressive language, whereas Wernicke's area is associated with receptive language.

8. Aphasia is the inability to use language, and agnosia is the inability to identify seen objects.

9. The limbic system (part of the lower brain) houses several neurological structures responsible for our emotions and memories (e.g., amygdala, hippocampus, and others).

10. Neurochemicals (brain chemicals):

    - **Dopamine**: This neurochemical is involved in producing positive moods and emotions. Dopamine is associated with reward, pleasure, and novelty seeking. It is implicated in Parkinson's disease and ADHD.

    - **Endorphins**: Endorphins are a natural opiate similar to morphine that are released to moderate pain.

    - **Serotonin** is associated with relaxation, sleep, and mood. An imbalance in serotonin is implicated in clinical depression.

    - **Glutamate** is a significant excitatory neurotransmitter that is released by nerve cells in the brain. It is responsible for sending signals between nerve cells. Under normal conditions, it plays an important **role in learning and memory. Glutamate** is one of the most prevalent neurochemicals in the brain and is related to a substantial number of disorders and neurodegenerative diseases.

II. Traumatic Brain Injury

A recent legal development is that federal law allows for traumatic brain injury (TBI) to be its own diagnostic category on individualized education plans (IEPs). Like learning disabilities, a brain injury must impair the functioning of a student to a marked degree and have an educational impact to qualify for special education services. Students who have brain injuries and receive special education services typically have a medical diagnosis of a moderate or severe brain injury. Mild brain injuries (mild traumatic brain injury [mTBI]), such as concussions, generally do not qualify children for IEP services due to their temporary nature.

There is neither a solitary test for a brain injury nor a typical profile for brain injury. Each brain injury manifests itself differently in individuals. With the previous statements in mind, common neurological functions that are sensitive to brain insults are processing speed, attention, and memory. After a brain injury, crystallized skills and knowledge generally return to a degree, whereas fluid abilities are prone to significant disruption.

It is important for school psychologists to note that pediatric concussion management (supports) in schools is a rapidly evolving need for students. This area of need provides psychologists with a novel and important role in schools. A leader in the field of school psychology and concussion management is Dr. Karen McAvoy and her key resource called the *REAP Manual*.

The following are brief concepts and information that might be useful to remember about children and brain injuries.

Key TBI Concepts

1. Two excellent resources for brain injury include the *Brain Injury Association of America* (www.biausa.org) and the *Brain Injury in Children and Youth: A Manual for Educators*, available for free at **www.cde.state.co.us/cdesped/ sd-tbi**. Brain injury assessment ideas and intervention ideas are available at **cokidswithbraininjury.com**

2. TBI is sometimes referred to as acquired brain injury. TBI may cause more than 50,000 deaths or disabilities a year. TBI is a leading cause of death in children younger than 18 years.

3. Research in the area of head injury is advancing at a very fast pace and some new theories are contradicting theories from just a few years ago. For example, it was previously believed it was better to have a brain injury as a child because a child's brain could heal itself more effectively than an adult's. Current thinking has significantly changed and now it is believed that a child's brain is more vulnerable to damage than an adult's.

4. Concussions are considered brain injuries and typically heal in 10 to 28 days. Despite the previous statement, even mild concussions (e.g.,

mild brain injury and mTBI) can cause persistent difficulties. If concussion symptoms do not resolve in several weeks, then the student may have postconcussion syndrome (PCS). Children may seem okay after a hit to the head, but damage and swelling may occur, which is why students should seek medical attention after any hit to the head that causes signs or symptoms.

5. A mainstream concussion management support framework is provided by Dr. McAvoy's *REAP Manual*. **REAP stands for Reduce, Educate, Accommodate, and Pace.**

6. Children with significant TBI require frequent assessments because they may show drastic changes in the first year of recovery. Both cognitive and personality changes could be evident after a TBI.

7. There is debate over neuroelasticity (plasticity), or how the brain heals itself. Current research illustrates that children are more at risk for permanent brain damage than adults. The younger the developmental age, the more at risk the person is for various types of long-term problems.

8. Cognitive tests can help determine the functioning of the brain (i.e., what the person can do) after a head trauma. Cognitive tests for older TBI victims typically show a large amount of variation among subtest scores. Processing speed, fluid abilities, and behavioral and emotional changes are typically noted postinjury. However, there is no "classic" profile of TBI.

9. Symptoms and signs of TBI include headaches, sleep disruptions, mood swings, personality changes, light or noise sensitivity, and balance problems.

10. Interventions for students with TBI should focus on what the child can do and build upon those strengths (i.e., capacity or strength-based approach). Half-day schedules have been effective in teaching students with TBI because low energy is a common symptom. Remember that **cognitive fatigue** is a primary trait of students with brain injuries.

11. In moderate to severe TBI cases, errorless learning techniques have proved effective. Visual charts, repetition of new information, and repetition of skills are also key strategies to employ with students who have TBI.

Models of Basic Information Processing (Cognitive Psychology)

1. Basic (Simplistic) Information Processing Model
Information (Input)_____Central Processing_____Expressive (Output)

2. Complex Model

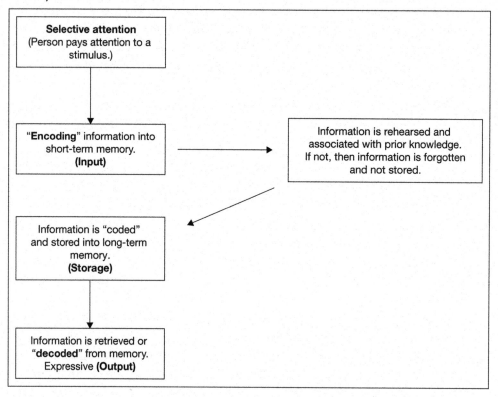

- *Note:* A breakdown or problem can occur at any level of the information-processing model. For example, people may have difficulty learning because they have not properly "encoded" the information. On the other hand, people may have properly encoded the information and understand concepts but cannot retrieve (decode) the details of the information.

- The average person can hold approximately **seven to eight bits of information in short-term memory**. Short-term memory should not be confused with working memory. In working memory, one must perform an activity while holding ideas, thoughts, and information *online*.

- People tend to remember the first and last aspects of new information they see or hear. This is called the **primacy memory effect** (referring to the first piece of information) and *recency* **effect** (referring to the last piece of information).

Learning Problems: Identifying Specific Learning Disabilities

1. **School psychology practices:** One of the most common issues that school psychologists are required to examine involves learning disabilities. The Individuals with Disabilities Education Act (IDEA) reauthorization increased

the options for identification of a specific learning disability (SLD) by permitting a number of different approaches beyond traditional IQ–achievement discrepancy comparisons. Primary areas to consider when school psychologists identify or diagnose an SLD involves a comprehensive, multidisciplinary evaluation that includes the assessment of a student's response to intervention (RTI) and an examination of a dysfunction in one or more of the basic psychological processes. The combination *of multiple sources of information, valid scientific RTI data, and mainstream cognitive testing* appears to be a sound approach to identifying learning disorders. It is also emphasized that *clinical judgment* plays an important role when dealing with complex diagnostic situations.

2. The *Diagnostic and Statistical Manual of Mental Disorders,* Fifth Edition (**DSM-5**; American Psychiatric Association, 2013) **and SLD**: The newest version of the *DSM* (i.e., *DSM-5*) includes changes to the category of SLD when compared to the *DSM-IV*—here are key points to remember:

- The *DSM-5* eliminates the use of the substantial discrepancy requirement.
- The *DSM-5* defines a learning disorder as academic difficulties that are well below average for age, and not better accounted for as an intellectual disability, but it does not require the use of intelligence testing.
- A new focus is on determining the extent of difficulties in academic areas.
- Learning disorders are specific instances of a single, overarching diagnosis instead of the *DSM-IV*'s provision of four separate disorders.
- The *DSM-5* utilizes a single diagnosis of specific learning disorder with specifiers that indicate the academic domain and specific skills that are impacted.
- The elimination of SLD—not otherwise specified (NOS).
- Addition of specifiers of degree of SLD: mild, moderate, and severe.

Additional Relevant Psychological Theories

Human Development

A. Piaget's Cognitive Developmental Stage Theory

This well-known theory is based on the premise that learning is active and children construct knowledge as they explore their environment and world.

- **Piaget's four stages of development**
  1. **Sensorimotor (0–2 years)**: Primarily involves motor actions and senses. Children eventually come to realize that objects exist separately from them and they can manipulate objects.
  2. **Preoperational (2–7 years):** Symbolic function emerges. Children develop the ability to make something stand for something else.

3. **Concrete operational (7–11 years):** Children begin to think about more than just one dimension of a problem or situation. They gain the understanding of *conservation*. Also gain the ability to think deeper and logically.

4. **Formal operational (11+ years):** Complex abstract thought emerges and hypothetical and deductive reasoning develops. Children perform mental operations on ideas or imagined situations.

B. Erik Erikson's Stages of Development

Erikson's theories are based on the notion that humans will confront a specific challenge at a given age range. Whether or not people successfully manage the challenge at a developmental stage directly influences their positive or negative outcome at that stage.

1. **Trust versus mistrust (0–18 months):** Attachment to a caregiver is important at this stage. A child must develop sufficient trust with the caregiver in order to explore the world. Mothers and fathers need to be warm, loving, and attentive to basic needs.

2. **Autonomy versus shame and doubt (18 months to 3 years):** Children start to develop a sense of confidence in their abilities to explore and to do things for themselves. Children begin to understand that they can control their behavior.

3. **Initiative versus guilt (3–5 years):** Children move from simple self-control, as in the previous stage, to taking initiative in play and in various tasks. Imaginary play and choosing activities are illustrated at this stage.

4. **Industry versus inferiority (6–12 years):** This stage covers the elementary school years, so know it well. Success or failure in school has lasting effects on self-efficacy and sense of adequacy. Children learn a sense of industry if they are recognized for various activities (e.g., painting, reading).

5. **Identity versus role confusion (13–18 years):** This stage covers the middle school and high school students. People develop a sense of identity, sense of self, and strong ego during this time. Peers, role models, and social pressures are factors associated with this stage.

6. **Intimacy versus isolation, generativity versus stagnation (or selfishness), and integrity versus despair:** The last few stages covered are important to review. However, the age ranges covered by these stages typically fall beyond the target population of school psychologists.

C. Bandura's Social Learning Theory

Albert Bandura's theory is a counterbalance to Skinner's strict behavioral theory of learning and development. Bandura's theory is based on children's ability to *observe* and learn vicariously. Children learn by their social interactions, which is why this theory is sometimes known as social cognitive theory.

1. Humans learn not only through reward and punishment conditioning, but also by observing and imitating others. For example, Bandura observed that children exposed to the aggressive behaviors of another person were likely to

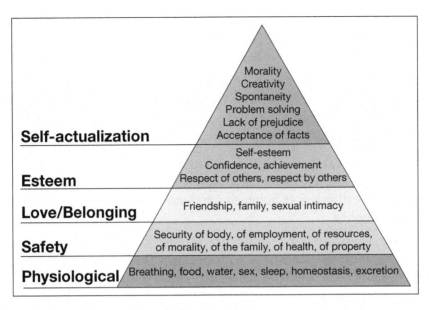

FIGURE 5.3   Maslow's hierarchy of needs (Finkelstein, 2006).

imitate that behavior (e.g., Bobo doll study). Although behavioral conditioning might take place, in some cases, no reinforcement is necessary to learn the behaviors.

2. Children imitate the behaviors of others and can select specific behaviors to imitate based on how they processed the information they observe.

D. Maslow's Hierarchy of Needs

Abraham Maslow, like other humanists such as Carl Rogers, offered a decidedly more positive view of human development than stage theories offered by Piaget and Freud. Maslow believed that if a student's lower level needs are supported, then higher levels in this hierarchy may be realized (see Figure 5.3).

E. Sigmund Freud's Psychodynamic Stages of Development

- **Psychodynamic theory:** A child's developing personality consists of three interrelated parts that are sometimes in conflict with each other:

  1. **Id:** Operates on the "pleasure principle." Maximizes pleasure and satisfies needs immediately.

  2. **Ego:** Is the rational, controlling part of personality that emerges and attempts to gratify needs through appropriate, socially constructive behavior.

  3. **Superego:** Emerges when the child internalizes (accepts and absorbs) parental or societal morals, values, and roles and develops a conscience.

- **Psychosexual stages:** Changes and outcomes in the organization and interaction of the id, ego, and superego involve five discrete stages. It is believed that lack of success in any stage could result in a child developing the primary traits of the stage as an adult. Although the following stages are now considered controversial due to the lack of empirical foundation, the major contribution of Freudian theory is the emphasis on how these early experiences shape later human development.

1. **Oral (0–1 year):** Infant is preoccupied with activities such as eating, sucking, and biting and with objects that can be put into the mouth.

2. **Anal (2–3 years):** The child learns to postpone personal gratification, such as "the pleasure of expelling feces" as he is trained to use the toilet.

3. **Phallic (3–5 years):** The child's sexual curiosity is aroused. He or she has a preoccupation with his or her own sexual anatomy that also alerts him or her to the differences between genders. This stage is critical for forming gender identity.

4. **Latency (6–12 years):** Sexual drives are temporarily submerged and children avoid relationships with peers of the other gender and instead become intensely involved with peers of the same gender.

5. **Genital (12+ years):** Sexual desires reemerge and are directed toward peers.

F. Kohlberg's Stages of Moral Development

Kohlberg's theory is based on the level of a child's cognitive capabilities, which influence moral reasoning and behavior.

- **Kohlberg's three stages of development**

1. **Preconventional:** Behavior is based on the desire to avoid punishment and gain rewards.

2. **Conventional:** Behavior is designed to acquire the approval of others and to maintain social relations. People accept societal regulations and conform to the rules. Children will conform to what parents say is right or wrong solely based on conforming to the rules. At this level, children generally do not consider higher order ethical standards.

3. **Postconventional:** Judgments about right and wrong are logical and behavior is controlled by an internalized ethical code that is relatively independent of the approval or disapproval of others.

G. B. F. Skinner's Behaviorism

Behaviorism is primarily based on consequences of behavior (rewards or punishments). The father of behaviorism, B. F. Skinner, believed that human behavior is largely shaped by the environment and through the consequences that immediately follow a behavior. Although behaviorism is a major theory of human development and it is heavily used in schools, experts assert that it is narrow and simplistic in scope. A criticism of strict behaviorism is that it does not consider the cognitive aspects of humans or the neurobiological features of behavior.

Critical NASP Resources to Review

- **Key Research Summaries on Various Relevant Concepts:** www.nasponline .org/research-and-policy/nasp-research-center/research-summaries
- **NASP Position Statements:** www.nasponline.org/research-and-policy/ professional-positions/position-statements

Insider Tip

This chapter contains supplemental, but relevant information that serves as important background information. Although there might be some actual exam items directly related to this chapter's content, most likely test questions will be indirectly related. As with some information found in other chapters, it is more appropriate to be highly familiar with this chapter's content rather than to memorize it. Exam questions related to human development, learning, or behavioral theory will typically start with a situational example, and then ask you to identify the specific theory or stage the example reflects.

Concepts to Remember

1. School neuropsychology is a growing field that is interested in *brain–behavior* relationships. Many of the tests that school psychologists employ can be interpreted through a neuropsychological lens.

2. The brain works as an integrated unit, with several brain areas sharing functions. While some brain regions share functions, there are some specific areas that have primary functions (e.g., the occipital lobe processes visual information).

3. Major brain areas to be familiar with include the following: The right hemisphere is typically related to simultaneous processing, spatial reasoning, and novel problem solving. The left hemisphere generally concerns language processes, sequential processing, and factual information. The frontal lobe is correlated to many traits associated with executive functioning, such as attention and behavioral regulation.

4. Brain injury is a leading cause of disability and death in youth. Currently, school districts are encouraging the formation of brain injury teams, where school psychologists are asked to take more of a leadership role. Many students with moderate to severe brain injuries require special education support. Be familiar with general supports provided for students to brain injuries.

5. Be familiar with mainstream information processing models proffered by cognitive psychologists. A common model includes the following key elements: attention, input-encoding, storage, output-decoding.

6. Be familiar with common disorders listed in the most current version of the *DSM* (i.e., *DSM-5*) and how such disorders are described. It might be helpful to be familiar with some of the issues related to the new *DSM*.

7. You do not necessarily have to memorize all the details related to theories of human development, behavior, and learning. However, be familiar with mainstream theories and the theorist that created them. Do not spend time with minor or controversial theories. Time is better utilized studying the tenets of behaviorism, such as response cost, schedules of reinforcement, and effective reinforcement principles.

Section II

Practice Tests

Note to the Reader

The following practice exams contain questions that are similar in both style and content to the actual items found on the *Praxis®* exam. However, it is important to note that several versions of this test are offered by the Educational Testing Service (ETS). Consequently, test questions and exam formats periodically change. For example, some students may be administered a test that contains a few questions with four response options, while some test takers may receive a version that includes test items with more response choices. Because the primary purpose of this guide is to help the student study effectively, but also in a time-efficient manner, these practice tests are designed with four response options instead of five or six. Having four response options does not significantly alter the difficulty of the sample test (25% vs. 20% correct guess rate), but it does allow the reader more time to study the complex content of test questions, which is the main point of taking practice tests. Questions that the reader answered incorrectly should be flagged as evidence of content that needs further review and study.

Most exam questions involve aspects that have myriad ancillary concepts associated with them. Therefore, the reader needs to fully understand all the related concepts each question addresses. Also, please note that some of the following mock test questions are associated with more than one test category as outlined in the Introduction of this guide. For example, questions regarding response to intervention (RTI) or Multi-Tiered System of Support (MTSS) can be linked to several categories such *as Direct and Indirect Services for Children, Schools, and Families* and *Systems-Level Services.*

During this trial run, ask yourself several questions about the underlying concept for each test item. You may even ask yourself how each test question could be asked differently. It is strongly recommended that you make notes regarding the questions you need to know more about. Notice the types of questions you miss the most. Are the missed questions the legal and ethical ones or the assessment ones? Also, be familiar with keywords and how those keywords are sometimes found in the correct response choice.

The benefit of taking practice tests is that it is an excellent way to study for the real test. Practice testing sharpens skills such as time management and response selection. It also decreases your anxiety because it takes some of the mystery out of the real exam.

A final comment and recommendation for the reader: As mentioned earlier, a high level of genuine effort has been made to ascertain the correct answers for each question. It is understood that some answers are open to debate and some experts might answer the following mock test questions differently. If the reader has concerns related to an answer provided in this guide, then it is important for him or her to conduct further research and discuss alternative responses with colleagues. A main point of this guide is to promote discussion of debatable items and for the reader to actively seek accuracy or clarity on areas of possible weakness. In the end, the test taker assumes responsibility for answering items correctly on the actual exam.

I personally wish you the best of luck and sincerely desire that aspiring school psychologists do well on the exam. Ready yourself as you would in an *actual testing situation*. Treat the following practice tests as real tests. Turn the page, read the directions carefully, and begin!

Practice Test I

DIRECTIONS: You have 2 hours and 20 minutes to complete the following 140-item test. Be mindful to keep *strict* time limits. Carefully examine the content of each response choice and select the option that is most closely aligned with the central aspects of the exam question. Do not leave any question blank. Answers and rationales for exam items are provided following Practice Test II.

Study and Test-Taking Strategies

Make a note of those questions that are very difficult to answer and move on to the next item. All questions carry the same score value, so do not spend too much time on one question. Remember to go back to difficult questions and complete them once you answer all other items.

Ready?   **Start Timing: 140 minutes**

1. Sue is a second-grade student who struggles with reading. It happens that Sue's teacher lives next door to a reading specialist in the same school district. Sue's teacher asked her neighbor to look at Sue's standardized reading test to offer some advice. What law has Sue's teacher violated?

   A. The Federal Confidentiality Act (FCA) of 1975

   B. No law was violated because the consultation was relevant for a reading specialist

   C. Individuals with Disabilities Education Act (IDEA) law provision for right to privacy

   D. Family Educational Rights and Privacy Act (FERPA)

2. Noam Chomsky is known for what psychological idea?

   A. Humans have a predisposition to acquire language

   B. Children who have impoverished backgrounds are more likely to have behavioral and emotional difficulties

C. Whole-word reading is innate

D. Children acquire language skills through explicit instruction

3. A school wants to adopt a new but controversial math curriculum. As a school psychologist, you are called in for a consultation. What do you tell the school's principal about best practices in this situation?

A. There will be resistance from some parents, so a meeting should be held with concerned parents

B. Parents need a way to voice their opinions during the adoption phase

C. The school should seek consensus on this issue because parents must agree on such an important topic

D. The school needs to consult with curriculum experts so that parents can make informed decisions

4. Which type of goal-setting approach is most appropriate when teaching teenage students?

A. Goal setting that is within the student's zone of proximal development

B. Mastery goal setting that increases performance and decreases anxiety

C. Performance goal setting based on classroom norms

D. High goals and standards to keep students striving for achievement

5. Which neurotransmitters are primarily implicated in depression?

A. Melatonin, serotonin, and dopamine

B. Serotonin, dopamine, and endorphins

C. Serotonin, norepinephrine, and dopamine

D. Glutamate, dopamine, and melatonin

6. A parent asks you to perform an emotional assessment on her daughter. When interviewing the parent for more background information on the situation, the mother mentions that her daughter has no friends and she appears withdrawn, sad, and anxious. Given the mother's observations, what is the most appropriate tool to initially use in your assessment?

A. The Behavior Assessment System for Children (BASC)

B. The Vineland

C. The Clinical Scales of Depression in Children-II

D. The Beck Depression Inventory

7. A child you recently tested with the Differential Ability Scales-II (DAS-II) had a General Conceptual Ability (GCA) standard score of 85. The student's Vineland assessment from the teacher illustrated an overall standard score

of 61, but the mother's Vineland resulted in an overall standard score of 87 and the father's Vineland revealed a score of 75. You determine that the discrepancy between the adaptive assessment scores is most likely due to:

A. Measurement error inherent in all tests, psychometrically referred to as standard error of measurement (SEM)

B. Differences in contextual factors; the child behaves differently in various settings

C. The subjectivity and different perceptions of raters

D. The difficulty associated with completing complex surveys

8. Which of the following is one of the first interventions employed for a child with attention deficit hyperactivity disorder (ADHD)?

A. Placing the student near the front of the classroom away from distractions (preferential seating)

B. Increasing the student's self-awareness and knowledge of the disorder

C. Having the student exercise before school to moderate hyperactive tendencies through natural dopamine production

D. Consistently reminding the student to take medication known to be effective in many cases (e.g., Ritalin, Adderall)

9. A 10th-grade teacher has a visually impaired student who is given an extensive assignment that requires a poster presentation. In this case, how should the teacher proceed?

A. Allow other students to help the impaired student

B. The teacher should set aside a special time to discuss optional accommodations for the assignment with the student

C. The visually impaired student should not be required to complete the entire assignment due to his or her handicapping condition and instead should be offered a relevant alternative

D. The task should be assigned as a joint effort between the teacher and the visually impaired student

10. You are a new school psychologist at a small public school. Your department leader gives you a new cognitive assessment to administer for which you have no formal training. The parents of the student you will be evaluating have hired an educational advocate. The advocate is formally requesting that you administer the new test because it uses the latest norms and it is culturally sensitive. From what you have read and heard from colleagues, the new test is highly regarded and should be used in this case. What should you do in this situation?

A. Ethically, you cannot administer the test and you should use a more familiar test

B. You can practice with the test first, and then administer it with supervision

C. You must to refer the case to another colleague who has more experience with the test

D. Ask a colleague to give the test, but be present during the administration

11. Your assistant principal notifies you that a seventh-grade student has made drawings depicting death. When you ask the student why she drew such pictures, the student stated she thinks people who commit suicide are cool. After intervening and speaking with the student, what should you do next?

A. Notify the parents of this situation and conduct a suicide evaluation

B. Notify administration and conduct a suicide assessment

C. Notify administration and a social worker to assist you with a suicide assessment

D. Call the student's parents and request that a suicide assessment be completed

12. You have just completed a multiday comprehensive assessment on a student initially referred for special education services. The student you tested has a Wechsler Intelligence Test for Children, Fifth Edition (WISC-V) Full Scale score of 67 and also has an Adaptive Behavior Assessment System (ABAS-III) score of 73. The student wants to know about his performance and asks you to explain the results. What is the best practice in this situation?

A. Tell the student that the test results give you information on how a student learns. The details should not be disclosed to the student, even with parent permission

B. Be truthful, but use developmentally appropriate language with the student when you discuss the results

C. First, secure permission from the parents before discussing assessment findings with the student

D. Discuss the results with the parent, student, and teacher at the same time

13. As a school psychologist, you work in a community where many parents use illegal drugs. You are concerned about one particular elementary school that you spend 2 days a week servicing. You have heard students talk about drugs and wanting to use drugs. What is an effective intervention in this case?

A. Present an antidrug intervention program to individual classes

B. Start a schoolwide antidrug campaign

C. Teach teachers how to talk with students about drugs

D. Gather parental, school, and community support to raise awareness and address the drug problem at school

14. What memory technique should students utilize to remember a long series of information?

   A. Chunking information

   B. Keyword note taking using personal technology

   C. Immediate multiple rehearsal trials with a 15-minute delayed review

   D. Teach students to remember patterns in information

15. According to the information processing model, incoming information is encoded into what first?

   A. The memory buffer

   B. The temporal lobe of the brain

   C. Conditional stimuli buffer

   D. Short-term memory (STM)

16. Diane is a sophomore at a large public high school. At the beginning of the year, Diane felt bullied by Sally. The first-year principal quickly intervened and stopped the bullying. A few months later, Diane reports to the administration that Sally is once again making aggressive comments at her. This time the principal suspends Sally for 2 days and calls Sally's parents. What is the most important recommendation you have for the principal?

   A. Call Diane's parents to notify them of the situation

   B. Make sure both Diane and Sally have mental health support

   C. Have Diane talk with the school psychologist or social worker about how to deal effectively with harassment in the future

   D. Recommend that Sally and Diane engage in a restorative practice to help prevent future incidences

17. Your school district wants to spend $10,000 to update its cognitive test library. For one particular test, the technical manual states the 6-week test–retest reliability coefficient is 0.79. You also make a note that the new test was correlated with a well-known test to determine convergent validity. The convergent correlation coefficient for the two tests was 0.62. Given the details of this case, you can tell your district which of the following:

   A. The new test has acceptable reliability and validity, but the validity is on the lower side of standard convention

   B. The new test's reliability coefficient supports the idea that the test measures what it is designed to measure, but the validity is unacceptable

   C. The correlation between the new and old test shows a moderate association and is typically not considered strong enough to recommend using the new test

   D. The new test can be used with confidence by the district as long as other measures are used as part of a comprehensive evaluation

18. Metacognition refers to what psychological and educational concept?

    A. Knowledge and self-awareness about one's own thoughts and abilities

    B. An effective reading technique

    C. A psychological counseling method used to help students think about their abilities and subsequent choices

    D. The ability to activate prior knowledge when trying to make a reading passage meaningful

Case example for questions 19 and 20: Seth is a ninth-grade student with a significant emotional disability (SED) identifying condition on his individual education plan (IEP). Seth was also diagnosed by a psychiatrist with several clinical disorders, including attention deficit hyperactivity disorder, combined type (ADHD-C) and anxiety disorder. During the school day, Seth is able to control most of his behaviors, but not all.

19. Despite Seth's above-average cognitive abilities, his grades are not stellar. However, he is passing all classes with Cs. Seth's teachers think he would benefit if he had more self-contained special education classes. What would you advise his teachers in this situation?

    A. Tell his teachers to keep data to track Seth's progress. The data will be used during his next annual review individual education plan (IEP) meeting to change his placement

    B. Tell the teachers that Seth's placement should be in the least restrictive environment and a more contained placement may not be warranted

    C. The special education team should discuss the issue with Seth's parents and then move him into more supportive classes once parental permission is secured

    D. Collaborate with the parents and ask them for their opinion in this situation

20. Seth's parents are very upset that he is making mostly Cs. Even though Seth is receiving special support services, his cognitive scores suggest that he should be making very high grades. The parents are threatening to file a lawsuit if Seth is not assigned increased direct support to address his needs more thoroughly. What most likely will happen in this situation?

    A. The school is providing "reasonable" education supports and does not have to supply all services. Therefore, the lawsuit will likely be unsuccessful

    B. The high cost of going to court will most likely force the school district to grant the parents' wishes

C. The parents and school district know that an individual education program (IEP) is a legal document and once a child is receiving special services, he is entitled to receive all services that a special education program offers

D. As stipulated under Individuals with Disabilities Education Act (IDEA, 2004), the parents will have to go to arbitration before a lawsuit can be filed

21. You have administered the Cognitive Assessment System (CAS-2) to evaluate a student's cognitive functioning. The student's overall (general) standard score is 50. How do you interpret this score?

A. The student's performance is considered average given the range of scores is 1 to 100

B. The student's score is roughly two standard deviations below the mean

C. The student most likely has a significant learning disability

D. The student's performance falls within the intellectual disability (ID) range of standardized scores

22. What is the approximate age range for the Wechsler Intelligence Test for Children, Fifth Edition (WISC-V)?

A. 5 to 16 years of age

B. 3 to 16.5 years of age

C. 5 to 17 years of age

D. 6 to 16.11 years of age

23. Cognitive behavioral therapy (CBT) is founded on which of the following principles?

A. Short-term, goal-oriented intervention focused on changing patterns of thinking and behavior

B. A person's behavior is maintained by consequences

C. Behavior is embedded in a dynamic environment. To change behavior, one must consider the individual's family, peer relations, and emotional needs

D. Behavior is driven by unconscious drives to ease anxiety and to be accepted unconditionally by peers

24. School "readiness" is related to which of the following?

A. A condition that exists when maturation is sufficiently developed to allow the rapid acquisition of basic academic skills

B. When a young child is able to control his or her behavior, he or she can start kindergarten

C. This is a term used to illustrate that a student is ready to advance to the next grade level

D. A student is considered in a state of "readiness" when that child can meet basic standards of his or her age group

25. On a cognitive assessment, a student has a 10-point difference between the verbal domain (standard score [SS] = 87) and nonverbal domain (SS = 97). The full-scale SS is 93. How would you interpret the student's assessment if the child had a suspected reading problem noted by his teacher?

A. The split between scores is statistically significant, but not necessarily clinically significant

B. It can be safely stated that the child has a learning disability

C. The full-scale score is invalid and cannot be used due to the large sub-test variability

D. It is considered best practice to administer a different cognitive test due to the difficulty of interpreting scores with such variations

26. When using standardized assessments with students from diverse cultural backgrounds, it is important to remember which of the following?

A. Some children are late bloomers and therefore most formal tests are not reliable for children younger than 6 years of age

B. Assume that a child's cultural background can mask her true abilities, which may not be fully illustrated on many tests

C. Minority populations are overrepresented in special education classrooms

D. Mainstream formal assessments should not be used with minority groups due to psychometric norming difficulties

27. When observing students, which type of bias should psychologists consider a confounding factor?

A. The halo effect

B. Observer bias

C. Interrater reliability

D. Cultural bias

28. Curriculum-based measurements (CBMs) are used for what purposes?

A. CBM measures a school's progress toward explicit academic standards

B. CBM is an effective tool used to evaluate a teacher's skills

C. CBM is used to find out how students are progressing in basic academic areas

D. CBM is a measurement and assessment method that can supplant standardized testing because it is considered an authentic tool

29. Which brain structure is usually associated with emotions?

    A. Parietal lobe

    B. Broca's area

    C. Prefrontal cortex

    D. Amygdala

30. A staff member is concerned about a student who does not answer questions in class and is unusually quiet. During a meeting with both the parents and the teacher, the student's mother states that her son is typically shy and unassertive across various environments. As you prepare to support the student, what is the most effective therapeutic intervention in this case?

    A. Rational-emotive therapy (RET)

    B. Person-centered (Rogerian) therapy

    C. Cognitive behavioral therapy that uses modeling and rehearsal

    D. Behavior therapy that rewards assertive behaviors

31. A school psychologist's duties are not solely devoted to special education students. When you are asked to counsel and/or assess the emotional status of a regular education student by a teacher or parent, it is best practice to do what first?

    A. Although a student may not be a danger to himself or herself or others, a school psychologist should always lend support to any student who needs help

    B. A psychologist should secure written permission from the parents/ guardian to perform therapeutic and diagnostic services

    C. Although important, it is not strictly necessary to secure permission to meet with students because such services are free to all public school students and fall under free and appropriate public education (FAPE) guidelines

    D. School psychologists who have a license from their state's department of education are considered public school employees. Therefore, a psychologist can counsel students because it falls within the scope of his or her licensed duties

32. You are asked to consult with a teacher regarding a classroom management problem. What is generally the best approach when starting a professional consultation?

    A. A nonhierarchal collaborative model is a good model to use

    B. A student-centered model is usually most effective

    C. A cognitive behavioral consultation model typically produces effective results

    D. The ecological collaboration model is commonly employed in initial consultation cases

33. Jack is a second-grade student who struggled academically last year. He is not a behavioral problem and he is somewhat reticent in class. At the end of the current school year, the parents are thinking that Jack should repeat the second grade because his grades are still very low. How would you advise Jack's parents?

    A. Interventions should be tried first and their effectiveness documented. Retention is typically not an effective strategy

    B. Jack, his parents, and teachers should be given the Light's Retention Scale as part of a comprehensive evaluation to help determine if he should be retained

    C. Talk with Jack's parents and teachers about placing him in the response to intervention (RTI) process and retain him only at the level he is struggling

    D. Jack's parents should be told that retaining students, although very difficult for the parents and child, is usually an effective means of helping students to build lagging skills

34. Which cognitive assessment is best suited for deaf students or students who do not speak English?

    A. The Differential Ability Scales-II (DAS-II)–Nonverbal

    B. The Wechsler Intelligence Test for Children, Fifth Edition (WISC-V) with an interpreter

    C. The Universal Nonverbal Intelligence Test (UNIT-II)

    D. The Stanford–Binet, Fifth Edition

35. For which disorder is flooding or "in vivo" therapy associated?

    A. Phobias and anxiety

    B. Depression and withdrawal

    C. Bipolar disorder

    D. Attention deficit hyperactivity disorder

36. According to Erikson, children in second grade are negotiating which stage of development?

    A. Initiative versus guilt

    B. Industry versus inferiority

    C. Trust versus mistrust

    D. Autonomy versus shame/doubt

37. When implementing a crisis intervention for an off-campus suicide, the second step is to do which of the following?

    A. Consult with administration about ongoing support for impacted students

B. Lend direct support to peers/friends of the deceased student

C. Perform a brief needs assessment for the school

D. Plan to have a brief assembly at school to show respect for the deceased student

38. The National Association of School Psychologists (NASP) is a strong proponent of providing supervision and mentoring for new school psychologists. The NASP recommends that school psychologists should directly supervise no more than how many interns at one time?

A. Two

B. Three

C. Four

D. Eight

39. Which law requires school districts to identify students with potential disabilities?

A. Section 504 of the Civil Rights Law

B. Free and Appropriate Education Act of 1977

C. Individuals with Disabilities Education Act (IDEA)

D. The Sousa–Hohnbaum Special Education Act of 1975

40. Which of the following is considered the first intelligence test made for children?

A. The Wechsler Intelligence Test for Children, First Edition (WISC-I)

B. The Stanford–Binet test

C. The Bellevue Test of Mental Abilities

D. The Scholastic Aptitude Test–Alpha Series

41. Projective tests (e.g., Rorschach, Draw a Person) are usually used for?

A. Building rapport with a student

B. Gathering supplementary information about a student

C. Determining if a student is prone to malingering and deception

D. These tests are rarely used by school psychologist due to poor psychometrics (e.g., reliability)

42. Parental complaints regarding Section 504 should be directed to which authority?

A. The Department of Education

B. The school district's administration office

C. The Office for Civil Rights (OCR)

D. The state's Board of Education

43. What is the primary difference between achievement tests and cognitive tests?

A. Intelligence tests are norm referenced and used to diagnose learning disabilities

B. Achievement tests are generally used to predict academic progress

C. Cognitive tests are typically used to predict future learning more than achievement tests

D. Cognitive tests use standard scores, whereas achievement tests use grade-equivalent scores

44. You find out that another school psychologist has violated an ethical rule. What should you do first?

A. Attempt to talk to the person directly and address the situation informally

B. Immediately report the situation to school officials because you have an ethical obligation to do so. Failure to report a known violation implicates you in the situation

C. Notify the school psychologist that if he or she does not report the violation, you will have to report it

D. Not all ethical violations are legal violations. Legally, you do not have to take any action

Case example for questions 45 and 46: A student was referred to you due to behavioral disruptions in class. After a series of interventions, the special education team and parents agree that formal assessments should be initiated. The results from your formal cognitive assessment demonstrated that the student has a very large verbal and nonverbal difference between scores. Other streams of information support the idea that the student has a learning disability, specifically a nonverbal learning disability.

45. The parents have difficulty accepting your findings and demand to see the test protocol. Your response should be to:

A. Show the protocol to the parents and give them a copy of only the test scores if they request it

B. Refuse to let the parents examine the protocol, citing copyright laws and the need to keep testing material strictly confidential. Refer the parents to your individual education program (IEP) report that details the results

C. Provide the parents with qualitative information and your reasoning when interpreting the test results. The protocol may be used in your explanation, but not copied

D. Reiterate for the parents that the identification of a learning disability is a team decision and multiple pieces of information were used in the determination. After your explanation, supply the parents with all the necessary scores

46. After a lengthy explanation about the student's evaluation, the parents in the aforementioned example are still refuting your results and want outside (private) testing done. Which of the following statements reflects what is most likely to happen?

A. The parents can have a private assessment done at the school district's expense if they complete the formal appeals process

B. Parents can have a private assessment completed, but the school district is not obligated to pay for outside testing if the results are congruent with the school's assessments

C. Private assessments are not typically paid for by a public school district

D. A judge can order private testing that is paid for by a school district, not considering whether the results are congruent with the school district's findings

47. A high school student is in your office requesting to see you. He is visibly upset because of a serious fight he had with his girlfriend the past night. You do not have permission to counsel him. What is the "best practice" in this situation?

A. You are not allowed to counsel a new student without parent permission

B. It is acceptable to perform a brief intervention in an emergency or crisis situation without permission

C. Refer the student to his counselor at school

D. Have the student wait in a supervised room until his parents can be contacted

48. At what point in a counseling relationship do you explain the limitations of confidentiality?

A. During your initial meeting

B. After a rapport has been established

C. When your sessions with the student are nearing completion

D. When you provide parents with informed consent

49. A parent and teacher complete an adaptive scales assessment (e.g., Vineland) on a child suspected of having a cognitive impairment. The parent's version is significantly different from the teacher's version. What do you do?

A. The results are said to be invalid and another type of survey should be administered

B. You should call the parent and teacher and ask questions regarding the survey. Ask about the child's functioning at home and school

C. Analyze and use other assessment sources for your evaluation instead of the survey. Although the survey was not used in your evaluation, you must make a notation in your report as to why the survey was not used

D. Interpret both the teacher and parent surveys separately and present the objective results to the special education team for consultation

50. The "stay-put" rule is implemented at what time?

A. When due process has started

B. When due process has been completed

C. When a student has been suspended

D. When it has been determined that a behavior was a manifestation of a child's disability

51. At what type of meeting are eligibility requirements discussed and interventions or modifications to the curriculum discussed?

A. During the initial staff meeting with parents and the special education team

B. During the initial referral meeting

C. During the student's annual meeting

D. During the formal assessment and testing phase

52. You are preparing to conduct a formal evaluation on a student for special education services. As part of your evaluation, you determine that you should administer a processing speed test due to fluency concerns voiced by the teacher. When is it considered best practice to administer this type of formal cognitive assessment?

A. During the student's typical school day and when the student is experiencing his or her normal routine

B. After you have observed the child in the classroom, in order to evaluate his or her true behavior

C. After you have examined authentic work samples and completed a file review

D. Research has demonstrated that the morning time frame is the most effective time for processing speed tests

53. The consumption of large amounts of alcohol during pregnancy can cause?

A. Intellectual disabilities (ID)

B. Executive functioning deficits

  C. Fetal alcohol symptoms (FAS)

  D. Fetal alcohol effects (FAE)

54. Autism is associated with which of the following?

  A. Abnormalities in brain structures and function

  B. Obsessive-compulsive disorder (OCD)

  C. Executive dysfunction

  D. Genetic disorder that is linked to the Y chromosome

55. According to mainstream researchers and experts, such as Sattler and Kaufman, the most valid and reliable score(s) on widely adopted cognitive test batteries are usually which score?

  A. The major cluster or domain score

  B. The individual subtest scores

  C. Ipsative score

  D. The global or full-scale standard score

56. According to educational theorists, when fostering intrinsic motivation, you should use:

  A. Variable reinforcement

  B. Tangible rewards

  C. Verbal praise

  D. Choice selection

57. Typically, block design subtests on major cognitive assessments primarily evaluate the functioning of the:

  A. Right hemisphere of the brain

  B. Left hemisphere of the brain

  C. Both hemispheres of the brain

  D. Cerebrum

58. If a student's misbehavior increases after the teacher takes away his recess time, this is called?

  A. Spontaneous behavioral burst

  B. Response cost

  C. Negative reinforcement

  D. Punishment

59. High school students who have dysgraphia should be given what type of accommodation and/or modification on tests?

  A. Extra time

  B. Frequent breaks

C. Multiple-choice tests

D. An alternative form version of the test

60. Which therapeutic method or therapy works best for selective mutism?

A. Behavior therapy

B. Cognitive therapy

C. Stimulus fading

D. Flooding

61. A second-grade teacher uses the removal of a desirable activity, such as music class, to shape the behavior of his special education students. The teacher does not think other interventions are practical or effective. As the school psychologist, how should you respond?

A. The welfare of the student comes first and the school psychologist has a duty to discuss the situation with the principal

B. It should be explained to the teacher that the method he is using might be working, but will most likely produce short-term results if no positive reward or feedback is used for compliant behavior

C. The teacher's intervention might be working in the short term, but you should suggest to the teacher that "feedback" is provided to the students when possible

D. Inform the teacher that such interventions usually foster an external motivation instead of an internal behavioral regulation skill in the student

62. In regard to the professional associations related to school psychology, which of the following statements is most valid?

A. The National Association of School Psychologists (NASP) is the primary accreditation body for the Nationally Certified School Psychologist (NCSP) credential

B. The American Psychological Association (APA) does not fully recognize master's- or specialist's-level school psychologists

C. There is no major difference between APA and NASP guidelines

D. The APA typically regulates psychologists working in clinical or research domains

Case example for questions 63 to 65: Parents gave signed permission for the special education team to complete a full evaluation. After the initial staffing meeting, the parents' lawyer demands that you supply them with copies of your protocols.

63. As a licensed school psychologist you should do which of the following?

A. As a lawyer is formally requesting the documents, you should supply all the necessary copies of the requested documents so you are in compliance with law

B. Collaborate with the parents by stating that all necessary information is in the individual education plan (IEP) report and review the IEP with the parents

C. Collaborate with the parents and review test information with the parents and lawyer, but you do not have to make copies at this point in the legal process

D. When legal matters initiate, you should inform the school district's lawyers and have them speak to the parent's lawyer before further communication with the parents continues

64. Which specific law or case law requires parental access to records?

A. Individuals with Disabilities Education Act (IDEA)

B. *Rowley vs. Hudson Board of Education*

C. *Brown vs. Board of Education*

D. Family Educational Rights and Privacy Act (FERPA)

65. If you copy protocols for parents or others, you might be violating what law(s)?

A. Federal copyright laws

B. Family Educational Rights and Privacy Act (FERPA)

C. Fair Testing and Assessment Act of 1990

D. Federal Communications Commission (FCC) laws

66. Executive function is primarily associated with which of the following traits?

A. Cognitive planning

B. Nonverbal learning

C. Spatial reasoning

D. Reading

67. Which is considered primary in crisis intervention?

    A. Leadership

    B. Community support

    C. Measured response

    D. Prevention

68. A teacher constantly sends disruptive and rowdy students to your office. By midyear, you are handling several students a week from this one particular teacher. You meet with the teacher in private to discuss the situation. You help the teacher implement a behavioral management plan for students with difficulties. Within a few weeks, referrals to you have dropped significantly. What consultation model did you employ?

    A. A direct service model

    B. A consultee-centered service model

    C. A teacher-centered model

    D. The Caplan model

69. A student is referred to the school psychologist's office because he consistently makes inappropriate comments and engages in disruptive behavior. What is your *first* approach to amending this problem?

    A. You figure out what is maintaining the behavior and stop the reinforcement

    B. You set clear expectations for the student and enforce natural consequences

    C. You perform a functional behavioral assessment (FBA) to determine the antecedent and consequence for the behavior so you can plan an intervention

    D. You collaborate with the teacher to write a proper behavior support plan

70. Authentic assessments are different from standardized assessments in which primary way?

    A. Standardized assessments use statistics to compare a student to a normative group, whereas authentic assessments are more criterion based

    B. Authentic assessments are considered informal methods

C. Standardized assessments are more time efficient

D. Authentic assessments are more time efficient

71. According to many functional behaviorists, what are the major reasons for a variety of common behaviors that school psychologists deal with in an educational setting?

A. Attention, affiliation, and control

B. Boredom, opportunity, and stimulation

C. Stimulation, approval, and reinforcement

D. Approval, control, and stimulation

72. An upper elementary school student constantly makes poor grades despite his concerted efforts. According to Erik Erikson, if this student does not feel a sense of industry, he will develop problems involving:

A. Shame

B. Doubt

C. Inferiority

D. Role confusion

73. A sophomore will not break the rules of his school because he does not want to face the disapproval of his peers and strict parents. According to Kohlberg, which stage of moral development is this student navigating?

A. Preconventional stage

B. Conventional stage

C. Postconventional stage

D. Concrete stage

74. Given a standard error of measurement (SEM) of 6 points, what can be said of a student who receives a standard score of 90 on a cognitive assessment?

A. The student's range of scores is within the average to below-average area

B. The student has an average score

C. The student score falls within the below-average range

D. The student's score is between the 84th and 96th percentiles

Case example for questions 75 and 76: A seventh-grade female student has a speech impediment and poor social skills. By the second month of school, the student is teased by a group of girls to the point she becomes despondent. Several other students are aware of the teasing, but do not do anything about it. One day, the student writes a detailed note to her teacher that she will kill the teasing students if they do not stop with the bullying.

75. In this situation, the school psychologist *must* do which of the following?

   A. Immediately determine which students are involved in the situation and conduct a threat assessment

   B. Mediate the situation and employ restorative practices with all the students involved

   C. Consult with your administration and recommend that the school resource officer be notified of the threat

   D. Notify the parents of the children who have been threatened

76. In this scenario, a school psychologist should also do which of the following?

   A. Seek to prevent a similar situation by instituting a schoolwide antibullying program

   B. Use an indirect collaboration consultation model to inform the principal about future interventions and effective supports

   C. Conduct a formal schoolwide needs survey to improve school climate and determine the extent of bullying and harassment problems

   D. Perform proactive interventions with identified bullies and intervene with repeat offenders

77. A student is referred to the school psychologist's office for poor self-confidence and negative self-talk. During the interview, you discover that the student believes she has always had bad luck and bad things just happen to her all the time. This student's belief is an example of:

   A. Negative metacognition

   B. Internal locus of control

   C. External locus of control

   D. Poor self-esteem

78. A caring single father constantly completes homework for his daughter. Despite suggestions from teachers and school staff, the parent continues to complete assignments for his child. The parent in this situation is doing which of the following?

   A. Instilling in the child a learned helplessness orientation

   B. Undermining the child's self-concept and self-confidence

C. Increasing the child's dependency on adult support

D. Modeling empathy and compassion

79. A teacher resides in the community where he teaches. One evening, he sees one of his students at a store. The student has visible marks on his face and arms. The father of this child is known to be strict. In this situation, the teacher should do which of the following?

A. Although not legally obligated to notify the authorities, the teacher should call social services and make a report of suspected abuse

B. The teacher needs to contact the school social worker immediately and collaborate to file a child abuse report

C. The teacher should ask the student about the marks and then make an informed judgment whether to call social services

D. As a mandated reporter, the teacher has a duty to notify social services or law enforcement about the marks

80. A parent comes to you and provides a written request that her son must be tested for special education services. After consulting with the teacher, it was discovered that the student has a history of very poor grades and seems to frequently daydream in class. What is the best practice in this situation?

A. Suggest to the parent that Multi-Tiered System of Support (MTSS) interventions be implemented before moving ahead with formal testing

B. Start the assessment process because parents who provide written requests for formal assessments have legal rights to testing under Individuals with Disabilities Education Act (IDEA) law

C. In a collaborative way, inform the parent that preliminary information provided by the teacher indicates attention problems and the parent should also talk with the student's pediatrician

D. Inform the parent that a formal evaluation will be completed by the school team, but the law gives schools 60 days to complete the assessment process

81. When should a school psychologist suggest exploring more information regarding medication for attention deficit hyperactivity disorder (ADHD) to parents?

A. After assessments have been completed and there are indications of ADHD

B. School staff should not typically recommend medication because it falls outside their scope of practice

C. Only after securing a confidential release of information to speak with the student's pediatrician about the child's difficulties at school

D. When the student's difficulties impact his or her development

82. A student is asked to dial a phone number while hearing the number for the first time. This is an example of what type of cognitive function?

    A. Short-term memory

    B. Working memory

    C. Encoding

    D. Transient memory

83. A student is diagnosed with mild autism. At school, it is common to observe which one of the following characteristics?

    A. Social skills difficulties

    B. Receptive language problems

    C. Inability to effectively use spatial and verbal information

    D. Emotional regulation difficulties

84. In regard to suspected child abuse cases, all school employees must do which of the following?

    A. Always notify the school administration of the suspected abuse

    B. Report cases of suspected abuse to police or social services

    C. Gather basic information about an abuse case and immediately contact the police or social services

    D. Report abuse cases to the school social worker and collaboratively report abuse cases

85. Traumatic brain injury (TBI) in children:

    A. Can cause learning disabilities and attention problems

    B. Is serious, but typically not as serious as TBI in adults because a child's brain has more neuroplasticity than an adult's brain

    C. In most cases will impact the cognitive development of children

    D. Typically produces a cognitive profile reflected by significantly higher nonverbal than verbal performance

86. During a formal assessment, you ask a child to say a word and then manipulate the word's sounds. What are you assessing when you ask a student to perform this task?

    A. You are testing for sound discrimination

    B. You are assessing word–sound associations

    C. You are evaluating phonemic awareness

    D. You are evaluating the student's verbal working memory

87. A teacher asks for your direct assistance regarding a disruptive student. You agree to observe the child. You discreetly sit in the class and observe what happens before, during, and after the targeted behavior. After your observation, you determine that the student was acting out when the student was working with a specific peer. What type of evaluation were you conducting to assist the teacher?

    A. You were performing a functional behavioral assessment (FBA)

    B. You were conducting a time sample observation

    C. You were assessing antecedents and consequences

    D. You were conducting qualitative observation

88. A student has significant difficulty perceiving visual symbols accurately. An inability to perceive visual stimuli accurately is typically associated with which part of the brain?

    A. Temporal lobe

    B. Parietal lobe

    C. Prefrontal cortex

    D. Occipital lobe

89. Cognitive psychologists hypothesize that the construct of "attention" can be categorized into different types. What are the primary types of attention?

    A. Selective and continuous

    B. Focused and continuous

    C. Selective and sustained

    D. Sustained and focused

90. When a preschool child imitates the aggressive behavior of an adult that he has recently observed in a movie, this behavior is based on which psychological construct?

    A. Modeling

    B. Latent aggression

    C. Observational learning

    D. Behavioral learning

91. Who is the theorist largely responsible for studying aggression in children and conducting experiments using a "Bobo" doll?

    A. B. F. Skinner

    B. Martin Seligman

    C. Albert Bandura

    D. Carl Jung

92. A colleague asks you to review a journal article that describes several studies and experiments. You are specifically asked to discern the strongest correlation coefficient from the following. Which one depicts the strongest correlation?

   A. 0.97
   B. −0.98
   C. 0.100
   D. −0.250

Case example for questions 93 to 95: In an experiment, you want to examine the effect background music has on learning. You form two groups. One group studies with soft classical background music, whereas the other group studies in a quiet area.

93. The group exposed to background music is called the:
   A. Experimental group
   B. Independent group
   C. Control group
   D. Dependent variable

94. The group not exposed to background music is called the:
   A. Experimental group
   B. Independent group
   C. Control group
   D. Dependent variable

95. In the experiment, the music is considered the:
   A. Experimental variable
   B. Manipulation variable
   C. Independent variable
   D. Dependent variable

96. When you assess a student for special services, best practice suggests that you do which of the following?
   A. Use at least two valid standardized measures before identifying a disorder or disability
   B. Present evaluation data to your special education team before formally identifying a disorder
   C. Use both valid formal and informal assessments to base your decisions
   D. Conduct at least one in-class observation of the student

97. Aphasia is normally associated with what type of problem?

    A. A speech–language disturbance

    B. A visual–motor disturbance

    C. An inability to write

    D. A difficulty with quantitative problem solving

98. A student employs a problem-solving method that reduces the number of options or alternatives to be considered. This student is using what type of problem-solving technique?

    A. Deduction

    B. Successive processing

    C. Logical reasoning

    D. A heuristic

99. A teacher asks you to assist with a student who has reading difficulties. You suggest that the student explicitly describe her reasoning and predict outcomes of selected paragraphs. Most likely, these suggestions are to improve the student's:

    A. Overall reading proficiency

    B. Decoding skills

    C. Comprehension skills

    D. Encoding skills

100. During a structured interview for a Canadian-born student, you notice that the interviewee is well groomed and has a quick but polite sense of humor. Care must be taken that your assessment results are not tainted by what psychological phenomenon?

    A. Halo effect

    B. Observer bias

    C. Cultural bias

    D. The Germain effect

101. You work as a school psychologist for a rural school district with a low socio-economic status (SES) population. Budget problems and personnel shortages are persistent in your district. The principal of your school informs you not to make recommendations for parents to seek community counseling services for their children. Additionally, the principal informs you that you must only conduct group counseling sessions, not individual sessions. Based on ethics and best practices, how do you respond to this situation?

    A. Given the practical and budgetary concerns of the situation, you should comply with the principal's directives

B. Explain your ethical obligations to the principal, but still comply with the directives

C. Notify the principal that you cannot completely comply with the directives because some situations warrant certain actions that are ethical

D. Consult privately with the district's attorney and follow the guidance of the district's lawyer

102. Curriculum-based measurement (CBM) enables a teacher to do which of the following?

A. Continuously monitor progress and adjust goals as necessary

B. Compare a student's performance to the norm group to determine what is typical

C. Provide evidence of teacher effectiveness in a given curriculum

D. Determine whether a curriculum is reliable and valid

103. When seeing a regular education student for the first time in a counseling meeting, a school psychologist should first secure:

A. Consent from the principal or school administration

B. Informed consent from parents

C. Consent from both the administration and parents

D. If licensed by a state government to work in public schools, no consent is necessary, but is considered best practice

104. A school district is mandated to formally identify children of all ages with suspected disabilities. According to educational law, this previous statement is known as:

A. No reject principle

B. Child find

C. Inclusion

D. Exclusion

105. Which standardized cognitive assessment is largely based on Lurian theory and the planning, attention, and simultaneous and successive processing (PASS) model?

A. Differential Ability Scales-II (DAS-II)

B. Wechsler Intelligence Test for Children, Fifth Edition (WISC-V)

C. Stanford–Binet, Fifth Edition

D. Cognitive Assessment System-2 (CAS-2)

106. A counseling approach that embraces the idea that behavior is guided by one's self-image, subjective perceptions, and the need for growth toward personal goals is called?

A. Psychodynamic counseling

B. Behaviorism

C. Humanistic counseling

D. Cognitive behavioral counseling

107. The Cattell–Horn–Carroll (CHC) theory of intelligence forms the basis for many current cognitive tests. According to this theory, which one of the following broad abilities is *not* part of the CHC model?

A. Fluid reasoning (*Gf*)

B. Quantitative knowledge (*Gq*)

C. Short-term memory (*Gsm*)

D. Simultaneous processing (*Gsp*)

108. To properly service all students and address the needs of a school, the National Association of School Psychologists (NASP) generally recommends how many school psychologists per student population?

A. 1 per 1,000 students

B. 2 per 1,000 students

C. 1 per school

D. 1 per 2,000 students

Case example for questions 109 to 111: An upper elementary school student is referred to the special team for unusual social and egocentric behavior. As a school psychologist, you first conduct an observation of the student and interview the teacher. Your inquiry reveals that the young boy has an uncanny ability to remember detailed facts about World War II military planes. You also find that the child is polite, but he has abnormalities in inflection when he speaks, few friends, and expressive language problems.

109. Based on the presenting symptoms, you decide to formally evaluate the student because you suspect?

A. Autism spectrum disorder

B. Nonverbal learning disorder (NVLD)

C. Social language disorder (SLD)

D. Asperger's syndrome

110. In the previous scenario, the parents have given you signed permission to directly support the student. You decide that social skills training is the best initial approach. Which of the following best reflects social skills training?

A. Self-awareness, positive reinforcement, and social praise

B. Direct instruction, modeling, and coaching

C. Metacognitive training, operant techniques, and language skills development

D. Perspective taking, response cost, and social praise

111. Your team feels that the student in this example needs special education services. In making the decision to offer the student special services, your team must demonstrate what critical finding?

A. The child meets the criteria for a disability as outlined in the *Diagnostic and Statistical Manual*, Fifth Edition (*DSM-5*)

B. Your testing results must show a significant and verifiable deficit within the school environment

C. The child's difficulty has a significant impact on his social development and/or academic progress

D. A developmental problem that is substantially below the student's age group must be based on formal and informal measures in a comprehensive evaluation

112. When conducting a formal behavioral observation, which of the following is important to document and analyze?

A. The frequency, intensity, and duration of the target behavior

B. How many times the behavior presents itself after the antecedent

C. The factors and consequences that reinforce the targeted behavior

D. The triggers for the behavior

113. According to the National Center for Learning Disabilities (NCLD) and other organizations, approximately what percentage of the public school student population aged 3 to 17 years has some form of learning disability?

A. 2% to 3%

B. 4% to 6%

C. 8% to 11%

D. 11% to 13%

114. On common cognitive test batteries, what is the generally accepted full-scale standard score that might signal a student is gifted?

  A. A standard score above 115

  B. A standard score above 120

  C. A standard score above 130

  D. A standard score above 140

115. A student who has a severe vision impairment is granted a formal waiver that excuses her from taking the state's annual assessment test. The parents of this student demand that the school accommodate her so that she can take the test. According to the law, what is the school's responsibility?

  A. The school must fulfill the needs of the student so she can complete the standardized state test

  B. The school is under no legal obligation since a waiver has been granted, but ethically the school should make the appropriate accommodations and allow the student to take the test

  C. The school should keep to its original plan and fully excuse the child from the test

  D. The school's decision to spend resources to accommodate the student depends on whether the student has the specific accommodations written in her individual evaluation plan (IEP)

116. Which of the following statements regarding threat assessment and school violence is *not* true?

  A. There is a general profile of a "school shooter" that is associated with bullying

  B. Most perpetrators of school violence have been bullied in the past

  C. Incidents of targeted school violence at school are rarely impulsive

  D. Most attackers engaged in behaviors that caused concern in others

117. One of the most effective intervention(s) for children with learning disabilities is which one of the following?

  A. Cognitive and behavioral

  B. Multifaceted or multimodal

  C. Experiential (hands-on) learning methods

  D. Neuropsychological interventions

118. The term "running record" is usually associated with which type of observational recording?

    A. Interval recording

    B. Narrative recording

    C. Event recording

    D. Continuous recording

119. What is the National Association of School Psychologists' (NASP) position regarding homeschooling?

    A. The NASP does not endorse the concept of homeschooling due to the lack of quality assurance and lack of licensed professionals providing instruction to students

    B. The NASP believes in collaboration between parents of homeschooled children and the public schools

    C. Due to lack of formal social programs and extracurricular opportunities, homeschooled children are most at risk of social developmental delays

    D. Psychoeducational assessments should be used with caution with children who are homeschooled because they typically have a different learning style and many tests are not normed on this population

120. The ability to analyze and synthesize several pieces of information is related to which type of cognitive processing?

    A. Sequential

    B. Nonverbal

    C. Metacognitive

    D. Simultaneous

121. It is best practice that all schools have a Multi-Tiered System of Support (MTSS). Which one of the following is not typically associated with an effective MTSS?

    A. Response to intervention (RTI) process

    B. Positive behavioral interventions and supports (PBIS)

    C. School-based mental health services

    D. After-school programs for students

122. Which of the following choices is most closely aligned with effective schoolwide policies and practices?

    A. An explicit and effective means to handle student suspensions

    B. High standards and rigorous curricula provided to all students

    C. Effective special education programs

    D. A defined threat assessment process

123. Your administration asks you to review the effectiveness of the school's behavior intervention and correction protocols. The first action you take is to perform a needs assessment. When you present the findings of your needs assessment to the staff, it is important that you discuss which one of the following topics?

A. Ways that parents can have a voice in the development of a new behavior management model

B. Cultural sensitivities and potential biases of staff

C. Common barriers to effective behavior intervention practices

D. The current school district's behavior policy and legal requirements

124. A systems-wide practice or policy that is generally endorsed by the National Association of School Psychologists (NASP) is:

A. Tracking

B. Threat assessment training

C. Zero tolerance

B. Retention

125. Student learning develops as target skills progress through phases. Which of the following choices describes this commonly held process?

A. Exposure → rehearsal → proficiency → adaptation

B. Acquisition → proficiency → generalization → adaptation

C. Acquisition → practice → proficiency → adaptation

D. Exposure → proficiency → adaptation → establishment

Case example for questions 126 to 128: A concerned parent calls the principal at your middle school and reports that she overheard a student talking about guns at a bus stop. The principal consults with the school psychologist and determines that the student should be formally interviewed. After the psychologist and principal's meeting with the student of concern, it is determined that a full threat assessment should be completed.

126. According to the Virginia Model and Safe School Initiative, what key sources of information should be used in an effective threat assessment?

A. Parents, staff interviews, peer interviews, and school records

B. Staff, parents, school records, and student of concern interview

C. Student of concern interview, parents, formal threat assessment measures, staff

D. Student of concern interview, parents, staff, and peers

127. During the student of concern interview, the school psychologist makes notes about the student's verbal and nonverbal communication. According to the threat assessment research, which of the following is a most concerning statement?

    A. The student admits to being a bully and is bullied

    B. The student is a "loner" and not connected to any staff member at school

    C. The student has struggled academically for many years

    D. The student has access to weapons at home

128. At the conclusion of the threat assessment, it was found that there are concerns with the student and the threat was substantive, but not imminent. The student of concern is allowed to attend school if a comprehensive threat and risk management plan is in place and implemented with fidelity. What should all effective threat and risk management plans contain?

    A. A provision that the parents seek mental health support for their child

    B. Increased supervision at school and home

    C. Restorative practice intervention

    D. Cognitive behavioral support at school

129. When talking to parents about bell-curve (e.g., normal curve) characteristics, one standard deviation from the mean encompasses how much of a given population?

    A. 50%

    B. 68%

    C. 75%

    D. 25%

130. Dialectical behavior therapy (DBT) attempts to build skills related to the following *four primary areas*:

    A. Mindfulness, stress tolerance, interpersonal skills, and emotional regulation

    B. Resilience, social skills, tolerance, and emotional regulation

    C. Resilience, social skills, tolerance, and behavioral regulation

    D. Social skills, self-advocacy, assertiveness, and problem solving

131. A student has witnessed an extremely violent act by another student at school. The exposed student has developed posttraumatic stress disorder (PTSD) symptoms. During the first few initial counseling sessions, the student is likely to engage in the following behaviors primarily related to PTSD?

    A. Self-soothing behaviors

    B. Blank staring

C. Inattention

D. Retelling the "story"

132. What is a common cultural barrier to a student's educational progress?

A. The parent's cultural values regarding formal education

B. The school's value placed on cultural sensitivity training

C. The parent's primary language

D. The use of interpreters

133. *Tatro v. Irving Independent School District* was a Supreme Court case that ruled:

A. Special education students have a right to the least restrictive environment

B. Special education students have a right to certain medical services and procedures

C. Schools are only required to provide adequate services, but not the best services

D. Students' records must be kept confidential and secured

134. What is an ecological assessment?

A. A comprehensive process in which data on how a child functions in different environments or settings are collected

B. Uses both formal and informal measures

C. An assessment that considers diversity and cultural factors

D. Uses functional behavioral assessment (FBA) data to form a hypothesis about a behavior

135. Which medication is commonly used to treat obsessive-compulsive disorder (OCD)?

A. Neurontin

B. Methylphenidate (Ritalin)

C. Fluoxetine (Prozac)

D. Abilify

136. When reviewing background information about a student for a formal assessment, which one of the following sources is *not* typically examined?

A. Medical/health records

B. Previous interventions

C. Developmental history

D. Parental socioeconomic status (SES)

Case example for questions 137 and 138: A high school student sustains a concussion during a football game on Friday night. The student attends school on Monday, but he is having difficulty focusing and processing information in class.

137. As a school psychologist, what should you do to support the concussed student at school?
    A. Send the student home, with administrative approval, and excuse absences until he can attend a full school day with little or no symptoms
    B. Create a temporary support plan that incorporates frequent breaks in the school day
    C. Do not allow the student to take tests until he is symptom free
    D. Collaborate with the school nurse to excuse the student from school until the student is symptom free

138. A concussion is commonly referred to in research and by medical experts as?
    A. Temporary brain injury
    B. Mild traumatic brain injury (mTBI)
    C. Mild brain dysfunction (mBD)
    D. Temporary brain dysfunction

139. Which legal case is most closely aligned to least restrictive environment (LRE)?
    A. *Honig v. Doe*
    B. *Larry P. v. Riles*
    C. *Oberti v. Cementon*
    D. *Rowley v. Hudson Board of Education*

140. Who is widely assumed to be the father of school psychology?
    A. Lightner Witmer
    B. Alfred Binet
    C. Francis Galton
    D. B. F. Skinner

End of Test: Go back and check your answers if time permits.

Practice Test II

DIRECTIONS: You have 2 hours and 20 minutes to complete the following 140-item test. Be mindful to keep *strict* time limits. Carefully examine the content of each response choice and select the option that is most closely aligned with the central aspects of the exam question. Do not leave any question blank. Answers and rationales for exam items are provided following this test.

Study and Test-Taking Strategies

Make a note of those questions that are very difficult to answer and move on to the next item. All questions carry the same score value, so do not spend too much time on one question. Remember to go back to difficult questions and complete them once you answer all other items.

Ready?   **Start Timing: 140 minutes**

1. When is response to intervention (RTI) data typically *not* used?

   A. To identify a student's learning problem or area of difficulty

   B. To target intervention strategies

   C. To help determine whether a student should be retained in a grade

   D. To decide whether interventions are related to positive student outcomes (effectiveness)

2. Interviewing is an important means to collect informal data. Which interview technique has a high degree of validity and allows for additional questioning?

   A. Semi-structured interview

   B. Structured interview

   C. Flexible interview

   D. Standardized interview

Case example for questions 3 and 4: As a school psychologist working for a large metropolitan school district, you have an extremely busy work schedule. Every month, you receive several referrals for special education evaluations from both parents and teachers. Your latest referral involves a second-grade student, but there is limited information about the student's difficulties. The referral you received states that the young male student is well behaved; however, he is struggling academically.

3. Given the previous situation, what would be your first step to address the referral question?

   A. Call the parents to ascertain more information and developmental history

   B. Talk with the teacher, or referral source, to better define the problem

   C. Ask the Multi-Tiered System of Support (MTSS) specialist about the types of interventions that have been employed

   D. Review student records to ascertain how long the student has been struggling

4. In the scenario described, you talk with the teacher and she mentions the student is periodically off-task and does not complete his assignments. However, the teacher cannot tell you precisely when the student is off-task. You decide that it is important to conduct a formal observation on the student's in-class behavior, but you are under time constraints. What observational technique is best to employ in this situation?

   A. Interval time sampling

   B. Latency

   C. Intermittent sampling

   D. Duration recording

5. Which analysis is *not* included in the three levels of an effective response to intervention (RTI) data analysis?

   A. Analysis of the trend of the data

   B. Analysis of the level of the data

   C. Analysis of the quality of data

   D. Analysis of the variability in the data

6. The pattern of change in a student's behavior *across time* can be best described as the

   A. Level

   B. Trend

   C. Variability

   D. Reliability

7. As a school psychologist, you are analyzing response to intervention (RTI) data that have been collected on a student's reading skills after the first 3 weeks of an intervention. You note that the RTI data indicate variability, with scores very low at certain times, but at other times the scores demonstrate significant gains. What is your initial evaluation of the data?

   A. The data are valid as students typically show variability with new interventions

   B. The data might be valid, but should be interpreted with caution

   C. The data are invalid and should not be used to make educational decisions

   D. The data should be screened for confounding variables that are helpful to consider

Case example for questions 8 and 9: Jack has been in a school's response to intervention (RTI) process for math difficulties. Students in this process are ranked on a 1 to 5 scale, with 5 being the highest classroom benchmark and 3 being the aim line. Jack's data indicate that he scored a 2, 3, and 2 on the last three learning sessions. Also, Jack's level of response to the instruction is about 15% correct per data set.

8. In the situation described, which of the following choices do you recommend to the teacher and support staff?

   A. Focusing more effort on increasing the student's rate of correct responses

   B. Modifying the intervention by providing better prompts, additional modeling, and corrective feedback

   C. Considering changing the type of intervention

   D. Gradually increasing the intervention using the last data point, which indicates a stalled trend and momentum

9. When examining data in this situation, which of the following does *not* need consideration?

   A. Is the percentage of correct responding below 85%?

   B. Are the data highly variable?

   C. Is the student from a low socioeconomic status (SES) community?

   D. Are there two to three consecutive data points that fall below the aim line?

10. During a special education evaluation, school psychologists are required to use which of the following items?

    A. Valid and reliable test data

    B. Multiple informal and formal sources of information

    C. Standardized and nonstandardized tests

    D. Response to intervention (RTI) and standardized data

11. As a school psychologist, you are asked to determine whether a child qualifies for special education services under the identification of intellectual disability (ID). You have already completed a cognitive assessment using the
Wechsler Intelligence Scale for Children, Fifth Edition (WISC-V); which one
of the following should you also complete to help in your formal evaluation?

   A. Woodcock–Johnson Test of Achievement

   B. Differential Ability Scales-II (DAS-II)

   C. Vineland-3

   D. Beery–Buktenica Developmental Test

12. What is the recommended guideline when collecting baseline response to
intervention (RTI) data?

   A. There should be no new highs (spikes) or lows for three consecutive data
points

   B. You should collect student baseline data for at least 2 weeks

   C. 85% of your baseline data should be at least 15% below the class average

   D. 15% of your baseline data should be at least 85% below the class average

13. Which brain-based process is considered a basal neurological process that
can be assessed with a neuropsychological test?

   A. Nonverbal reasoning

   B. Verbal reasoning

   C. Visual–spatial reasoning

   D. Processing speed

14. You are asked to perform a social and emotional assessment for a fifth-grade
student. Which procedures will be most effective in your assessment?

   A. Give the Behavior Assessment System for Children-III (BASC-III) behavior assessment and the Differential Ability Scales-II (DAS-II) cognitive
assessment

   B. Interview the parent to gather key developmental history and conduct
a student behavioral observation

   C. Conduct a functional behavioral assessment (FBA) and student interview

   D. Give the BASC-III behavior assessment and conduct an FBA

Case example for questions 15 and 16: Sally is a third-grade student who has
difficulty with task persistence and work completion. She is respectful to staff
and does not have a history of behavioral problems. Parents report that her
father recently lost his employment and the family may have to move. Sally's
teacher and mother have requested assistance from the school psychologist.

15. As the school psychologist, you decide to conduct a functional behavioral assessment (FBA) on Sally to help inform a comprehensive intervention strategy. What are the initial steps in the FBA process?

    A. Interview the parents, perform an observation, formulate an intervention plan, and evaluate the plan

    B. Define the problem, perform an observation, develop a hypothesis, and formulate a plan

    C. Develop a hypothesis, perform an observation, consult with the teacher, and formulate a plan

    D. Interview the teacher, perform an observation, develop an intervention, and evaluate the plan

16. In the previous scenario, you carefully craft an intervention plan that is based on your functional behavioral assessment (FBA) results. Your data suggest that Sally is socially motivated and she enjoys socializing with the friends she sits by during class. Which of the following intervention strategies is endorsed as an effective first strategy to use?

    A. Implement an individually tailored response cost plan

    B. Employ a behaviorally based point and level system

    C. Modify the immediate environment to promote on-task behavior

    D. Provide immediate corrective feedback for off-task behavior

17. What is the primary difference between a curriculum-based assessment (CBA) and a curriculum-based measurement (CBM)?

    A. CBM is a term used to describe a specific type of measurement used for reading intervention programs in a response to intervention (RTI) process

    B. CBA is a term used to describe a broad assessment program or process, which may include CBMs or structured observations

    C. A CBM is an assessment designed to measure the effectiveness of class-wide intervention programs

    D. A CBA is designed to measure a student's progress in a remedial program

18. Which of the following is the best example of a curriculum-based measurement (CBM)?

    A. A student is given a nationally standardized test such as Dynamic Indicators of Basic Early Literacy Skills (DIBELS). A standard score is derived and compared to national norms

    B. A student is given a math test at the beginning of a semester, then given the same test at the end of the semester. Results are compared for growth

C. A student reads aloud for 2 minutes. The number of words read correctly and incorrectly are counted and compared to the class average

D. A student is given a classroom reading test and the results are compared to the state's standards for proficiency

19. Generally speaking, a student might have an intellectual disability (ID) if the student has subaverage scores on an adaptive functional assessment and a full scale standard score of _____ or below on a mainstream cognitive test battery.

A. 85

B. 80

C. 75

D. 70

20. A school psychologist is asked to test a female student suspected of having a learning disability. The female student only speaks a few words of English, but she is fluent in Spanish. When the psychologist conducts an assessment, it is prudent to do which of the following?

A. When using an interpreter, the interpreter should be certified by the National Association of Interpreters (NAI) and speak both languages proficiently

B. If a cognitive test battery is employed, only use tests that are normed on a Spanish normative group

C. Use informal measures as well as appropriately normed standardized assessments

D. Place an emphasis on parent interviews, teacher data, and developmental history

21. During a behavioral assessment, psychologists typically conduct student observations. What type of confounding factor should psychologists consider?

A. The halo effect

B. Examiner bias

C. Teacher bias

D. Thorndike effect

22. Although projective measures can be useful as part of a comprehensive assessment, many projective tests have been criticized for which of the following?

A. The need for the examiner to have extensive and specialized training to administer such tests

B. The length of time to administer such tests is significantly longer than standardized tests

C. Reliability, such as interrater reliability, is sometimes lower than mainstream standardized measures

D. Projective tests are not considered valid for school purposes

23. When collecting and analyzing data on student behavior, which three aspects of the target behavior should you emphasize in your analysis?

A. Intensity, variability, and duration

B. Intensity, duration, and frequency

C. Duration, quantity, and quality

D. Duration, frequency, and quality

24. A fourth-grade student was referred to you due to overall low academic performance. In addition to Multi-Tiered System of Support (MTSS) data and informal measures, you decide a full cognitive battery is appropriate to administer. At the initial special education meeting, you meet with the parents. What is best practice when you describe your Wechsler Intelligence Scale for Children, Fifth Edition (WISC-V) results to the parents?

A. Start with interpreting the individual subtests, and then explain the global score

B. Start with interpreting the global score, and then explain major index scores

C. Only provide and interpret the global score

D. It is generally good practice only to describe areas of concern and below-average scores

25. You are asked to design a positive behavior support (PBS) plan for your school. Which one of the following PBS aspects is *not* an effective plan feature?

A. Establish and define clear and consistent expectations

B. Acknowledge students for demonstrating the expected behaviors

C. Staff uses objective data to make informed decisions about interventions

D. Parents should feel welcome to help supervise students at school

Case example for questions 26 to 28: Bullying and harassment are major problems in schools. As a psychologist, you are asked to help mitigate bullying in your school.

26. One of the first steps you take to address bullying issues in your school is to educate your staff. When you present to staff, you state that research indicates what percentage of students have reported being bullied?

A. 50% to 60%

B. 20% to 30%

C. 80% to 90%

D. 10% to 25%

27. Effective antibullying programs include all of the following *except*:

    A. Widespread staff supervision of students

    B. Programs to address bystander beliefs and behavior

    C. Strict consequences for bullying behavior and zero-tolerance policies

    D. Systems to build social skills and to address social skill deficits

28. A student is caught harassing a group of students in a younger grade. You, as a school psychologist, are asked to intervene. What is an effective approach to this situation?

    A. It is best to start individual counseling, but maintain student confidentiality

    B. Seek parental permission and then start counseling

    C. Recommend a restorative practice approach to the parents and administration

    D. Recommend group interventions, such as group counseling

29. When initially entering into a mental health counseling situation with a student, a school psychologist needs to carefully explain the limitations of confidentiality. When is it *not* appropriate to breach confidentiality with a student?

    A. When the student mentions that she has thoughts of scratching herself to relieve tension

    B. When the student gives permission to breach confidentiality

    C. When the student is thinking about spray painting her gang sign on the school's front door

    D. When another staff member engages the psychologist in consultation about how to help the student in the classroom

30. Which type of counseling technique has a substantial amount of research to support its effectiveness and is widely adopted by mental health practitioners?

    A. Cognitive behavioral therapy (CBT)

    B. Cognitive-emotional therapy (CET)

    C. Rational-emotive therapy (RET)

    D. Psychoeducational support (PES)

31. Schools generally favor behavioral techniques based on B. F. Skinner's theories. Which one of the following statements best describes Skinner's beliefs?

    A. Behavior is shaped by rewards

    B. Behavior is influenced by a person's family environment

    C. Behavior is shaped by consequences that follow the behavior

    D. Punishment is not an effective means to modify behavior

32. Jack is a ninth-grade student participating in a program that requires him to assist students with Down syndrome. With supervision from the special education teacher, Jack tutors other students in their life skills curriculum and attends field trips to the store so the students can learn in the authentic environment. Which intervention strategy is being employed to help Jack build his empathy?

   A. Behaviorism

   B. Cognitive behavioral intervention

   C. Authentic environmental intervention

   D. Service learning

Case example for questions 33 and 34: You are working with a first-grade student named Bill. Bill has a moderate level of autism and he is also suspected of having attention deficit hyperactivity disorder (ADHD). Your current task is to teach him a classroom routine that involves several transitions. During your intervention, you conduct a task analysis and break the correct behavior down into multiple smaller steps. You follow a systematic instructional technique called discrete trial instruction (DTI), with several repeated trials in a highly structured environment.

33. In this situation, which behavioral technique are you following?

   A. Applied behavior analysis (ABA) and intervention

   B. Applied behaviorism

   C. Discrete behavioral analysis and intervention

   D. Discrete behavioral modification (DBM)

34. Which one of the following choices is a key feature of an effective behavioral intervention?

   A. The use of positive reinforcers with prompts

   B. Use of negative reinforcers only after positive reinforcement has been attempted

   C. The use of prompts during the initial training stages, then gradual employment of fading techniques

   D. The use of response cost techniques after target behavior is rehearsed and taught

35. As a psychologist, you will be consulted on crisis topics, plans, and interventions. Which one of the following statements is regarded as the best approach to crisis preparation?

   A. Crisis interventions should address individuals, groups, and systems

   B. Crisis prevention measures should be emphasized, developed, practiced, and put in place

C. Postvention measures should be rehearsed and considered part of a systematic response to crisis

D. Building-level crisis teams should be created and work seamlessly with district-level crisis teams

36. During a traumatic event, children may experience a wide variety of emotions and reactions. When actively intervening with students who may have been exposed to a trauma or a crisis situation, school psychologists should screen for what type of mental health issue?

A. Contagion effects

B. Posttraumatic stress disorder (PTSD)

C. Depression

D. Anxiety

37. A teacher alerts you to a high school student who has made suicidal comments during a class assignment. You meet with the student and decide a full suicide assessment is prudent. Given this situation, it is critical to do which of the following?

A. Secure parent permission immediately and start a student interview

B. Inform your school administrator that you are engaged in a priority assessment

C. Do not leave the student unsupervised during the process

D. Immediately notify the parent(s) and conduct a suicide assessment with a mental health team member

Case example for questions 38 and 39: You are a school psychologist practicing in an affluent public school district. You are notified by the district's crisis team that an unfortunate situation has occurred. A seventh-grade student died from a self-inflicted injury late at night. The next morning, you are called to assist the crisis team at the student's school. The administration has already been notified of the situation and they are awaiting support from the district crisis team.

38. In the situation just described, your initial and primary concern is which of the following?

A. Your attention should be to support and provide resources for the student's family

B. It is critical to locate the student's friends within the school and provide them support

C. You must debrief all staff about the situation before school starts

D. You must discuss and plan for contagion effects with school staff

39. Which one of the following postvention intervention strategies is valid?

A. Provide students with verifiable facts and several details about the suicide to mitigate rumors

B. It is important to make a special early morning announcement to all students and staff to prevent rumors

C. With mental health staff on-site, a special schoolwide assembly should be conducted to address contagion factors

D. Provide in-school resources and counseling spaces for students who need additional support

40. You are performing a formal evaluation on a 6-year-old student. During your teacher consultation, the teacher mentions that the student has difficulty with simple symbolic thinking, which should have already started to emerge. According to Piaget, this student should be in which stage of development?

A. Preoperational stage

B. Concrete stage

C. Operational stage

D. Preconcrete stage

41. As a school psychologist, you provide evaluations for gifted and talented students. As you interview a gifted high school student, you find the student is highly opinionated and wants to follow a defined occupational path as a criminal lawyer. According to Erik Erikson, this student is navigating which stage of development?

A. Adolescent versus preadolescent stage

B. Initiative versus shame and guilt

C. Identity versus role confusion

D. Industry versus inferiority

42. You are training school staff on the topic of school violence. A staff member asks you about the role of violent television shows and video games. Your response to the question is that you believe children can learn aggressive behaviors by watching violent movies or by observing the actions of others. Your comments are based on research conducted by which psychological researcher?

A. Abraham Maslow

B. B. F. Skinner

C. Albert Bandura

D. Jean Piaget

Case example for questions 43 to 46: You are evaluating a sixth-grade male student, named Cameron, for special education services. As part of your comprehensive assessment, you administer a full cognitive test battery (e.g., Wechsler Intelligence Scale for Children, Fifth Edition [WISC-V]) and various social–emotional measures. The preliminary results are as follows: The full-scale standard score on Cameron's cognitive test battery is 113 (SS-113). All major cognitive domains (indexes) were found to be within two standard points of each other. The Behavior Assessment System for Children-III (BASC-III) indicates that both the teacher and parent forms have T-scores above 65 within the Attention domain. Your semi-structured student interview reveals that Cameron follows the rules of the school, but he appears to follow these rules only to avoid punishment or gain rewards.

43. Given the previous scenario, what preliminary statement can you make about Cameron's overall cognitive ability?

   A. Cameron's standardized test score suggests that he might be gifted, but further information is needed to confirm this initial finding

   B. Cameron's cognitive ability is considered well within the average range

   C. Cameron's cognitive abilities are considered low average

   D. Cameron's cognitive abilities are situated within the high-average to above-average range

44. Based on the provided Behavior Assessment System for Children-III (BASC-III) results, what is your initial impression regarding Cameron's attention?

   A. Cameron's attention scores are within the high-average range and indicate he might have attention deficit hyperactivity disorder (ADHD)

   B. Cameron's BASC-III T-scores place him in a category for significant attention problems, but more information is needed to confirm the presence of a disability

   C. Cameron's scores on the BASC-III are elevated slightly above normal and it is prudent to monitor his level of attention throughout the school year

   D. Cameron's scores on the BASC-III are well within the average range and both the teacher and parent forms confirm each other's observations in two environments

45. In addition to the assessment tools used in the previous example, what other assessments should you complete as part of a comprehensive evaluation?

   A. A review of student records and a student observation

   B. A parent interview and behavioral checklist

   C. A behavioral checklist and response to intervention (RTI) data review

   D. RTI data review and review academic performance

46. In the previous scenario, which stage of Kolhberg's moral development is Cameron most likely situated?

    A. Preadolescent

    B. Conventional

    C. Preconventional

    D. Adolescent

47. As a school psychologist, you must discuss with parents a wide variety of behavioral and emotional disorders listed in the *Diagnostic and Statistical Manual (DSM)*. In one particular case, you have evaluated a student who has significant attention problems. Both formal and informal measures have indicated that the student you evaluated has difficulty sustaining his concentration and has been observed to fidget across multiple domains. During the parent meeting, you mention to the parents that their son has characteristics of attention deficit hyperactivity disorder (ADHD). The parents want to know the research on ADHD. Which of the following choices is an appropriate research-based statement about ADHD?

    A. You state that ADHD is diagnosed in approximately 15% of a school's population

    B. You respond by saying ADHD is overdiagnosed, but the parents could benefit from a consultation with their pediatrician

    C. You state that school psychologists do not diagnose ADHD, but rather school psychologists identify students with attention difficulties

    D. You state that ADHD is diagnosed more in males than in females

48. For which of the following disorders is anxiety a prevalent characteristic?

    A. Bipolar disorder

    B. Personality disorder

    C. Posttraumatic stress disorder

    D. Mood disorder

49. Several years ago, autism spectrum disorders (ASD) used to have a prevalence rate of approximately 1 in every 2,500 people. Current research indicates the prevalence rate for ASD has dramatically increased to which of the following levels?

    A. 1 in every 186 people

    B. 1 in every 55 people

    C. 1 in every 1,000 people

    D. 1 in every 88 people

50. Deb was referred to your special education team for a full evaluation. The referral centered on Deb's below-average performance in reading and her lack of an age-expected response to reading interventions. While reviewing academic records and Deb's performance on the Woodcock–Johnson Test of Achievement, you notice that Deb struggles with quantitative concepts as well as reading. Due to your findings, it would be appropriate to screen Deb for which specific disorder?

    A. Dyslexia

    B. Dyscalculia

    C. Math disability

    D. Learning disability

51. Landon is a seventh-grade student suspected of having mild autism. When shown pictures of people engaging in various social interactions, you ask him how each person in the picture feels. Landon has difficulty with this task and provides atypical responses. This informal task provides information related to which one of the following choices?

    A. Theory of the Mind

    B. Perspective taking

    C. Theory of Subjectivity

    D. Social skills deficit

52. Students who have an external-locus-of-control perspective typically have difficulty in school and in life. An external locus of control is most closely aligned with which of the following?

    A. Display of helplessness

    B. Learned helplessness

    C. Low self-esteem

    D. Depression

53. A teacher tells her class that they can have 10 minutes of free computer time to play recreational games if they complete their short math assignment first. What behavioral principle is this teacher employing to motivate her students?

    A. Positive reinforcement

    B. Skinner's Principle

    C. Premack Principle

    D. Contingency reward

54. What is the primary difference between punishment and negative reinforcement?

    A. Punishment increases a desired behavior by decreasing undesired behavior, whereas negative reinforcement does not

    B. Negative reinforcement increases behavior, whereas punishment decreases behavior

    C. Negative reinforcement decreases desired behavior, whereas punishment decreases undesired behavior

    D. Punishment and negative reinforcement are functionally the same terms

55. Which of the following behavioral reinforcement schedules has shown to be effective, but it is difficult to modify the behavior once established using this technique?

    A. Fixed-ratio reinforcement

    B. Mixed-ratio reinforcement

    C. Variable-ratio reinforcement

    D. Fixed-interval reinforcement

56. Several current mainstream cognitive test batteries are theoretically based and statistically derived. What is the name of the modern psychometric test theory that includes such components as *Gf* (fluid intelligence) and *Gc* (crystallized intelligence)?

    A. Thurstone theory

    B. Spearman theory

    C. PASS theory

    D. Cattell–Horn–Carroll theory

57. School psychologists typically consult with several educational specialists and must know some of the concepts and terms of other professional disciplines. In one situation, a school psychologist is told by a speech–language pathologist that a fifth-grade student frequently makes grammatical mistakes in class. For example, during a conversation, the student said, "To car we the go." The speech–language pathologist is concerned about the student's:

    A. Semantics

    B. Syntax

    C. Phonological awareness

    D. Phonemic awareness

58. Which theorist is associated with language acquisition and is known for creating the term "language acquisition device (LAD)?"

    A. Arthur Jensen

    B. Mihály Csíkszentmihályi

    C. Noam Chomsky

    D. Paul Broca

59. A fourth-grade teacher has been instructing her students how to add and subtract fractions. Her self-made tests are based on classroom standards and mastery of a defined skill. What type of test is this teacher using?

    A. Criterion-referenced test

    B. Norm-referenced test

    C. Local norm-referenced test

    D. Standards-based test

Case example for questions 60 and 61: Michele is a student engaged in a school's response to intervention (RTI) process. She is given weekly assessments to gauge her progress with reading comprehension. Michele's scores are based on a 1 to 10 scale, with 10 being the highest score possible. Her scores for the past several weeks are 1, 5, 7, 7, and 10.

60. What is the mean score in the given set of numbers?

    A. 7

    B. 5.5

    C. 5

    D. 6

61. What is the mode in the given set of numbers?

    A. 7

    B. 5.5

    C. 5

    D. 9

62. You are asked to evaluate a new cognitive abilities screening test for your school. In the technical manual, you notice the full-scale standard score of the new test has a statistical correlation of 0.68 with another well-respected cognitive test. Given these details, you can make which of the following assumptions?

    A. The new test has acceptable reliability

    B. The new test has unacceptable reliability

C. The new test shows a moderate effect size

D. The new test shows moderate convergent validity

63. Brooke is a first-year psychologist practicing in a small public school district. A struggling teacher asks Brooke for a consultation regarding effective teaching practices. During her consultation, Brooke should *not* make which of the following statements to the teacher?

   A. Try activating students' prior knowledge before teaching new concepts

   B. Provide corrective feedback to students during frequent practice sessions

   C. Give additional homework items when new concepts are introduced

   D. Try to place new concepts within the students' zone of proximal development

64. Student learning develops as targeted skills progress through phases. Which of the following processes is an accurate depiction of student learning?

   A. Acquisition → proficiency → generalization → adaptation

   B. Acquisition → practice → generalization → adaptation

   C. Acquisition → proficiency → application → adaptation

   D. Practice → proficiency → generalization → adaptation

65. Best practices in pedagogy involve which of the following broad concepts?

   A. Explicit and incremental approach to presenting information

   B. Explicit and systematic approach to presenting information

   C. Repetition and practice of new information

   D. Exposure and rehearsal of new concepts

66. An effective high school teacher is able to respond to the individualized needs and abilities of all learners. Other staff observe this teacher to improve their practices. Which of the following important pedagogy concepts is the teacher using?

   A. Small-group instruction

   B. Individualized instruction

   C. Differentiated instruction

   D. Cooperative learning

67. In addition to student motivation, school climate, and school policies, what is another factor in student success or failure?

   A. Family involvement

   B. Socioeconomic status (SES)

   C. Family dynamics

   D. Standardized curriculum

68. A middle school administrator calls the school psychologist into a conference with a student's parents at the end of the school year. The student in question has been struggling this year and has failed most classes. On state assessments, the student has scored significantly below the standards for her grade level. The parents are worried about moving their daughter to high school if she does not have the academic skills and she is not adequately prepared. What would be a good recommendation for the school psychologist to make?

   A. Administer the Light's Retention Scale to see if the student qualifies for grade retention

   B. Recommend remediation in core subject areas at the high school and allow the student to take a few elective courses

   C. Seek additional information to determine whether other factors are involved in the student's struggles that may necessitate Multi-Tiered System of Support (MTSS) or special education services

   D. Recommend summer school to make up for failed courses instead of grade retention

69. Which of the following choices are *not* typically associated with schoolwide zero-tolerance policies?

   A. Racial disproportionality

   B. An increasing incidence of suspensions and expulsions

   C. Elevated dropout rates

   D. Behavioral management

70. Cooperative learning is an effective teaching method. A chief benefit of cooperative learning is:

   A. Students increase their prosocial skills

   B. Students increase their own learning by helping others and gain a greater understanding of individual learning differences

   C. Cooperative learning techniques are more time efficient than other teaching methods

   D. Cooperative learning increases empathy as well as academic skills

71. Although token economies are effective systems to use in behavioral modification programs, what is a complaint often stated by teachers regarding these methods?

   A. Token economies need relevant reinforcers to work effectively

   B. Token economies are generally effective for younger elementary students, not older students

   C. Token economies are sometimes cumbersome to implement and maintain

   D. Token economies do not maintain the target behavior once withdrawn

72. A teacher who typically gives students large projects and assignments asks the school psychologist for help with two struggling students. The students are well behaved and do well in other classes, but they have difficulty completing work in her class. The psychologist's observation and recommendation should include which of the following?

    A. A task analysis to recommend where to break larger tasks into smaller steps

    B. A time interval observation and recommendation to the school's Multi-Tiered System of Support (MTSS) process

    C. The psychologist should review academic records first, and then consult with the teacher

    D. A narrative observation and recommendation to the school's response to intervention (RTI) process

73. A second-grade teacher asks you to help with a student named Amy. Amy needs to develop her reading skills. The teacher stated that Amy is a fluent reader, but her comprehension is below her peers. Which comprehension reading strategy would you recommend?

    A. Lindamood-Bell Reading Intervention

    B. Survey, question, read, recite, and review (SQ3R)

    C. Wilson Reading Remediation Program

    D. Woodcock–Johnson Reading Intervention Program

74. What is an example of an *accommodation* for a student who struggles with reading?

    A. Having the student point to pictures of answers instead of writing answers about an assigned reading text

    B. Having the student take a reading test that is more aligned with his or her level of reading

    C. Allowing extra time for the student to read a text during assignments or tests

    D. Allowing the student to read books at his or her level of cognitive ability

75. According to cognitive behavioral theorists, learning is supported by mental representations of new concepts merging with a person's existing mental concepts. In this example, existing mental concepts are called:

    A. Visualizations

    B. Neurocognitive representations

    C. Imprints

    D. Schemata

76. When engaged in a professional consultation situation, which of the following personality traits are important elements for success?

    A. Empathy and trustworthiness

    B. Expertise and knowledge

    C. Knowledgeable and professional

    D. Efficient and respectful

77. A psychologist is asked to collaborate and consult on a student with behavioral problems in the classroom. What are the basic steps of the Behavioral Model of consultation?

    A. Consult with stakeholders—create a plan—implement the plan—evaluate the plan

    B. Consult with stakeholders—create a plan—implement the plan—monitor the plan

    C. Identify the problem—implement a plan—monitor the plan—evaluate the plan

    D. Identify the problem—consult with stakeholders—implement a plan—evaluate the plan

78. Which model of consultation focuses on building the teacher's skills to address student problems in the future?

    A. Consultee-centered model

    B. Student-centered model

    C. Strength-based model

    D. Client-centered model

79. You are asked to help address a kindergartener's difficult behavior. The teacher is new and you decide to address the problem yourself. You directly teach the student self-regulation skills. In this particular case, you are engaged in which type of consultation model?

    A. Consultee-centered model

    B. Student-centered model

    C. Strength-based model

    D. Client-centered model

Case example for questions 80 to 83: A first-grade teacher asks for a consultation with the school psychologist. The teacher is concerned about a student named Jack. Jack has difficulty interacting with his peers, teases girls in class, and he is frequently off-task.

80. In this example, you decide to call a meeting for all relevant parties such as the teacher, parents, and administrator. This type of special consultation is called a:

   A. Conjoint behavioral consultation

   B. Client-centered consultation

   C. Consultee-centered consultation

   D. Multisystemic consultation

81. During your consultation with the staff and parents, your first step is to do what?

   A. Review Multi-Tiered System of Support (MTSS) data on the problem

   B. Define the problem as specifically as possible

   C. Review interventions that have been previously implemented

   D. Review the student's records

82. All of the following are common barriers to effective consultation *except*:

   A. Adversarial relationship with outside agencies

   B. Communication difficulties among parties involved in the consultation situation

   C. Unclear or unfocused goals

   D. Financial and time considerations

83. Of all the consultation models, which model is generally considered a best-practice model?

   A. Conjoint behavioral consultation

   B. Client-centered consultation

   C. Consultee-centered consultation

   D. Multisystemic consultation

84. When is it legal to disclose the confidential records of a student to a third party (e.g., outside the school)?

   A. When a medical doctor requests student records and a student health issue exists

   B. When your school administrator directs you to disclose confidential records

   C. When you are ordered to do so by a police officer

   D. When there is a safety issue involved

85. You are a school psychologist employed by a large public school district. A portion of this school district is very wealthy. During the summer months when the schools are closed, a parent asks you to complete a full cognitive assessment for her child. The parent needs a full-scale cognitive test score so she can register her son at a private school. The parent is willing to pay you for your service. What should you do in this situation?

    A. Refer the parent to the school psychologist at the student's home school

    B. A psychologist can accept this work if he or she is licensed and qualified to do so as a private practitioner

    C. Inform the parents that the service she seeks is provided free of charge by the public school district her son attends

    D. A school psychologist cannot accept this type of work

86. What is the appropriate number of interns that a school psychologist *supervisor* can oversee?

    A. 1

    B. 2

    C. 3

    D. 4

87. Jackie is a school psychologist who has been practicing for 3 years. She shares a job with another psychologist named Mike. Jackie recently discovered that Mike has been giving money to other staff for referrals to his private counseling practice. Many of the students Mike counsels for a fee are regular education students at the high school. What should Jackie do in this situation?

    A. File a grievance with National Association of School Psychologists' (NASP) ethical board

    B. Inform the school's administrator

    C. Discuss the situation with Mike directly and file a grievance if the practice does not cease

    D. Remind Mike that support services can be provided for free by the school

88. When a formal ethical complaint is filed against a National Association of School Psychologists (NASP) member, the NASP can take several potential actions. Which one of the following actions is *not* valid?

    A. Expel the member from the NASP

    B. Recommend to the member to seek additional training and skill building

    C. Require the member to provide a formal apology

    D. Revoke the license of the practitioner

89. Aversive behavior modification techniques and restraining are legal in many states. What is considered best practice regarding aversive techniques such as restraining?

   A. It is best practice not to employ aversive techniques in any situation

   B. Aversive techniques should only be employed when safety is an issue

   C. Only use aversive techniques if such techniques comply with strict state laws and regulations and the staff member is properly trained

   D. It is best practice to rarely use aversive techniques and on a case-by-case basis

90. During a confidential counseling situation, a high school student informs you that his uncle uses illegal drugs. The uncle does not live with the student, but visits the student monthly. What should you do as the school's psychologist?

   A. You should ask the student more questions to determine whether the student is in danger

   B. You should notify law enforcement

   C. You should consult with social services, without using names, to secure guidance about what you should do and to stay in compliance with local laws

   D. You are not required to do anything since there is no immediate danger. It is best practice to call the parents, with student approval, and discuss the situation openly

91. A student who receives special education services brought a knife to school. The student claims that he forgot the pocket knife was in his backpack, which he had taken on a fishing trip with his father over the weekend. It is important to note that the student has been suspended earlier this year for bullying issues. In the current situation, the student was suspended for 10 days. What violation of this student's rights occurred?

   A. A special education student cannot be removed from school for more than 10 days

   B. A special education student cannot be suspended for more than 7 consecutive days without a manifestation review

   C. A special education student must have a special review meeting if suspended 10 days or more

   D. Special education students cannot be expelled or suspended for more than 10 days, but they can be enrolled in another school that better addresses their needs

92. A student is receiving special education services for a mild dyscalculia disability. The special education team leader has placed this student in a class designed for students with significant math needs. The special education teacher reasons that it is better to "overserve" a student with mild needs than it is to underserve such students. In this case, which legal aspect of special education law does the teacher run the risk of violating?

    A. Every Student Succeeds Act (ESSA)

    B. Least-Restrictive Environment

    C. Individuals with Disabilities Education Act (IDEA)

    D. Family Educational Rights and Privacy Act (FERPA)

93. Which law mandates that schools must keep strict and confidential records?

    A. Individuals with Disabilities Education Act (IDEA)

    B. Federal Education Confidentiality Law of 1974

    C. Family Educational Rights and Privacy Act (FERPA)

    D. The Individuals with Disabilities Education Improvement Act of 2004 (IDEIA 2004)

94. According to the law, what is the primary difference between special education law (Individuals with Disabilities Education Act [IDEA]) and Section 504?

    A. Functionally, there is no difference as both laws regulate services for students with disabilities

    B. Section 504 is for students who have physical disabilities, not learning disabilities

    C. Section 504 is for students who have handicaps diagnosed by medical professionals

    D. Section 504 is a part of the Rehabilitation Act of 1973 that prohibits discrimination based on disability

95. A parent of a sixth-grade student is suing a school district because the school psychologist tested the student 3 years back without parental consent. At the time of the initial evaluation, the psychologist called and left several messages for the parent asking her to provide consent for the child's triennial review (reevaluation), but the parent never returned the calls. The calls were documented in the student's file. At a subsequent meeting, the parent was concerned about the testing, but she allowed services to continue for another 2 years. What is the most likely reason the parent's lawsuit will not succeed?

    A. The parents were informed of their rights at the meeting 3 years ago

    B. The student did not demonstrate harm from the services provided

    C. You do not need parental consent to test for triennial reviews

    D. The psychologist made documented attempts to contact the parents and proceeded with typical services

96. According to the Individuals with Disabilities Education Improvement Act of 2004 (IDEIA 2004), how much time does a special education team have to complete a formal evaluation if signed permission to proceed with an evaluation has been provided?

    A. 45 days

    B. 60 days

    C. 30 days

    D. 90 days

97. Although the roots of school psychology date back to the late 1800s, the first school psychologist was officially recognized in 1915. Pioneers in school psychology developed and used assessments to evaluate development in children. Of the options provided, who is considered the first school psychologist?

    A. Arnold Gesell

    B. B. F. Skinner

    C. Carl Young

    D. Charles Spearman

98. The field of psychology has grown increasingly more scientific since its origins over 100 years ago. Psychometric testing, which scientifically measures human traits, has helped to establish psychology as a legitimate discipline. Despite its roots in science, psychology is not without controversy. A famous psychological researcher, known for his work in behavioral genetics, was criticized for his assertion that intelligence has a strong genetic basis. Who was this famous psychological expert?

    A. Raymond Cattell

    B. Charles Spearman

    C. David Wechsler

    D. Arthur Jensen

99. A rural school district has two curriculum tracks. One track is for college-bound students and one track is for vocational training. The vocational track is typically for students with limited financial means. This school district was sued because it violated the law regarding ability of tracking students and denying access to courses for some students. In the final legal decision, the judge based his opinion on which landmark case?

    A. *Diane v. State Board of Education*

    B. *Brown v. Board of Education*

    C. *Hobson v. Hansen*

    D. *Larry v. Riles*

100. A district-level school psychologist is asked to lead a threat assessment on a high school student. The student was caught at school with pepper spray and a list of students targeted for revenge. The threat assessment team was thorough during the inquiry and confidential student information was shared with the administration and law enforcement. Parents were not present during the student of concern interview. Because a violent incident was averted and strict disciplinary action was taken against the student of concern, the parents of the targeted students were not notified. What potential legal violation is involved in this situation?

    A. Since law enforcement was given confidential student information, Family Educational Rights and Privacy Act (FERPA) may have been violated

    B. A duty-to-warn infraction occurred

    C. Informed consent by the parents was not secured before the threat assessment

    D. A psychologist cannot conduct a threat assessment on a student without the student's parents or legal representation present

101. What famous landmark case ruled that public schools could not segregate based on race? This law is also known as the antisegregation law.

    A. *Hobson v. Hansen*

    B. *Brown v. Board of Education*

    C. *Rowley v. Board of Education*

    D. *Larry P. v. Riles*

102. A student was in a car accident and sustained substantial damage to the left temporal lobe, especially to the Broca's area. Given this information, it is reasonable to assume that the student may have difficulty with which of the following cognitive abilities?

    A. Spatial reasoning

    B. Receptive language

    C. Auditory long-term memory

    D. Expressive language

103. Neuropsychology is related to school psychology, but the primary focus of a school neuropsychology assessment is which of the following?

    A. Neuropsychology is concerned with brain–behavior relationships

    B. Neuropsychology focuses on the neurological aspects of learning

    C. Neuropsychology gives practitioners neurological information that can be used to predict student achievement

    D. Neuropsychology evaluates a student's higher level reasoning and problem-solving skills

104. As a school psychologist, you have knowledge of basic psychopharmacology and brain chemicals. Which of the following brain chemicals is thought to be implicated in producing positive moods and emotions, especially those associated with rewards? Parkinson's disease and attention deficit hyperactivity disorder (ADHD) are also associated with an imbalance of this neurochemical.

A. Serotonin

B. Dopamine

C. Endorphins

D. Cortisol

105. Cognitive-psychology researchers use the term "executive function" to describe a constellation of behaviors or functions necessary for success. School neuropsychologists are most likely to describe the same executive functions, such as initiation, impulse control, organization, and attention, by using which of the following terms?

A. Neurocognitive function

B. Frontal lobe function

C. Global neurocognitive function

D. Temporal lobe function

106. A child who has significant neurological impairments in the right hemisphere of the brain due to a stroke would most likely have which of the following learning problems?

A. Difficulty with memory for previously learned skills

B. Phonological processing problems

C. Reading and spelling difficulties

D. Difficulty with novel problem solving

107. The information-processing model, originally created by cognitive psychologists, helps practitioners conceptualize how humans think and learn. Which of the following choices best illustrates the cognitive processing model?

A. Attention→ input → processing → long-term storage

B. Attention → decoding → processing → output

C. Attention→ processing → encoding → decoding

D. Attention → encoding → storage → decoding

108. A T-score of 64 is considered to be within which range?

A. Above average

B. Average

C. Below average

D. Significantly below average

109. Colette, a third-grade student, has a documented history of reading problems. Colette's family is supportive of her learning, but they struggle financially and had to move twice in the past 2 years. The parents and teachers are worried that Colette will fall further behind in her reading development. In a consultation situation, what should the school psychologist recommend?

A. The psychologist should recommend a special education evaluation based on the Child Find law

B. The psychologist should recommend an after-school tutoring program and connect the family with community support services

C. The psychologist should make a formal recommendation to the school's Multi-Tiered System of Support (MTSS) process

D. The psychologist should consult with the student's team and parents, then formulate a support plan

110. You are counseling a second-grade student who is significantly concerned about her father's recent unemployment. From Abraham Maslow's perspective, you could say this student is coping with the aspects found at which level?

A. Love and belonging

B. Safety needs

C. Self-actualization

D. Primary needs

111. Modeling and role playing are key intervention techniques that are used to address various student difficulties. Of the following choices, modeling and role playing are considered important interventions for which type of problem?

A. Depression

B. Trauma

C. Attention deficit hyperactivity disorder (ADHD)

D. Social skills deficits

112. You are counseling a regular education high school student who has been caught using his brother's attention deficit hyperactivity disorder (ADHD) medication. The parent believes her son is distraught because he was denied admission to a selective college that he wanted to attend. When you meet with the student, you tell the student that he has control of how he chooses to respond to the situation. Which counseling theorist emphasizes that people can choose how to respond to difficult situations?

A. Viktor Frankl

B. Sigmund Freud

C. Carl Rogers

D. Abraham Maslow

113. In which of the following situations would a school psychologist tell a teacher that the technique of "time-out" is appropriate to employ?

A. When a child blurts out answers in class despite being told twice to stop

B. When a student with attention deficit hyperactivity disorder (ADHD) starts to have difficulty focusing on the task at hand

C. When a student with oppositional defiant disorder (ODD) is socializing during a test

D. When a student moves around the room without permission during a teacher's presentation of a new concept

114. In a response to intervention (RTI) process, Tier 2 (Level 2) interventions are generally associated with which of the following?

A. Intensive interventions

B. Benchmark interventions

C. 5% to 8% of the student population

D. Strategic interventions for "at-risk" students

115. When conducting a problem-solving and ecological assessment, what four components should psychologists emphasize?

A. School environment, student records, formal assessments, and student learning styles

B. School environment, home environment, community environment, and interpersonal skills

C. Instruction, curriculum, environment, and learning style

D. Informal assessments, formal assessments, student records, and student interview

116. A parent is demanding that her son be placed on an individual education plan (IEP) because he has a formal diagnosis of schizophrenia. The student's pediatrician has also recommended an IEP and wrote a prescription for one. Despite the mother's concern, the student's medication appears to be effective in managing his disorder and he is able to make educational progress. As a school psychologist, what is your response to the parent?

A. If there is no educational or social impact, then a formal special education IEP may not be appropriate

B. Legally, a medical diagnosis and recommendation from the doctor must be honored

C. Although the school is not legally obligated to provide an IEP in this situation, it is good practice to provide special education support

D. Students with schizophrenia should be provided formal supports and an IEP, especially to prevent the student's difficulties from getting worse within the school environment

117. From a historical perspective, which is a new role for schools?

A. Reading interventionist for response to intervention (RTI) programs

B. Brain injury resource specialist for school districts

C. Threat assessment team leaders for schools and law enforcement

D. Autism evaluation specialist

118. What type of behavioral intervention would you recommend for a student with a phobia involving insects?

A. Flooding

B. Cognitive behavioral therapy

C. Systematic desensitization

D. Functional behavioral analysis and intervention

119. According to psychological research, students who sacrifice sleep to play hours of continuous video games might develop which of the following problems?

A. Antisocial personality disorder

B. Traits normally associated with attention deficit hyperactivity disorder (ADHD)–inattentive type

C. Aggressive tendencies and poor social skills

D. Difficulties with memory and learning

120. Before administering a new psychological assessment, it is reasonable for a school psychologist to do which of the following?

A. Complete a formal training course on the new test

B. Give the new test to students but report the scores as informal measures until proficiency is achieved

C. Practice with the new test and be supervised by a colleague familiar with the test until proficient

D. Watch a training video and practice with the new test until proficient

121. A school psychologist is reviewing research about several new assessments for reading fluency. As the psychologist reviews the reliability data, he or she notes there is significant variability in the correlations. Which of the following correlation coefficients depicts strongest reliability?

    A. 0.96

    B. −0.97

    C. 0.100

    D. −0.450

122. Informal and formal data are required to inform professional judgments regarding an individual student at the four response to intervention (RTI) levels. Which one of the following is *not* a level typically required to inform professional judgment?

    A. Background data collection and problem identification level

    B. Screening level

    C. Analysis and determination level

    D. Formal assessment level (special education evaluation)

123. Two mainstream cognitive test batteries are the Wechsler Intelligence Scale for Children, Fifth Edition (WISC-V) and the Stanford–Binet, Fifth Edition (SB-V). When these tests were being constructed, their overall full scale scores were statistically analyzed and found to be highly correlated. What is the purpose of correlating overall scores on similar tests when creating them?

    A. To establish validity

    B. To establish convergent validity

    C. To establish reliability

    D. To establish predictive validity

124. School psychologists are increasingly asked to support students with several different types of difficulties, especially mild brain injuries (e.g., concussions). If a student sustains a hit to the back of the head, what difficulties should you expect and how should you support the student within the school environment?

    A. The student will most likely have visual difficulties and light sensitivity. The school psychologist should allow for frequent rest breaks and allow the student to wear sunglasses at school

    B. The student will most likely have headaches. The school psychologist should allow the student to stay at home until the student's headaches have fully resolved

C. The student will most likely have cognitive fatigue and short-term memory problems. The school psychologist should allow for frequent breaks in the health room and a late school start as needed

D. The student will most likely have difficulty focusing and experience headaches. The school psychologist should collaborate with parents to create a support plan for the student

125. According to the Virginia Model of Threat Assessment, what are the three qualitative identification levels for threats?

A. Low, medium, and high

B. Nonsignificant, significant, and imminent

C. Transient, substantive, and imminent

D. Low, medium, and significant

126. In crisis situations, there are several ways that students cope with stress and trauma. According to the Belief, Affect, Social, Imagination, Cognitive, and Physiological (BASIC-Ph) model of coping, which of the following is *not* a coping style?

A. Belief

B. Avoidance

C. Social

D. Imagination

127. According to Epstein's Model of Parent Involvement, which one of the following is a key element of the model?

A. Communicating

B. Community opportunities

C. Parent opportunities

D. Staff–parent collaboration

128. A school psychologist may evaluate research for school districts (systems level). One of the most common means to evaluating research variables has been through analysis of variance (ANOVA). Which type of ANOVA moderates bias in the dependent variable to increase the validity of the researcher's conclusion?

A. Multivariate ANOVA

B. Mixed factorial ANOVA

C. Repeated-measures ANOVA

D. Analysis of covariance (ANCOVA)

129. Multilevel modeling (MLM) is an important method to know because it may offer an alternative to analysis of variance (ANOVA) techniques. What choice best defines MLM?

    A. MLM is a statistical model of parameters that vary at more than one level

    B. MLM is a statistical method that controls biases at all levels of analysis

    C. MLM is a technique that controls biases in the dependent variable

    D. MLM is a method that analyzes covariances between variables

130. Suicide among school-aged children and adolescents is a significant and serious concern. According to the National Association of School Psychologists (NASP), suicide in the school-aged population is:

    A. The first leading cause of death

    B. The second leading cause of death

    C. The third leading cause of death

    D. The fourth leading cause of death

Case example for questions 131 and 132: As a school psychologist, you are asked to perform a focused assessment on a student suspected of having attention deficit hyperactivity disorder, combined type (ADHD-C). You have already formally observed the student in two classes, given a standardized broad-spectrum assessment, and interviewed the parents for developmental information.

131. What other formal measure would you employ as part of your comprehensive evaluation?

    A. Behavior Assessment System for Children-III (BASC-III)

    B. Conners Rating Scales–Revised

    C. Conners-3

    D. Attention Deficit Hyperactivity Disorder (ADHD) Test

132. In the situation provided, the Behavior Assessment System for Children-III (BASC-III) Teacher and Parent Forms show significant score variability. The Teacher Form reveals a T-score of 66, while the Parent Form illustrates a T-78. How would you interpret these results?

    A. While both forms show significant score differences, both sets of scores suggest the student has indications of a substantial attention problem

    B. Due to the significant score discrepancy, best practice is not to interpret the BASC results and put more emphasis on other measures to make a professional impression about attention deficit hyperactivity disorder (ADHD)

    C. Both sets of scores, while discrepant, are still within the normal (average) range and do not indicate clinical concerns

    D. The teacher form does not indicate high-level attention concerns, but the parent shows substantial concerns

133. When talking to parents about bell curve (e.g., normal curve) characteristics, two standard deviations from the mean encompasses approximately how much of a given population?

    A. 50%

    B. 68%

    C. 95%

    D. 25%

134. A systems-wide practice or policy that is generally endorsed by the National Association of School Psychologists (NASP) is:

    A. Tracking

    B. Positive behavioral interventions and supports (PBIS) training

    C. Zero tolerance

    D. Retention

135. Which critical law or case law states that special education students must have a manifestation hearing to review placement if they are suspended for more than 10 days?

    A. *Buckley Amendment to the Family Education Act*

    B. *Lau v. Nichols*

    C. *Larry P v. Riles*

    D. *Honig v. Doe*

136. Prior written notice must be given to parents for which of the following?

    A. When a special education student is assessed for suicide

    B. Change of service, or educational programming

    C. When a special education student is suspended

    D. When a special education student is assessed for threat

137. Which academic practice/method is most closely aligned with Vygotsky's cooperative learning theory?

    A. Tell-Show-Do-Practice-Generalize (TSDPG)

    B. Classwide Peer Tutoring (CWPT)

C. Peer-to-peer instruction (PTPI)

D. Systematic and direct instruction

138. School psychologists must know facts related to various disorders. What is the name of the disorder that is believed to be caused by an extra chromosome, afflicts 1 out of 700 people, and is sometimes referred to as Trisomy 21?

A. Fragile X

B. Autism

C. Pervasive developmental disorder

D. Down syndrome

139. An important role of school psychologists is to implement antibullying programs in schools. During a schoolwide training, the school psychologist tells staff that bullying is conceptualized as a type of which of the following?

A. Violence that is characterized by a consistent abuse of power

B. Relationship aggression that is characterized by an imbalance of power

C. Violence that is characterized by consistent harassment of others

D. Harassment that is unwanted and chronic

140. What is the current National Association of School Psychologists' (NASP) opinion regarding *no-harm* or *no-suicide* contracts with students who may be suicidal?

A. Having students sign a no-harm contract raises the student's awareness that others are willing to provide support and has shown moderate effectiveness in practice

B. No-harm contracts have moderate effectiveness, but should be used with caution and a part of a comprehensive support plan

C. No-harm contracts have little utility, but may be used with high school-aged students

D. No-harm contracts have shown little effectiveness and are not generally recommended

End of Test: Go back and check your answers if time permits.

Practice Tests: Answers and Explanations

Each of the following explanations is keyed to the test category where the information can be found and the corresponding chapter in this book:

- *Professional Practices, Practices That Permeate All Aspects of Service Delivery*—first test category (Chapter 1)
- *Direct and Indirect Services for Children, Families, and Schools*—second test category (Chapter 2)
- *Systems-Level Services*—third test category (Chapter 3)
- *Foundations of School Psychological Service Delivery*—fourth test category (Chapter 4)

Practice Test I

1. **D.** The Family Educational Rights and Privacy Act (FERPA) governs student information and confidentiality related to educational records. *Foundations of School Psychological Service Delivery*

2. **A.** Noam Chomsky is known for concepts related to language development and language acquisition device. *Foundations of School Psychological Service Delivery*

3. **B.** During a professional consultation situation, parents (not just concerned parents) must have an avenue to express themselves and feel as if their opinions are considered. *Professional Practices, Practices That Permeate All Aspects of Service Delivery*

4. **A.** Although a few other choices are valid, answer "A" is the best response because it has a specific basis in pedagogy. While it is important to have high and realistic goals when teaching students, students perform best

when goals are individualized. Educational goals need to be within a student's specific and attainable limits, which is called the zone of proximal development. *Direct and Indirect Services for Children, Families, and Schools*

5. **C.** Serotonin is *the* major brain chemical that is implicated in clinical depression. Although other brain chemicals, such as glutamate, might also play a role in depression, the other answer choices do not support its combination with other neurochemicals. Of the combinations provided, norepinephrine and dopamine are the other two neurotransmitters primarily supported by research. Always choose answers that take precedence in the current body of mainstream research. *Foundations of School Psychological Service Delivery*

6. **A.** Despite the two traits associated with possible depression (e.g., withdrawal and sadness), the additional comment about anxiety indicates that a broad-spectrum tool such as the Behavior Assessment System for Children (BASC) is a valid assessment to initially use. Most likely, supplemental narrow-band tools will be employed to illuminate more information on this case, but the BASC is a common assessment starting point. *Professional Practices, Practices That Permeate All Aspects of Service Delivery*

7. **C.** This is a very difficult question to answer because other answer choices could be correct. Also note the superfluous information (Differential Ability Scales-II [DAS-II] score), which has little influence on the right answer. Despite other tempting responses, the *best* answer is C. Given the presenting facts of this case, it is unlikely that a student would score more than 20 standard points higher at home than at school because the interrater reliability is very good with the Vineland. Note the discrepancy between the parents. While behaviors certainly vacillate between environments, it is acceptable to assume there may be a problem of perception between the raters when scores are extremely discrepant. *Professional Practices, Practices That Permeate All Aspects of Service Delivery*

8. **B.** Although exercise and student placement in the classroom are effective interventions, raising a student's awareness of her difficulty is a key *first* step in treatment. *Direct and Indirect Services for Children, Families, and Schools*

9. **B.** When students feel they have a voice in their own learning, they tend to perform better. Students with certain types of difficulties can complete full assignments and should not be denied the opportunity to be aligned with their classmates if collaborative accommodations can mitigate a person's disability. *Direct and Indirect Services for Children, Families, and Schools*

10. **B.** In practice and in real-world settings, it is permissible to study new tests and administer such tests with supervision or guidance from a qualified practitioner colleague. *Professional Practices, Practices That Permeate All Aspects of Service Delivery* and *Ethical, Legal, and Professional Foundations*

11. **A.** It is best practice to share important information with parents about their children as soon as possible, even if further investigations suggest the issue is not life-threatening. In suicide and threat assessment situations, parental

permission for assessment is desirable, but not strictly necessary (answer "D"). Parents will have to be notified early in all cases of suicidal ideation. However, police or social services do not necessarily have to be notified in all cases. *Professional Practices, Practices That Permeate All Aspects of Service Delivery* and *Direct and Indirect Services for Children, Families, and Schools*

12. **C.** To prevent a difficult situation from developing, parental notification about cognitive assessment results should be secured first before talking with students or teachers about formal results. *Professional Practices, Practices That Permeate All Aspects of Service Delivery* and *Foundations of School Psychological Service Delivery*

13. **D.** This question is one that seems easy to answer at first, but then you find all answers are correct. Your task, as mentioned earlier, is to find the *best* answer. In this case, the most encompassing answer choice is "D" because it covers items found in other choices. *Professional Practices, Practices That Permeate All Aspects of Service Delivery* and *Systems-Level Services*

14. **A.** Chunking is a well-known psychological technique that is a common memory aid, such as when people memorize or repeat phone numbers. Phone numbers are a series of numbers broken up into chunks by hyphens so that they can be easily memorized. *Direct and Indirect Services for Children, Families, and Schools*

15. **D.** Straightforward factual answer. *Direct and Indirect Services for Children, Families, and Schools*

16. **A.** Legally, it is important to notify parents when aggressive actions are involved between students (e.g., duty to warn). All other answer choices are good response choices and valid, but you *must* perform the actions provided in "A." *Foundations of School Psychological Service Delivery*

17. **C.** Although there are slight differences of professional opinion about what is best practice related to validity and reliability cutoff coefficients, a test's psychometrics should be, in general, above 0.70. It is suggested by this author that test psychometrics be above 0.80. *Professional Practices, Practices That Permeate All Aspects of Service Delivery*

18. **A.** The definition of metacognition is defined by answer choice A. Note that choices B and C may also be valid responses based on their applied nature, but the best response for the definition is "A." *Foundations of School Psychological Service Delivery* and *Direct and Indirect Services for Children, Families, and Schools*

19. **B.** Least restrictive placement is a legal issue that must be honored if a student is making reasonable progress. Note that a student making Cs is considered reasonable academic progress. *Foundations of School Psychological Service Delivery* and *Direct and Indirect Services for Children, Families, and Schools*

20. **A.** As noted earlier, the least restrictive environment (LRE) concept is a legal issue and should be honored. Students do not have to make the highest

grades to make academic progress and schools are not obligated to make sure students make the highest grades possible. Key terms to note are "reasonable educational progress." *Foundations of School Psychological Service Delivery*

21. **D.** A standard score of 50 is significantly below average and suggests a high level of cognitive impairment. The new term used to describe significant cognitive difficulties is intellectual disability. *Professional Practices, Practices That Permeate All Aspects of Service Delivery*

22. **D.** The answer to this question is factual. While it is unlikely you will have such a specific question, some exams may have such an item. Students who answer such questions correctly are most likely well prepared to answer questions within this domain. *Professional Practices, Practices That Permeate All Aspects of Service Delivery*

23. **A.** Cognitive behavioral therapy (CBT) is a common psychological technique that takes a hands-on, practical approach to problem solving. Once patterns of behavior and thinking are modified, the person feels better and confident to cope with challenges. *Direct and Indirect Services for Children, Families, and Schools*

24. **A.** School readiness is a broad term that encompasses both behavior and cognitive aspects of a child. Look for a keyword association with the concept of school readiness, which is "maturation." *Foundations of School Psychological Service Delivery*

25. **A.** Differences between scores are observed in the general population. Although such splits between scores should always be considered, it is important not to jump to conclusions. Follow-up testing to confirm the suspected disability and more information are warranted to fully examine the given situation. *Professional Practices, Practices That Permeate All Aspects of Service Delivery*

26. **B.** Although other choices are good responses, answer B is the best answer. Note that choice D is not a good choice and it is not fully accurate. Current cognitive assessments are better developed to account for cultural issues than previous assessments. Despite improvements, cultural issues are still very important to consider as confounding factors when testing minority students. *Data-Based Decision Making* and *Ethical, Legal, and Professional Foundations*

27. **A.** The answer to this question is based on a well-known psychological theory called the halo effect. The halo effect is a confounding factor when people are engaged in formal observations. The other option choices are not valid responses. *Foundations of School Psychological Service Delivery* and *Professional Practices, Practices That Permeate All Aspects of Service Delivery*

28. **C.** Curriculum-based measurement (CBM) is a measurement tool and is often confused with curriculum-based assessment (CBA). CBMs are effective tools to track student progress. CBMs supplement, not replace,

standardized measures. *Professional Practices, Practices That Permeate All Aspects of Service Delivery*

29. **D.** The amygdala is a neurological structure that is found in the limbic system and plays a pivotal role in emotions. *Foundations of School Psychological Service Delivery*

30. **C.** Cognitive behavioral therapy (CBT) is one of the most common and effective psychological interventions. Although other options are valid choices and debatable, CBT is the best answer for this question due to its support in mainstream research. *Direct and Indirect Services for Children, Families, and Schools*

31. **B.** It is best practice to secure parental permission before counseling. Securing permission helps prevent conflict and builds collaboration. *Foundations of School Psychological Service Delivery* and *Direct and Indirect Services for Children, Families, and Schools*

32. **A.** This question has distracter options that appear to be good choices. Remember that *collaboration* is a key term and many choices that have this term are usually the correct answer. *Professional Practices, Practices That Permeate All Aspects of Service Delivery*

33. **A.** Although there are exceptions, the National Association of School Psychologists (NASP) typically does not endorse grade retention. *Direct and Indirect Services for Children, Families, and Schools*

34. **C.** The Universal Nonverbal Intelligence Test (UNIT) is a mainstream nonverbal test battery that is appropriate for many deaf students or English as a second language (ESL) students. *Professional Practices, Practices That Permeate All Aspects of Service Delivery*

35. **A.** This answer is straightforward and fact based. Even if you have never heard of "in vivo" therapy, the words "flooding techniques" should give you the best clue to the correct answer. *Direct and Indirect Services for Children, Families, and Schools*

36. **B.** To answer this question, you have to know Erikson's stages of development. It might be helpful to know the associated age ranges for these stages and especially the key traits of each stage. *Foundations of School Psychological Service Delivery* and *Direct and Indirect Services for Children, Families, and Schools*

37. **B.** The first step in this situation is to lend support to the family members of the deceased student. The second step is to provide support to classmates and friends. *Direct and Indirect Services for Children, Families, and Schools*

38. **A.** The answer is two and fairly straightforward. Typically, the lower the number of students a supervisor must manage the better. *Foundations of School Psychological Service Delivery*

39. **C.** Individuals with Disabilities Education Act (IDEA) outlines Child Find services. *Foundations of School Psychological Service Delivery*

40. **B.** Alfred Binet is credited as creating one of the first standardized intelligent tests for children. *Foundations of School Psychological Service Delivery*

41. **B.** Projective tests are effective measures, but a high degree of skill and training are involved. It is good practice to supplement test results when using projective measures. *Professional Practices, Practices That Permeate All Aspects of Service Delivery*

42. **C.** Section 504 is an Americans with Disabilities Act (ADA) law and governed by the Office for Civil Rights (OCR). *Foundations of School Psychological Service Delivery*

43. **C.** One of the primary reasons cognitive assessments are administered to students who are struggling academically is to predict academic performance and to help determine the appropriate level of curriculum. *Professional Practices, Practices That Permeate All Aspects of Service Delivery*

44. **A.** In low-level cases of an ethical violation, it is acceptable to address the situation at the direct level with the person. *Foundations of School Psychological Service Delivery*

45. **C.** This is a difficult question to answer. Note that test protocols cannot be copied and parents cannot be allowed to copy some types of information from a test protocol. Psychologists should fully *explain their reasoning* and educate parents about what scores mean without violating laws. *Data-Based Decision Making, Professional Practices, Practices That Permeate All Aspects of Service Delivery* and *Foundations of School Psychological Service Delivery*

46. **B.** Parents can use private testing, but schools do not always have to pay for such testing. Only in special circumstances are schools required to pay for outside testing. *Foundations of School Psychological Service Delivery*

47. **B.** When safety or crisis situations arise, psychologists have more flexibility to meet with students. You do not need permission in this situation. *Foundations of School Psychological Service Delivery* and *Direct and Indirect Services for Children, Families, and Schools*

48. **A.** It is best practice to set your rules and limitations of counseling as early as possible in the therapeutic relationship. *Direct and Indirect Services for Children, Families, and Schools*

49. **B.** Asking clarifying questions, when differences in results are discovered, may illuminate the reasons for the differences. Results are not necessarily invalid just because differences exist, but you should explore *why* significant differences exist. *Professional Practices, Practices That Permeate All Aspects of Service Delivery*

50. **A.** A child cannot change schools or placement when a due process proceeding has commenced. *Foundations of School Psychological Service Delivery*

51. **A.** The only other possible answer to this question is C, but annual meetings are typically for reviewing goals and progress toward goals. The student's eligibility for special education services is discussed during the initial staffing (not referral) meeting. *Foundations of School Psychological Service Delivery*

52. **A.** This simple question might be difficult to answer because it suggests that a processing speed test has unique administration criteria, when the main point is that the test is a formal cognitive test that follows standard administration practices. Although option "C" might also be a good answer, the point of a school psychologist's assessment is to determine how a child functions in a *typical* school day. Additionally, authentic fluency evaluations are usually done in real-time reading situations, not via a work sample review. *Professional Practices, Practices That Permeate All Aspects of Service Delivery*

53. **D.** The answer is factual. You must know the correct terms to describe specific disorders. For example, do not be misled by official-sounding terms, such as fetal alcohol symptom, because there is no such disability. Fetal alcohol effects (FAE) is the correct terminology. *Direct and Indirect Services for Children, Families, and Schools*

54. **A.** Sometimes you will have a few easy questions. Through a process of choice elimination, the best answer to this question is a neurologically based issue that is implicated in autism. The majority of disorders that psychologists deal with are brain-based dysfunctions. *Foundations of School Psychological Service Delivery*

55. **D.** The broader the score the more valid and reliable it is to interpret, given little intra/intersubtest variability. *Professional Practices, Practices That Permeate All Aspects of Service Delivery*

56. **D.** This is a difficult question to answer if you do not know the research related to *intrinsic* motivation. Note that tangible rewards, while effective in some situations, may hinder the development of intrinsic motivation. Cognitive approaches are best to use to build intrinsic motivation. "Choice" is a cognitive approach that gives students control to develop preferences. *Foundations of School Psychological Service Delivery* and *Direct and Indirect Services for Children, Families, and Schools*

57. **A.** Block design tasks can measure several different cognitive functions, but from a neuropsychological perspective, novel visual perception tasks (e.g., block design) usually activate the right regions of the brain. *Foundations of School Psychological Service Delivery* and *Professional Practices, Practices That Permeate All Aspects of Service Delivery*

58. **C.** Punishment and negative reinforcement are commonly confused. Remember, any intervention that *increases* a behavior is related to negative reinforcement. *Foundations of School Psychological Service Delivery* and *Direct and Indirect Services for Children, Families, and Schools*

59. **C.** Children who have dysgraphia have difficulty in writing coherently. Multiple-choice tests are a typical and appropriate accommodation for this disorder. *Direct and Indirect Services for Children, Families, and Schools* and *Foundations of School Psychological Service Delivery*

60. **C.** Although the answer to this question could be debated, stimulus fading is a specific and effective method used with students who demonstrate

selective mutism. Stimulus fading is related to gradual desensitization techniques. *Foundations of School Psychological Service Delivery* and *Direct and Indirect Services for Children, Families, and Schools*

61. **B.** The best answer to this question is "B," although "D" is also a possibility. Choice "B" is the better answer because it addresses both the positive and negative interventions involved in shaping behavior. *Foundations of School Psychological Service Delivery* and *Direct and Indirect Services for Children, Families, and Schools*

62. **A.** This question is fairly straightforward. The *best* choice for this question is that the National Association of School Psychologists (NASP) is the primary accreditation body for the Nationally Certified School Psychologist (NCSP) credential. *Foundations of School Psychological Service Delivery*

63. **C.** This is a difficult situation and a difficult question to answer. Only a judge can legally order a psychologist to turn over protocols that are copyright protected. In this situation, it is best to collaborate with the parents and explain your results to them. Although "B" is a valid choice, if a lawyer is demanding access to school records and protocols, it is best to review test results, but not copy them ("C") unless subpoenaed to do so. If parents and the lawyer persist in their demands, contact the school's lawyer. *Foundations of School Psychological Service Delivery* and *Professional Practices, Practices That Permeate All Aspects of Service Delivery*

64. **D.** Family Educational Rights and Privacy Act (FERPA) is related to confidentiality issues and parent access to school records. *Foundations of School Psychological Service Delivery*

65. **A.** This is not a common test question, but psychologists must be aware that copyright laws impact their practices as much as educational laws. *Foundations of School Psychological Service Delivery*

66. **A.** Planning is one of the major traits associated with the concept of executive functioning. Organization, emotional regulation, and behavioral regulation are other traits of executive functioning. *Foundations of School Psychological Service Delivery*

67. **D.** Prevention is primary in crisis intervention. Use the alliteration "Prevention is primary" to help you remember this concept. *Direct and Indirect Services for Children, Families, and Schools* and *Systems-Level Services*

68. **B.** The consultee is typically the teacher and is the proper terminology in the research. When you employ a consultee-centered model, you are building a person's skills to address situations without your direct help. *Professional Practices, Practices That Permeate All Aspects of Service Delivery*

69. **C.** Although other choices may seem like good answers, the better response is "C" because it incorporates the key aspects of other choices. "C" is a more thorough response in this situation. *Direct and Indirect Services for Children, Families, and Schools*

70. **A.** Answer "A" is factual and the best answer given the choices. Authentic assessments generally do not use standardized psychometrics and they lend themselves to professional judgment more than standardized measures. *Professional Practices, Practices That Permeate All Aspects of Service Delivery*

71. **A.** Although there are several motivations for behavior, choice "A" provides the primary reasons for common student behavior. *Attention* from peers, *affiliation* with valued others, and to *control* for anxiety are illustrated in venerable school psychological literature. All other options might be included in some research, but they are not widely accepted by experts. *Foundations of School Psychological Service Delivery* and *Direct and Indirect Services for Children, Families, and Schools*

72. **C.** The two key terms in Erikson's stages are "industry versus inferiority." You should be familiar with the five stages of development that center on school-aged students. Note that the answer to this question could be found on an earlier item on this test (question 36). *Foundations of School Psychological Service Delivery* and *Direct and Indirect Services for Children, Families, and Schools*

73. **B.** The approval of others and social pressure are hallmark traits of the conventional level of moral reasoning. *Foundations of School Psychological Service Delivery*

74. **A.** On most mainstream cognitive assessments, a standard score of 90, with a commensurate standard error of measurement (SEM) of 6 points, is considered to be within the average and to below-average range. *Professional Practices, Practices That Permeate All Aspects of Service Delivery*

75. **D.** Although the student in this situation needs interventions due to her harassment, a threat of violence warrants specific legal obligations and actions from school staff. The duty to warn is a key obligation psychologists must fulfill. A threat assessment will most likely follow. *Foundations of School Psychological Service Delivery* and *Systems-Level Services*

76. **C.** Although choice "A" is a good option, the *best* choice would be "C" because it is a more comprehensive intervention that uses data to focus a systems-level intervention. This question has links to various domains. *Systems-Level Services, Professional Practices, Practices That Permeate All Aspects of Service Delivery,* and *Direct and Indirect Services for Children, Families, and Schools*

77. **C.** People with an external-locus-of-control attitude do not believe they have control over events that happen to them. Students with this orientation often develop a learned-helplessness disposition. *Direct and Indirect Services for Children, Families, and Schools*

78. **B.** Due to the parent's actions, the child will have difficulty developing confidence in her abilities. Only through concerted effort can genuine achievement and confidence be created. *Direct and Indirect Services for Children, Families, and Schools*

79. **D.** School staff are mandated reporters and *must* notify police or protective services when they suspect abuse. *Foundations of School Psychological Service Delivery*

80. **A.** In the spirit of Multi-Tiered System of Support (MTSS) and response to intervention (RTI), interventions should be implemented before a formal special education evaluation is started. Although formal testing may be concurrent with MTSS interventions, many times students will respond appropriately to interventions and are not found to be disabled. *Direct and Indirect Services for Children, Families, and Schools* and *Professional Practices, Practices That Permeate All Aspects of Service Delivery*

81. **A.** Although some practitioners may debate the answer to this question, it is appropriate to let parents know about the research regarding medication if your assessment data support your comments. As long as the psychologist is recommending that the parent only speak with a doctor and is not giving a directive to take medications, then this action is permissible. *Foundations of School Psychological Service Delivery* and *Professional Practices, Practices That Permeate All Aspects of Service Delivery*

82. **B.** Working memory is the ability to hold information "online" while performing another task. *Foundations of School Psychological Service Delivery*

83. **A.** Students with mild autism may also have some of the traits listed in the other choices, but the best response for this question is "A." A hallmark trait of autism is social skills deficits and social language problems. *Foundations of School Psychological Service Delivery* and *Direct and Indirect Services for Children, Families, and Schools*

84. **B.** Mandated reporters must notify police or social services. Even if mandated reports "tell" the school social worker or principal, they are ultimately responsible to report suspected abuse to the proper authorities. *Foundations of School Psychological Service Delivery* and *Direct and Indirect Services for Children, Families, and Schools*

85. **A.** Although a child's brain can make a complete recovery after a brain injury, it is more vulnerable to permanent damage than an adult's in most cases. Brain injuries can produce learning, behavioral, emotional, and attention problems. Traumatic brain injury (TBI) assessment is a growing responsibility for school psychologists. *Foundations of School Psychological Service Delivery* and *Professional Practices, Practices That Permeate All Aspects of Service Delivery*

86. **C.** This question has several distracter answers. Phonemic awareness is the ability to manipulate sounds. For example, say cat, then say it again without the /c/ sound. *Direct and Indirect Services for Children, Families, and Schools*

87. **A.** A Functional behavioral assessment (FBA) is the standard formal evaluation that specifically evaluates the antecedents, behavior, and consequences. *Foundations of School Psychological Service Delivery* and *Direct and Indirect Services for Children, Families, and Schools*

88. **D.** The occipital lobe is considered the primary anatomical region of the visual cortex. *Foundations of School Psychological Service Delivery*

89. **C.** There are several types of attention described in mainstream research. Attention can be divided into selective, sustained, and divided subtypes. The previous terms are technical in nature and are used with precision. *Foundations of School Psychological Service Delivery*

90. **A.** Modeling is the proper psychological term to describe learning through observation. Reference Albert Bandura's work related to modeling. *Foundations of School Psychological Service Delivery*

91. **C.** This question is factual and straightforward. See question 90. *Foundations of School Psychological Service Delivery* and *Direct and Indirect Services for Children, Families, and Schools*

92. **B.** Remember that a negative correlation can be stronger than a positive correlation. Note that a −0.98 is almost a perfect (i.e., highest possible) correlation. *Professional Practices, Practices That Permeate All Aspects of Service Delivery*

93. **A.** Test takers are typically confused by this question. The experimental group is the one that is exposed to the conditions of the experiment. *Foundations of School Psychological Service Delivery*

94. **C.** The control group is *not* exposed to experimental factors. See question 93 as a comparison. *Foundations of School Psychological Service Delivery*

95. **C.** The correct term is *independent variable*, not *experimental variable*. Make sure you know the subtle differences between terms with these types of questions. Most students misunderstand the terms independent and dependent variables. *Foundations of School Psychological Service Delivery*

96. **C.** The National Association of School Psychologists (NASP) endorses and encourages the use of both formal and informal measures when evaluating a student for special education services. Note that option "D" is valid, but subsumed by answer "C" because an observation is considered an informal measure. *Professional Practices, Practices That Permeate All Aspects of Service Delivery*

97. **A.** The term *aphasia* is associated with a range of language problems, such as word-retrieval difficulties and verbal comprehension trouble. *Foundations of School Psychological Service Delivery* and *Direct and Indirect Services for Children, Families, and Schools*

98. **D.** Although "A" and "C" are reasonable answers, the best answer is a "D" heuristic. A heuristic is a tool used in problem solving and is based on reducing the number of factors to consider. *Direct and Indirect Services for Children, Families, and Schools*

99. **C.** When students are asked to describe their reasoning, they are forced to interrogate their thoughts and to think deeply. Such techniques increase understanding and comprehension. *Direct and Indirect Services for Children, Families, and Schools*

100. **A.** The halo effect is a well-known psychological effect. Note that this question, or concepts related to it, was asked in a previous question on this test. Sometimes, you can answer questions by remembering previous items. Reference question 27. *Foundations of School Psychological Service Delivery*

101. **C.** School psychologists cannot be asked to violate their ethical code of conduct. Handling this case at the lowest level first, before higher level actions are pursued, is best practice. *Foundations of School Psychological Service Delivery*

102. **A.** Curriculum-based measurement (CBM) is not a norm-referenced measurement tool. It is effective in the response to intervention (RTI) process and allows staff to monitor progress toward educational goals. *Direct and Indirect Services for Children, Families, and Schools*

103. **B.** When meeting with students, you only need permission from the parents and should secure such permission before counseling starts. Although it might be important to notify relevant staff and administration, it is not required. *Foundations of School Psychological Service Delivery* and *Direct and Indirect Services for Children, Families, and Schools*

104. **B.** Child Find is a provision and terminology used in the Individuals with Disabilities Education Act (IDEA) that mandates schools to actively seek out children with disabilities. *Foundations of School Psychological Service Delivery*

105. **D.** The Cognitive Assessment System-2 (CAS-2) is based on A. E. Luria's theory and his landmark work. Luria's work forms the basis for many neuropsychological theories. *Professional Practices, Practices That Permeate All Aspects of Service Delivery*, and *Foundations of School Psychological Service Delivery*

106. **C.** Humanists, such as Rogers and Maslow, are central figures who believed people have an innate desire for growth. *Direct and Indirect Services for Children, Families, and Schools*

107. **D.** The Cattell–Horn–Carroll (CHC) theory is a well-established and accepted statistical theory used for the foundation of many mainstream cognitive tests. Simultaneous processing is not part of the CHC model, but rather the planning, attention-arousal, and simultaneous and successive processing (PASS) theory. *Professional Practices, Practices That Permeate All Aspects of Service Delivery* and *Foundations of School Psychological Service Delivery*

108. **A.** Although the lower ratio of students to school psychologist is better, the National Association of School Psychologists (NASP) generally recommends that psychologists should serve no more than 1,000 students. *Foundations of School Psychological Service Delivery*

109. **A.** It is important to remember that the *Diagnostic and Statistical Manual of Mental Disorders*, Fifth Edition (*DSM-5*) has placed Asperger's syndrome under the primary domain of autism spectrum disorder. Many features

of Asperger's syndrome are similar to autism, but not as severe as autism. *Direct and Indirect Services for Children, Families, and Schools*

110. **B.** There are aspects of each choice that are valid, such as self-awareness and perspective training, but only choice "B" contains the correct combination of common social skills training elements. The best answer for this question is "B." *Direct and Indirect Services for Children, Families, and Schools*

111. **C.** Children with autism often qualify for special education services because their social skills deficits impede their ability to make and maintain social relationships. Most special education services are predicated upon whether the student's area of difficulty significantly impacts academic progress or social development. *Direct and Indirect Services for Children, Families, and Schools*

112. **A.** It is the best practice to evaluate the frequency, intensity, and duration of a behavior when asked to conduct formal observations or functional behavioral assessment (FBA). *Direct and Indirect Services for Children, Families, and Schools*

113. **B.** According to the National Center for Learning Disabilities (NCLD, 2014), the prevalence rate for learning disabilities is approximately 4% to 8% (Centers for Disease Control and Prevention [CDC] = 7.6%). Note that a range of statistics is provided in the choices because some research organizations vary slightly in their stated rates. *Foundations of School Psychological Service Delivery* and *Direct and Indirect Services for Children, Schools, and Families*

114. **C.** The standard convention related to the gifted range of standard scores is approximately 130 (125–135). *Professional Practices, Practices That Permeate All Aspects of Service Delivery*

115. **A.** Legally, the student in this example must be afforded the same opportunities and activities as a general education student. *Foundations of School Psychological Service Delivery*

116. **A.** Research in this area suggests there is no definitive profile of a school shooter, although there are traits and incidences to consider as risk factors. Reference the *Safe School Initiative* provided by the U.S. Secret Service and the U.S. Department of Education. *Systems-Level Services* and *Direct and Indirect Services for Children, Families, and Schools*

117. **B.** In most cases, the best approach to teaching students is by using an array of different approaches that hold their interest and may cover their learning preferences. *Direct and Indirect Services for Children, Families, and Schools*

118. **B.** This answer is factual and straightforward. Narrative recording contains a running record and notes on a student. *Professional Practices, Practices That Permeate All Aspects of Service Delivery*

119. **B.** The National Association of School Psychologists (NASP) has a positive view of homeschooled children, but also supports a healthy collaboration among all parties involved in a child's learning. *Foundations of School Psychological Service Delivery* and *Professional Practices, Practices That Permeate All Aspects of Service Delivery*

120. **D.** Simultaneous processing is a neurocognitive process and term used by school neuropsychologists. *Professional Practices, Practices That Permeate All Aspects of Service Delivery*

121. **D.** After-school programs are not typically linked to Multi-Tiered System of Support (MTSS) because this response choice is too broad and may not be linked to positive academic or behavioral outcomes. *Systems-Level Services*

122. **B.** This question might be difficult to answer because all options seem appropriate. However, the answer that covers the broadest area is "B," the other choices are too narrow (i.e., specific). According to systems theory, schoolwide practices that promote learning have high expectations and a challenging curriculum taught by supportive staff. *Systems-Level Services*

123. **C.** According to best practice for needs assessments, it is important to review common barriers to effective practices as well as effective practices and ineffective practices. Other choices may be valid, but a review of Chapter 3 details the points of a needs assessment. *Systems-Level Services*

124. **B.** Although not explicitly stated, the National Association of School Psychologists (NASP) and other professional organizations support a research-based and formal approach to dealing with school violence and serious threats. The Virginia model and the U.S. Secret Service's Safe Schools Initiative are two models that are widely adopted by public school systems. Note that the other choices are certainly not endorsed by the NASP. *Systems-Level Services*

125. **B.** As noted in Chapter 2, *Foundations of Effective Pedagogy and Instruction*, a widely accepted model of student skill acquisition, is noted in choice B. *Direct and Indirect Services for Children, Families, and Schools*

126. **D.** Most widely adopted models of threat assessment recommend that a multitude of sources be used to gather relevant threat assessment information. While the student of concern interview is critical, other sources, such as peer and staff interviews, can illuminate information that is sometimes deliberately not disclosed by the parents or the student of concern. Note that student records and information from the community are also important; however, these sources were not included in the correct combination of the choices offered. Only "D" offers the best combination of sources. *Systems-Level Services* and *Direct and Indirect Services for Children, Families, and Schools*

127. **D.** While aspects of the other choices are important considerations, a school shooting cannot take place if the student of concern does not have ready access to weapons. Of the choices provided, it is first and foremost importance to secure weapons access, then focus on the other related threat assessment factors. *Systems-Level Services* and *Direct and Indirect Services for Children, Families, and Schools*

128. **B.** Although there are several important items common to all effective management plans, two of the most important interventions that can be implemented without complication are increased supervision and

restricted access to weapons. Although mental health support, restorative practices, and various psychotherapeutic methods (e.g., cognitive behavioral therapy [CBT]) are effective, sometimes the student of concern can resist engaging with the previous interventions. *Systems-Level Services* and *Direct and Indirect Services for Children, Families, and Schools*

129. **B.** One standard deviation from the mean on the bell curve encompasses 68% of the population. *Professional Practices, Practices That Permeate All Aspects of Service Delivery*

130. **A.** Reference Chapter 2, section "Major Types of Individual Counseling Approaches and Theories." Although dialectical behavior therapy (DBT) is not as common as other counseling approaches, it is gaining in popularity and has proven effective for various groups of people with special needs. *Direct and Indirect Services With Children, Families, and Schools*

131. **D.** All of the other choices are valid symptoms of posttraumatic stress disorder (PTSD). However, the primary trait of PTSD is the urge to retell the personal perception and interpretation of the traumatic event. The retelling of a traumatic event is hypothesized to be a natural way for the mind to make sense of the event and integrate the event into the person's experience. *Direct and Indirect Services for Children, Families, and Schools*

132. **A.** While schools need to endorse cultural sensitivity trainings and use interpreters when necessary, the parents' involvement with school and the value placed on formal education is typically a major influence not only on a student's progress, but also on the student graduating from high school. The primary language spoken at home is also a key factor in academic progress, but many children immersed in school start to learn a second language in addition to the home language. *Foundations of School Psychological Service Delivery*

133. **B.** Schools must provide health services to students, but not medical services that require a licensed medical doctor to perform. *Foundations of School Psychological Service Delivery*

134. **A.** An ecological assessment can use a variety of methods to assess a student, but a central component of this type of assessment is the influence of multiple environments and factors considered in behavioral/developmental analysis. *Professional Practices, Practices That Permeate All Aspects of Service Delivery*

135. **C.** Prozac is a commonly prescribed medication for depression, posttraumatic stress disorder (PTSD), and obsessive-compulsive disorder (OCD). While school psychologists do not prescribe medication, they can encourage parents to talk to their doctors about medication options and make available credible medical research on the topic. For the exam, you should be familiar with major trade name medications for common disorders such as attention deficit hyperactivity disorder (ADHD), depression, seizure

disorder, bipolar disorder, and anxiety. Only a few questions of this type are usually on the test. *Foundations of School Psychological Service Delivery* and *Direct and Indirect Services with Children, Families, and Schools*

136. **D.** While parental socioeconomic status (SES) might impact a student, the first three choices are the *most* common areas that are examined for a typical formal special education assessment. Student behavioral and academic (e.g., transcripts) records are also reviewed. *Professional Practices, Practices That Permeate All Aspects of Service Delivery*

137. **B.** This question might be difficult for some people to answer if they are not familiar with best practices in concussion management. Although there is still some disagreement among experts, school psychologists are playing an increased role in this area to support students. Currently, most experts agree that students should attend school if they have mild symptoms and a support plan. Students should rarely stay at home until symptom free. Rather, students should have a support plan that allows them frequent access to the health room for rest breaks. Reference the *REAP* (Remove/Reduce, Educate, Adjust/Accommodate, Pace) *Manual* by Dr. McAvoy for more information. *Direct and Indirect Services for Children, Families, and Schools*

138. **B.** Concussions are considered by the majority of medical and allied medical experts as a mild brain injury or mild traumatic brain injury (mTBI). Although some experts are beginning to use other terms and they are reluctant to use the term "brain injury" or "temporary brain injury," mTBI is still the most prevalent term used interchangeably with concussion. *Direct and Indirect Services for Children, Families, and Schools*

139. **C.** *Oberti v. Cementon* (1993) is a legal case that affirmed the rights of a special-needs student to be included in regular education classes and activities. The courts also underscored that schools must adhere to the Individuals with Disabilities Education Act (IDEA) requirements, especially those related to the least restrictive environment (LRE) clause. *Foundations of School Psychological Service Delivery*

140. **A.** Most scholars believe that the father of *school* psychology is Lightner Witmer. Dr. Witmer established a clinic at the University of Pennsylvania in 1896. He combined educational and psychological services to help students with learning and behavioral problems. *Foundations of School Psychological Service Delivery*

Practice Test II

1. **C.** Although all choices could be valid, the National Association of School Psychologists (NASP) does not generally endorse grade retention. *Professional Practices, Practices That Permeate All Aspects of Service Delivery* and *Direct and Indirect Services for Children, Families, and Schools*

2. **A.** Semi-structured interviews have high validity because the interview questions are standardized and asked of all interviewees. This method also allows for the interviewer to ask follow-up questions, unlike the structured interview method. Note that option C sounds legitimate, but this response is not a valid term. *Professional Practices, Practices That Permeate All Aspects of Service Delivery*

3. **B.** In the scenario, the referral question is vague and the student's specific area of struggle is unknown. It is good practice to define the problem as specifically as possible before targeting interventions or assessments. Note that "A" and "D" are good choices, but are not generally utilized until the referral problem is better defined. The student may not be in the response to intervention (RTI) process and the referral may be a step in placing the student in the RTI system once areas of difficulty are defined. *Professional Practices, Practices That Permeate All Aspects of Service Delivery* and *Direct and Indirect Services for Children, Families, and Schools*

4. **A.** Interval sampling is a good choice because it is a time-efficient method, especially when it is difficult to determine when a behavior begins or ends. Option "C" is not a common term. *Professional Practices, Practices That Permeate All Aspects of Service Delivery*

5. **C.** Generally, there are three levels of analysis: variability, level, and trend. *Professional Practices, Practices That Permeate All Aspects of Service Delivery* and *Direct and Indirect Services for Children, Families, and Schools*

6. **B.** A *trend* is a collection of data points that show a decrease or increase in performance across time. *Professional Practices, Practices That Permeate All Aspects of Service Delivery*

7. **D.** Although it could be argued that any other response is a good answer, the best answer is "D" because confounding variables should always be considered when analyzing any type of collected data. A confounding factor could be related to the student's learning and development. *Professional Practices, Practices That Permeate All Aspects of Service Delivery*

8. **B.** This is a difficult question to answer because the other responses could be correct. However, the *best* answer for the given scenario is "B." Modifying instruction is acceptable because the last data point does show positive movement. An appropriate response for this question involves specific techniques (unlike option "D"). Specific interventions would be a modification in the intervention that includes corrective feedback and effective prompts. *Professional Practices, Practices That Permeate All Aspects of Service Delivery* and *Direct and Indirect Services for Children, Families, and Schools*

9. **C.** Although socioeconomic status (SES) can be a confounding factor in some academic cases, it is typically not a solitary factor and it is considered with several other confounding variables. It is important to examine how the other three correct answers focus narrowly on the analysis of the response to intervention (RTI) data set. *Professional Practices, Practices That Permeate*

All Aspects of Service Delivery and *Direct and Indirect Services for Children, Families, and Schools*

10. **B.** Best practice and legal mandates clearly state that practitioners must use a variety of sources that include formal and informal measures. Although valid and reliable data (choice "A") is a good choice, such statistical terms are generally used to describe standardized and formal measures. Also, choice "C" has the word "tests" and informal measures are typically not tests. *Professional Practices, Practices That Permeate All Aspects of Service Delivery*

11. **C.** School psychologists typically provide a cognitive assessment *and* adaptive-functional assessments. Note that you do not have to know the names of these tests if other terms in the choices describe the nature of the test. *Professional Practices, Practices That Permeate All Aspects of Service Delivery*

12. **A.** Baseline data should not have significant variability in performance. Baseline data collection is not time driven, as seen in response option B, but one should collect at least three data points. Note that the last two options are not valid. *Professional Practices, Practices That Permeate All Aspects of Service Delivery* and *Direct and Indirect Services for Children, Families, and Schools*

13. **D.** Although all the other processes listed might be included on major neuropsychological assessments, processing speed is considered a basal neurological function and is considered an ability rather than a skill. Remember, if you see the term "reasoning," this implies a higher order process. *Professional Practices, Practices That Permeate All Aspects of Service Delivery*

14. **D.** Given that your focus is a social/emotional evaluation, a psychologist should use a formal social/emotional measure, such as the Behavior Assessment System for Children (BASC), and conduct a functional behavioral assessment (FBA). This combination will provide formal and informal data that are necessary to address the referral question. Note that answer "C" does not provide formal data. *Professional Practices, Practices That Permeate All Aspects of Service Delivery*

15. **B.** Although only a few steps are listed for each choice, the functional behavioral assessment (FBA) process starts with defining the problem, then other steps follow. Also, the hypothesis for the behavior is based on observational data and only option "B" has this step in the correct order. *Professional Practices, Practices That Permeate All Aspects of Service Delivery*

16. **C.** Current guidelines encourage an emphasis on the antecedent and environmental modifications over consequences to modify student behavior. This is not to state that consequences are not important to consider, but many times it is easy and effective to modify a student's immediate environment before more complex strategies are used. *Professional Practices, Practices That Permeate All Aspects of Service Delivery* and *Direct and Indirect Services for Children, Families, and Schools*

17. **B.** Curriculum-based assessment (CBA) is broader than a curriculum-based measurement (CBM), which may include specific measurements such as

CBM. CBMs can be used for reading, math, or spelling, not just for reading in the response to intervention (RTI) process. *Professional Practices, Practices That Permeate All Aspects of Service Delivery*

18. **C.** Curriculum-based measurement (CBM) is a measurement tool that typically references a class (i.e., local) norm and the test material is taken directly from the child's curriculum. *Professional Practices, Practices That Permeate All Aspects of Service Delivery*

19. **D.** For special education purposes, the criteria for an intellectual disability are deficient adaptive functional scores and a standard score that is two standard deviations (30 points) below the mean on cognitive test measures. As always, a psychologist can use professional judgment if there are other sources of data that support such a diagnosis. *Professional Practices, Practices That Permeate All Aspects of Service Delivery*

20. **C.** Although choice "B" is correct, the best response is "C" because it includes critical informal data as well as information taken from formal tests that are normed appropriately. *Professional Practices, Practices That Permeate All Aspects of Service Delivery* and *Foundations of School Psychological Service Delivery*

21. **A.** The halo effect is a well-known observer bias that is a confounding factor when observing people. This factor was heavily researched by Edward Thorndike. *Professional Practices, Practices That Permeate All Aspects of Service Delivery*

22. **C.** Although choices "A" and "B" are sometimes true, there are some brief projective measures that do not involve lengthy training or time to administer. Some research indicates that reliability statistics are generally lower on some projective measures compared to standardized tests. Despite some reliability considerations, projective tests, in the hands of a skilled psychologist, have utility and provide valid information. *Professional Practices, Practices That Permeate All Aspects of Service Delivery*

23. **B.** All other responses have one term that is not a valid response choice. *Professional Practices, Practices That Permeate All Aspects of Service Delivery*

24. **B.** Test interpretation should begin from broad scores because these scores are the most valid and reliable. Item and subtest interpretation generally do not have the validity of broader scores. "C" and "D" are not good choices because it is important to report the pattern of strengths and weaknesses. *Professional Practices, Practices That Permeate All Aspects of Service Delivery*

25. **D.** All of the other choices are effective features of positive behavior support (PBS). While choice D has some validity, it is not the best response. *Direct and Indirect Services for Children, Families, and Schools* and *Systems-Level Services*

26. **B.** While a large number of students are harassed, recent research indicates it is not more than 50% but more than 10%. *Systems-Level Services*

27. **C.** Zero-tolerance policies are discouraged. Schools should try to reeducate students who harass and bully other students. A psychologist's role is to remediate and educate, not punish. *Direct and Indirect Services for Children, Families, and Schools* and *Systems-Level Services*

28. **C.** While counseling is effective and may be part of a corrective measure, the bully should make amends with the victims in a positive manner. Restorative practices are a highly recommended and current intervention strategy. *Direct and Indirect Services for Children, Families, and Schools* and *Systems-Level Services*

29. **D.** Option "D" does not provide information about confidentiality during the consultation. Danger and safety to self or others are *primary* causes to breach confidentiality ("A" and "C"). Also, a student can give you permission to talk with others (B). *Direct and Indirect Services for Children, Families, and Schools* and *Foundations of School Psychological Service Delivery*

30. **A.** Note that choice "B" is not a real therapy. "C" is not widely practiced in schools and choice "D" is a general approach rather than a specific counseling technique. Cognitive behavioral therapy (CBT) is widely regarded as an effective counseling method. *Direct and Indirect Services for Children, Families, and Schools*

31. **C.** Although all of the response choices are valid, answer "C" best describes Skinner's belief. Note that answer "C" is broader than the other choices and the word "consequences" covers both positive and negative reinforcements that may shape behavior. *Direct and Indirect Services for Children, Families, and Schools* and *Foundations of School Psychological Service Delivery*

32. **D.** Service learning includes teaching students in the authentic environment and is typically used to build empathy in students. *Direct and Indirect Services for Children, Families, and Schools*

33. **A.** Applied behavior analysis (ABA) is an effective approach with students who have autism. ABA includes the key aspects of task analysis, a highly structured environment, and systematic means of teaching new skills. The other choices may contain valid terms, but the other choice options are not completely valid names of the correct method. Note that the question has extraneous information that acts as a distracter (e.g., attention deficit hyperactivity disorder [ADHD]). *Direct and Indirect Services for Children, Families, and Schools*

34. **C.** The first three choices are all valid, but choice "C" is the best choice because it includes fading techniques. Once an appropriate behavior is taught using a highly structured and systematic means, the prompts must be slowly removed so the student can be independent. *Direct and Indirect Services for Children, Families, and Schools*

35. **B.** All responses to this question are valid; however, the best way to approach crisis is to work to prevent a crisis situation from happening in the first place. Practice and preparation are key aspects of crisis plans. *Systems-Level Services*

36. **B.** Posttraumatic stress disorder (PTSD) is a primary concern after exposure to a traumatic event. PTSD symptoms are varied, but center on hyperarousal, overalertness, anxiety, avoidance, and obsessive thoughts about the incident. *Direct and Indirect Services for Children, Families, and Schools*

37. **C.** While it is important to notify parents and your school administrator of the assessment, it is *most* critical that you never leave a potentially suicidal student alone. *Direct and Indirect Services for Children, Families, and Schools* and *Systems-Level Services*

38. **D.** Although it is important to talk to staff as soon as possible and provide support to the family and peers of the student, it is primary to first plan for contagion effects and *prevent* dangerous copycat actions by others that are sensitive to suicidal topics. Typically, a discussion with key staff will yield names of sensitive students that should be monitored and supported. Note that option "C" may not be practical because holding a meeting before school for *all* staff is very difficult. *Direct and Indirect Services for Children, Families, and Schools* and *Systems-Level Services*

39. **D.** Choice "A" may seem like a good answer—only facts should be provided to others. However, too many details about a suicide are not necessarily a good idea, especially for younger students. Although rumor control is an important consideration, a general morning announcement to all students and all staff is not a common practice, especially in very large schools. Option "C" is not a valid choice. *Direct and Indirect Services for Children, Families, and Schools* and *Systems-Level Services*

40. **A.** The preoperational stage covers the age range between 2 and 7 years. The hallmark feature of this stage is the emergence of simple symbolic thinking. For example, a picture of a cat is known by the student to represent a real cat. Option "D" is fictitious. *Foundations of School Psychological Service Delivery* and *Professional Practices, Practices That Permeate All Aspects of Service Delivery*

41. **C.** The typical age range for students within the identity versus role confusion stage is 13 to 18 years. Although the age range for stage theories is important to consider, it is most important to consider the aspects that define particular stages. In the question, the gifted and talented description is not a significant consideration. It can be inferred that the student's occupational path provides a sense of identity. *Foundations of School Psychological Service Delivery* and *Professional Practices, Practices That Permeate All Aspects of Service Delivery*

42. **C.** Albert Bandura believed in the cognitive component of learning and he believed that people can learn by watching others. His beliefs were in contrast to the principles of strict behaviorism. Bandura is also known for his famous Bobo doll study involving violence. *Foundations of School Psychological Service Delivery* and *Systems-Level Services*

43. **D.** Given a common standard error of measurement of ±5 points, a full-scale standard score of 113 would situate the true score within the average

to above-average range (108–118). Most major tests have a standard average score range of 85 to 115. Standard scores typically near 110 are considered high average. *Professional Practices, Practices That Permeate All Aspects of Service Delivery*

44. **B.** A T-score of 65 or more is near the clinically significant range (e.g., 1.5 standards above the mean). Although the two scores are cause for concern, more information from observations and other measures is necessary to make professional judgments regarding attention deficit hyperactivity disorder (ADHD). The Behavior Assessment System for Children (BASC) is a good tool, but it is only one source of data, and the National Association of School Psychologists (NASP) endorses multiple sources of information in formal situations. *Professional Practices, Practices That Permeate All Aspects of Service Delivery*

45. **A.** Although all choices could be valid, the choice that would complete a comprehensive evaluation is choice "A." A review of student records involves both previous academic and behavioral information. Also, choice "A" is the only choice that involves a student observation, which is key for initial evaluations. *Professional Practices, Practices That Permeate All Aspects of Service Delivery*

46. **C.** Kohlberg used the term "preconventional" to describe the stage of moral development that is based on the desire to avoid punishment and gain rewards. It is important to remember that stage theories might have age ranges attached to them, but in this case, it is better to understand the defining characteristics of a particular stage than it is to memorize age ranges. Note that choices "A" and "D" are invalid terms. *Foundations of School Psychological Service Delivery*

47. **D.** This question might seem simple at first, but each option has a slight error that invalidates selection. The prevalence of attention deficit hyperactivity disorder (ADHD) is approximately 3% to 7% of the population, not 15%. Although ADHD might be overdiagnosed, this statement is debatable and partly based in professional opinion rather than a solid research-based response. Answer "C" might be a valid response, but option "D" is the best answer because it is supported by long-standing research. *Direct and Indirect Services for Children, Families, and Schools* and *Foundations of School Psychological Service Delivery*

48. **C.** Anxiety is a central feature of posttraumatic stress disorder (PTSD). Most individuals with PTSD relive traumatic events that trigger a fight or flight response that is based on fear. Fear and lack of control over events cause anxiety. Although the other choices might also have anxiety components, it may not be the prevalent feature in all cases. For example, some people diagnosed with a personality disorder might experience anxiety, but some people with this diagnosis may not experience it. *Direct and Indirect Services for Children, Families, and Schools*

49. **D.** Although prevalence rates will vary every few years, autism spectrum disorders (ASDs) are said to be about 1 in every 88 people (Centers for

Disease Control and Prevention, 2012). Keep in mind that ASD includes pervasive developmental disorder (PDD). *Direct and Indirect Services for Children, Families, and Schools* and *Foundations of School Psychological Service Delivery*

50. **B.** It is inferred that Deb is already being screened for dyslexia due to the formal referral related to reading. The new information indicates that she may also have a quantitative reasoning problem that is the hallmark feature of dyscalculia. Note that math disability is not a formal term. The *Diagnostic and Statistical Manual of Mental Disorders*, Fifth Edition (*DSM-5*) identifies learning disorders with classifiers under the umbrella term "Specific Learning Disorder With Impairments in Math." *Professional Practices, Practices That Permeate All Aspects of a Service Delivery* and *Foundations of School Psychological Service Delivery*

51. **A.** "Theory of the Mind" is the appropriate name of a specific theory associated with the perspective-taking difficulties associated with autism. Of the choices offered, "A" is the *best* answer. *Foundations of School Psychological Service Delivery* and *Direct and Indirect Services for Children, Families, and Schools*

52. **B.** Learned helplessness is a term created by Dr. Martin Seligman. People who believe that they have little control over events in life typically develop a learned helplessness perspective. Some children with learned helplessness attitudes typically have depressive symptoms and do not have positive life outcomes. *Direct and Indirect Services for Children, Families, and Schools* and *Foundations of School Psychological Service Delivery*

53. **C.** The Premack Principle is a well-known behavioral tenet related to B. F. Skinner's theories. The Premack Principle states that a higher desired behavior can shape a lower desired behavior. *Foundations of School Psychological Service Delivery* and *Direct and Indirect Services for Children, Families, and Schools*

54. **B.** Negative reinforcement can increase a target behavior and is typically confused with the term *punishment* because punishment also uses negative means to achieve its goal. On the other hand, punishment uses negative means in an attempt to decrease a behavior (e.g., punishing a child to decrease stealing). To help with the distinction between terms, think of the annoying seatbelt reminder noise in a car. The noise is a negative stimulus designed to *increase* your seatbelt-buckling behavior. *Foundations of School Psychological Service Delivery* and *Direct and Indirect Services for Children, Families, and Schools*

55. **C.** Variable reinforcement schedules are effective because the participants do not know when they will be rewarded. Once established, the participants are likely to continue the behavior because they do not know when the specific behavior will be reinforced, so they will continue the behavior in the hope that each behavior will result in a reward. Variable reinforcement

behaviors are difficult to extinguish once established. *Foundations of School Psychological Service Delivery* and *Direct and Indirect Services for Children, Families, and Schools*

56. **D.** Major cognitive tests, such as the latest versions of the Wechsler Intelligence Scale for Children (WISC) and Differential Ability Scales (DAS), are constructed on a sophisticated statistical theory known as the Cattell–Horn–Carroll (CHC) theory. The first two choices are named after famous psychometricians, but their names are not used as terms for specific theories. *Foundations of School Psychological Service Delivery*

57. **B.** Syntax is related to the rules governing how words and sentences are constructed, including the order of words. Semantics involves word meanings and is not a correct response. The correct syntax in the given example should be, "We go to the car." Phonological and phonemic concepts involve the sound structure of words and language, not the order of words. *Foundations of School Psychological Service Delivery*

58. **C.** This question is one of the few test items that straightforwardly asks for the name of a specific person. All choices are well-known psychological theorists, but Noam Chomsky is known for his work on language acquisition. *Foundations of School Psychological Service Delivery*

59. **A.** Criterion-referenced tests are also known as standards-referenced tests and are defined by mastery of standard or defined skills. Norm-referenced tests are the opposite of criterion-based tests. Choice "C" is a fictitious and invalid response. *Professional Practices, Practices That Permeate All Aspects of Service Delivery*

60. **D.** The mean, or average, is found by adding all the numbers in a set of numbers, and then dividing by the total numbers given in the set. In the case provided, the sum of the set is 30. There are five numbers given. Dividing 30 by 5 equals 6. *Professional Practices, Practices That Permeate All Aspects of Service Delivery*

61. **A.** The mode is the most frequently occurring number in a set of numbers. Choices "B" and "C" are not valid, whereas "D" is considered the range. Although not given, the median is the middle number of a data set. *Professional Practices, Practices That Permeate All Aspects of Service Delivery*

62. **D.** The first two choices are not valid responses to this question because reliability involves the consistency of scores and performance across time. One method of determining validity is found by comparing a test to another test that measures the same underlying trait. It is important to understand the difference between validity and reliability. *Foundations of School Psychological Service Delivery*

63. **C.** All of the other choices are valid responses. Choice "C" might be a common practice, but the research regarding homework is variable and is not the best response given the other choices for this test question. *Direct and Indirect Services for Children, Families, and Schools*

64. **A.** The terms *practice* and *application* are not valid terms for this question. The previous terms are found in the other choices and therefore are not valid responses. *Direct and Indirect Services for Children, Families, and Schools*

65. **B.** This question is difficult to answer because it is specific. Key terms to remember are **explicit** and **systematic**. *Direct and Indirect Services for Children, Families, and Schools*

66. **C.** When teachers differentiate instruction, they directly address the individual differences, abilities, and needs of individual learners. *Direct and Indirect Services for Children, Families, and Schools*

67. **A.** Although other choices are valid and might be good responses, the *best* response would be choice "A." Family involvement and educational support provided by parents can offset factors such as those associated with socioeconomic status (SES). *Direct and Indirect Services for Children, Families, and Schools* and *Foundations of School Psychological Service Delivery*

68. **C.** Grade retention in general is not an endorsed practice. Although "D" is a good choice, it should be only given after additional information is gathered on the problem. *Systems-Level Services* and *Direct and Indirect Services for Children, Families, and Schools*

69. **D.** "D" is an invalid response item. All other choices are correct responses. Remember, the role of school is to educate students, not punish them harshly. *Systems-Level Services* and *Direct and Indirect Services for Children, Families, and Schools*

70. **B.** "B" is the best choice because it includes both an increase in personal learning and knowledge of other skills. "A" is also a good choice, but it does not include an increase in academic skills. Choice "C" is not necessarily accurate because some cooperative lessons are more time intensive than other methods. Option "D" is a good response, but research related to cooperative learning does not necessarily focus on increasing empathy. *Direct and Indirect Services for Children, Families, and Schools*

71. **C.** Token economies are effective in changing behaviors, but busy teachers have difficulty collecting data and rewarding students immediately after a desired behavior. Token economies are effective with all ages and are typically not too expensive to employ. If fading is done properly with a cognitive component, then the target behavior can be maintained after tokens are withdrawn. *Direct and Indirect Services for Children, Families, and Schools*

72. **A.** The keywords in the question are large projects. If students do not have problems in other classes and behavior is not a concern, then it should be suspected that the students have difficulty with long, complicated information or tasks. A task analysis is a critical component that is necessary to know where to break assignments into easier steps. Referral to the Multi-Tiered System of Support (MTSS) or response to intervention (RTI) process is generally an involved process. A full intervention program, such as RTI, may not be appropriate in this situation if a simple fix will suffice. *Direct and*

Indirect Services for Children, Families, and Schools and *Professional Practices, Practices That Permeate All Aspects of Service Delivery*

73. **B.** SQ3R stands for survey, question, read, recite, and review. This method asks the reader to activate his or her prior knowledge of the text and to create questions before reading. The previous steps increase metacognition and comprehension. Lindamood-Bell and Wilson programs are well-known reading interventions but are not necessarily focused on reading comprehension as is SQ3R. Also, psychologists initially recommend specific strategies for particular learning difficulties rather than comprehensive remediation programs. *Direct and Indirect Services for Children, Families, and Schools*

74. **C.** It is important to know the difference between an accommodation and remediation. Remediation typically changes the task or level of curriculum, whereas accommodation changes the environment and/or conditions under which the task is completed. However, there is some debate about the exact nature of these concepts. Allowing for extra time does not change the academic task to be completed, but rather it accommodates for the time in which it must be finished. If you allow a student to read a lower level passage, this intervention changes the task that is required to be completed by other students. Answer "A" might be construed as a writing intervention, not a reading accommodation. *Direct and Indirect Services for Children, Families, and Schools*

75. **D.** This answer is straightforward. All other choices are invalid. *Direct and Indirect Services for Children, Families, and Schools* and *Foundations of School Psychological Service Delivery*

76. **A.** Although all the other choices are valid, the best choice would be option "A." The keywords in the question are "personality traits." As Carl Rogers states, the ability to develop *trust* in both counseling and consultation situations is the foundation for success. Choices "B" and "C" are more aligned with skills rather than personality traits. *Professional Practices, Practices That Permeate All Aspects of Service Delivery*

77. **C.** This is one of those seemingly simple questions that takes time to answer. Although all choices may seem valid, it is critical to *identify and define* the problem first. A problem must be circumscribed to better focus on the consultation conversation and interventions within a behavioral plan. The first two choices do not contain the "identification" term and therefore are not appropriate responses. Choice "D" is close, but does not have the critical "monitor" phase of the model. For the exam, it is important to be familiar with behavioral models, mental health models, instructional models, and organizational models of consultation. As mentioned previously, models that focus on building the consultee's skills (indirect consultee-centered model) is an endorsed practice. *Professional Practices, Practices That Permeate All Aspects of Service Delivery*

78. **A.** "*Consultee*" is a term that generally describes the teacher. The consultee-centered model is a favored model of consultation because it allows the

teacher to solve future problems once skills are developed. *Note:* In a "client-centered" model of consultation, the client is a student. *Professional Practices, Practices That Permeate All Aspects of Service Delivery*

79. **D.** When the consultant provides direct services to the client (e.g., student), this is an example of the client model. *Professional Practices, Practices That Permeate All Aspects of Service Delivery* and *Direct and Indirect Services for Children, Families, and Schools*

80. **A.** In the conjoint behavioral model, the focus is on the behavior of the student and the consultation involves a joint effort among all parties. Choice "D" may sound valid, but it is a fictitious term. *Professional Practices, Practices That Permeate All Aspects of Service Delivery*

81. **B.** The behavioral consultation model starts with clearly defining the problem. Once a problem behavior is defined, the next steps can be implemented, such as data collection and creating a plan. *Professional Practices, Practices That Permeate All Aspects of Service Delivery*

82. **D.** There are many barriers to effective consultation and other professional relationships that school psychologists face. The first three are valid choices. Consultation sometimes involves a heavy time commitment for all parties involved; however, school psychological consultations do not directly cost money for parents or teachers. Financial considerations are not typical concerns in most cases. *Professional Practices, Practices That Permeate All Aspects of Service Delivery*

83. **C.** Teaching other staff members how to solve problems for themselves is an effective and time-efficient practice in the long term. Consultee-centered models are endorsed by the National Association of School Psychologists (NASP). *Professional Practices, Practices That Permeate All Aspects of Service Delivery*

84. **D.** The first two choices are invalid as the student's parents or guardian must also give permission to disclose confidential records as indicated in the Family Educational Rights and Privacy Act (FERPA). Note that in option "A," a health issue could be mild and not serious. If a health issue is serious, then it would be appropriate to disclose student information. Choice "C" is a more difficult consideration, but a police officer cannot make a psychologist disclose confidential information that may not be pertinent to a situation at hand. Only a judge (not law enforcement) can order the release of student records without parent permission, unless there is an immediate danger issue. Answer "D" involves safety and harm, which always trumps confidentiality laws. *Foundations of School Psychological Service Delivery*

85. **B.** If the psychologist in this situation is qualified and licensed to engage in private practice, then she can accept this type of work. One of the reasons this type of private practice work is ethical to accept is because public school districts are not required to test students who do not have suspected problems. If the student had a suspected disability, then the psychologist might

not be able to accept this work because such issues are covered by public schools. School psychologists in private practice can test students for a variety of reasons, such as applications to a private school. Ethical questions can be very difficult to answer, so it is important to review the ethical guidelines of the National Association of School Psychologists (NASP). *Foundations of School Psychological Service Delivery*

86. **B.** The answer to this question is straightforward. The National Association of School Psychologists (NASP) recommends that supervisors manage no more than two interns at a time. *Foundations of School Psychological Service Delivery*

87. **C.** In cases that do not involve danger or safety, practitioners should try to solve the problem at the lowest level possible, but they are obligated to file a formal complaint if the issue is not resolved. *Foundations of School Psychological Service Delivery*

88. **D.** Only state authorities can revoke the license of a legally licensed practitioner. Although the National Association of School Psychologists (NASP) has authority that governs membership privileges, it does not have law enforcement powers. *Foundations of School Psychological Service Delivery*

89. **B.** Although aversive techniques should be avoided, there are some circumstances that involve safety in which such techniques are appropriate. For example, a student is actively cutting himself in your office and you must physically restrain the child for his safety. *Foundations of School Psychological Service Delivery*

90. **C.** Although choice "A" is also a valid response, to make sure you are following state laws regarding child abuse reporting, it is good practice to seek consultation with a state agency while maintaining anonymity for the student. *Foundations of School Psychological Service Delivery* and *Direct and Indirect Services for Children, Families, and Schools*

91. **C.** Special education students can be suspended, but if the suspension totals more than 10 days, a review meeting must be held to determine whether the behavior plan is appropriate and other needs of the student are being properly addressed. *Foundations of School Psychological Service Delivery*

92. **B.** Least restrictive environment (LRE) is a legal clause within the Individuals with Disabilities Education Act (IDEA) that states, "To the maximum extent appropriate, children with disabilities should be educated with children who are not disabled, and special classes, separate schooling, or other removal of children with disabilities from the regular educational environment should occur only when the nature or severity of the disability is such that education in regular classes with the use of supplementary aids and services cannot be achieved satisfactorily." Note all other choices are related to special education law. *Foundations of School Psychological Service Delivery*

93. **C.** Choice "C" is correct. The Family Educational Rights and Privacy Act (FERPA) was created to safeguard educational records. Note that FERPA was established in 1974 and option B was an invalid distracter. *Foundations of School Psychological Service Delivery*

94. **D.** Section 504 is an antidiscrimination, civil rights statute and contains a broad definition for the terms *handicap* or *disability*. Special education laws, such as Individuals with Disabilities Education Improvement Act (IDEIA), have narrow definitions of disability and more specific criteria that must be met to be identified with a particular disability compared to Section 504. *Foundations of School Psychological Service Delivery*

95. **D.** As with many legal questions, the answer to this question can be debated. If a psychologist makes documented "good-faith" efforts to contact a parent for a student's reevaluation, then the psychologist may proceed cautiously if parent contact fails. Additionally, the parent's complaint takes place 3 years after the event, but the law only provides a 2-year window to file a complaint. When answering legal or ethical questions, look for the *best* answer and be aware that some response choices will have elements of truth in them. *Foundations of School Psychological Service Delivery*

96. **B.** The answer to this question is factual and straightforward. Once a parent signs permission to evaluate, the special education team has 60 days to complete the evaluation. *Foundations of School Psychological Service Delivery*

97. **A.** Gesell is widely regarded as the *first* school psychologist, whereas Witmer is known as the father of school psychology. All of the other choices provided are famous experts in related psychological fields. *Foundations of School Psychological Service Delivery*

98. **D.** Jensen is a prominent contributor to the field of psychology as it relates to intelligence. Jensen received some controversial criticism for his work, but current mainstream theory holds to his view that there is a genetic component to intelligence. *Foundations of School Psychological Service Delivery*

99. **C.** In the case of *Hobson v. Hansen*, the court ruled that schools must provide equal educational opportunities despite a family's socioeconomic status (SES). *Foundations of School Psychological Service Delivery*

100. **B.** Anytime safety or danger is an issue, confidentiality laws are trumped. Parents do not need to give consent or be present in a student interview if other students are in danger. However, if a list was found with student names on it and a weapon was found, the parents of the students who were listed must be notified. Precedent for this situation is based on the Tarasoff case. *Foundations of School Psychological Service Delivery*

101. **B.** In the field of educational law, the famous *Brown v. Board of Education* is one of the most important cases and was responsible for addressing discriminatory practices. All other choices are also important educational legal cases, but do not directly influence segregation. *Foundations of School Psychological Service Delivery*

102. **D.** Language, in general, is largely influenced by the left hemisphere and the temporal lobe of the brain. A specific area in the temporal lobe, called Broca's area, plays a critical function in expressive language. *Professional*

Practices, Practices That Permeate All Aspects of Service Delivery and *Foundations of School Psychological Service Delivery*

103. **A.** Neuropsychology is concerned with brain–behavior relationships. Although a neuropsychologist can use tests that measure higher level reasoning skills, generally speaking, neuropsychological instruments evaluate basal neuropsychological processes such as memory, attention, and processing speed. Full-scale scores from school psychology tests, such as the Wechsler Intelligence Scale for Children (WISC) or Differential Ability Scales (DAS), are very good at predicting student achievement, while neuropsychologists can pinpoint subtle areas of neurological difficulties. *Professional Practices, Practices That Permeate All Aspects of Service Delivery* and *Foundations of School Psychological Service Delivery*

104. **B.** The brain contains several neurochemicals that are usually maintained in a tight balance. Dopamine is a well-known and critical neurochemical that must be in balance for the brain to function. Several research studies suggest that attention deficit hyperactivity disorder (ADHD) and Parkinson's disease are related to low levels of dopamine. *Direct and Indirect Services for Children, Families, and Schools*

105. **B.** The frontal cortex of the brain plays a pivotal role in the regulation and management of behaviors associated with executive functions. *Foundations of School Psychological Service Delivery*

106. **D.** The right hemisphere of the brain is associated with new learning and processing novel information. The left hemisphere, in general, helps with memory for learned facts, logic, and details. *Foundations of School Psychological Service Delivery* and *Direct and Indirect Services for Children, Families, and Schools*

107. **D.** There are more elaborate depictions of the information processing model, but in its simplest form, option "D" best represents this cognitive process. Although the information processing model is still used by practitioners, some researchers caution that the model is too simplistic. Brain processes illustrated by computer models are useful, but not entirely accurate. *Foundations of School Psychological Service Delivery*

108. **A.** The answer is factual and straightforward. Make sure you do not confuse T-scores with standard scores (SSs). If this question asked about an SS of 64, then the answer would be substantially different (e.g., SS = 64 is significantly below average). *Professional Practices, Practices That Permeate All Aspects of Service Delivery*

109. **C.** Because the student has a *history* of reading problems, an intervention should be recommended. Special education might be an option at a later time, but because Colette has moved twice at a young age, it is likely that there is an environmental factor influencing her learning. Choice "D" is valid, but "C" is specific and likely to lead to formal supports for the student. *Professional Practices, Practices That Permeate All Aspects of Service Delivery* and *Direct and Indirect Services for Children, Families, and Schools*

110. **B.** Family health and employment stability are aspects of Maslow's lower level of needs, called *safety needs*. Safety needs come after physiological needs, which are the most basic needs. *Direct and Indirect Services for Children, Families, and Schools*

111. **D.** Although modeling and role-playing could be useful in all of the choices, it is most likely to be employed with students who need to develop appropriate social skills. *Direct and Indirect Services for Children, Families, and Schools*

112. **A.** Of all the choices provided, Viktor Frankl emphasized that people have a choice in how they respond to events, even in the most difficult situations. *Direct and Indirect Services for Children, Families, and Schools*

113. **B.** Time-out techniques are frequently used as punishment when they should be employed as preventive measures. In choice "B," a student with attention deficit hyperactivity disorder (ADHD) might possibly need a cognitive rest break to help with his concentration and prevent negative behaviors that may develop. *Direct and Indirect Services for Children, Families, and Schools*

114. **D.** There are three levels typically illustrated within the response to intervention (RTI) pyramid. At the bottom level, screening and universal measures reside. Level 2 RTIs are associated with more targeted interventions for at-risk students. At the highest RTI level, the most intensive interventions are found, usually for 5% to 8% of a school's population. *Direct and Indirect Services for Children, Families, and Schools* and *Systems-Level Services*

115. **C.** This item might be difficult to answer because other choices are valid or have components that are valid. Remember the acronym ICEL when answering ecological types of questions. ICEL stands for instruction, curriculum, environment, and learner style. *Direct and Indirect Services for Children, Families, and Schools* and *Professional Practices, Practices That Permeate All Aspects of Service Delivery*

116. **A.** Special education qualifications have strict criteria that a special education team must consider. A primary consideration by the special education team is to determine whether a student cannot access the general curriculum and if there is negative educational and/or social impact from the suspected disability. In this case, it is implied that the student is making "reasonable educational progress." There may be other ways to address the concerns of the parent and the needs of the student outside of the special education progress (e.g., Multi-Tiered System of Support [MTSS]). Medical doctors that are not employed by a school district have no authority to dictate educational services. *Professional Practices, Practices That Permeate All Aspects of Service Delivery*

117. **B.** A new role for psychologists is brain injury specialist because psychologists are trained in measuring brain-based functions. Although options "C" and "A" might also be valid choices, psychologists have been involved

in providing professional consultation regarding reading problems and threatening behaviors longer than brain injury management issues (which is a new development). *Foundations of School Psychological Service Delivery*

118. **C.** Although this question and answer is not common to the field of school psychology, be prepared to answer such questions. Systematic desensitization is a well-known behavioral technique that is typically associated with helping people with various irrational fears. *Direct and Indirect Services for Children, Families, and Schools*

119. **D.** Lack of sleep has been scientifically correlated with poor memory performance. Video game playing by teens is a growing concern as it is addictive to school-aged students, especially males. *Foundations of School Psychological Service Delivery* and *Direct and Indirect Services for Children, Families, and Schools*

120. **C.** The answer to this test item is difficult because all but "B" are valid responses. The best answer is "C" because this choice includes practice and supervision. A colleague can provide insight and feedback when learning new psychological tests and practices. It is not always feasible to take a full training course on a new test. Watching a video of a new assessment is helpful, but it does not provide an opportunity for interactive questions. *Foundations of School Psychological Service Delivery* and *Professional Practices, Practices That Permeate All Aspects of Service Delivery*

121. **B.** Remember that a negative correlation can be stronger than a positive correlation. Note that a −0.97 is almost a perfect (i.e., highest possible) correlation. *Professional Practices, Practices That Permeate All Aspects of Service Delivery*

122. **C.** Option "C" is not a valid level, but all other choices are correct levels. The level that is missing is the *progress monitoring and response to intervention (RTI) level*. At this level, data are used to determine effectiveness of the interventions (RTI) once a student is identified as having a problem. *Professional Practices, Practices That Permeate All Aspects of Service Delivery* and *Systems-Level Services*

123. **B.** When two similar measures are purposely correlated, this is done to establish *convergent* validity. Two similar, but different tests should correlate highly. If two purportedly similar measures did not correlate, then one of the tests might be an invalid measure of the construct being assessed. Correlation coefficients for tests should be within the 0.80 to 0.90 range to be endorsed for use. *Professional Practices, Practices That Permeate All Aspects of Service Delivery*

124. **A.** School psychologists do not have extensive training in neuropsychology, but they should be aware of basic brain-based functions. A basic knowledge of neuropsychology can increase a school psychologist's understanding of student learning and behavior. In this question, a hit to the back of the head typically impacts the occipital lobe of the brain. The

occipital lobe is the primary visual cortex. When the occipital lobe is dysfunctional due to a concussion, students commonly have problems with visual processes (reading, writing) and they experience light sensitivity. *Direct and Indirect Services for Children, Families, and Schools*

125. **C.** The Virginia Model of Threat Assessment (see Dr. Cornell's work) uses three qualitative categories for threats. The classifications are *transient, substantive, and imminent*. The older classifications, offered by the U.S. Secret Service, are *low, medium, and high*. *Systems-Level Services*

126. **B.** The BASIC-Ph Model of Coping is an acronym that stands for Beliefs, Affect, Social, Imagination, Cognitive, and Physiological. Note that avoidance (option "B") is not valid and should have been termed "affect" according to the model. *Direct and Indirect Services for Children, Families, and Schools* and *Systems-Level Services*

127. **A.** Epstein's Model of Parental Involvement includes the following specific elements: parenting, communicating, volunteering, learning at home, decision making, collaborating with community. *Foundations of School Psychological Service Delivery*

128. **D.** The key benefit of analysis of covariance (ANCOVA) is that it mitigates bias in the dependent variable(s). This type of analysis of variance (ANOVA) increases the accuracy of conclusions regarding the independent variable because it accounts for covariates related to within-group variance or group error. *Systems-Level Services* and *Foundations of School Psychological Service Delivery*

129. **A.** Multilevel modeling (MLM) is a statistical model of parameters that vary at more than one level. If there are multiple levels or variables to consider in research, then MLM is a useful alternative to analysis of variance (ANOVA). *Foundations of School Psychological Service Delivery*

130. **B.** According to the National Association of School Psychologists (NASP), suicide is the second leading cause of death. A total of 17% of high school students have contemplated suicide. *Systems-Level Services*

131. **C.** Although the Behavior Assessment System for Children-3 (BASC-3) is an effective formal measure to aid in an attention deficit hyperactivity disorder (ADHD) identification, it is considered a broad-spectrum assessment, which has already been administered. The Conners Rating Scales–Revised is a narrow brand tool, but it is older than the Conners-3. The Conners-3 is the most current version of a narrow band ADHD tool that is widely utilized by school psychologists. *Professional Practices, Practices That Permeate All Aspects of Service Delivery*

132. **A.** Behavior Assessment System for Children-3 (BASC-3) T-scores above 65 are clinically significant. Although there is significant score differences, both the parent and teacher forms are signifying that the student has problems with attention. In other words, both scores are within the same range

of concern and there is no discrepancy in the "range." *Professional Practices, Practices That Permeate All Aspects of Service Delivery*

133. **C.** A review of the bell curve illustration in this guide reveals that two standard deviations account for the majority of the bell curve population (approximately 95%). Note that one standard deviation would encompass about 68% of a population. *Professional Practices, Practices That Permeate All Aspects of Service Delivery* and *Foundations of School Psychological Service Delivery*

134. **B.** Positive behavioral interventions and supports (PBIS) is a well-known systems-wide practice. PBIS is an effective practice endorsed by the National Association of School Psychologists (NASP). All other choices are not endorsed practices. *Systems-Level Services*

135. **D.** *Honig v. Doe* affirmed the "stay put" rule and prevents a special education student from being removed from school without a proper review. *Foundations of School Psychological Service Delivery*

136. **B.** If a special education student has any formal change of service or programming, the school must secure parent approval before changes are made. Note that any student can be assessed for suicide or threat without formal consent due to extreme safety concerns. *Foundations of School Psychological Service Delivery*

137. **B.** Classwide Peer Tutoring (CWPT) is a proactive intervention to help all students. It is similar to Vygotsky's theory on collaborative learning. *Direct and Indirect Services for Children, Families, and Schools*

138. **D.** Down syndrome is a low-incidence chromosomal disorder. The Centers for Disease Control and Prevention (CDC) states that roughly 1 out of every 700 people may have some degree of Down syndrome. *Direct and Indirect Services for Children, Families, and Schools*

139. **A.** Bullying is conceptualized in various ways by many experts and researchers. Although the answer to this question may be debatable, many experts would agree that bullying is a form of aggression, not necessarily violence, which also involves an abuse of power. Note that some aspects of each choice may be true, but option "A" is the best choice given the options provided. *Systems-Level Services*

140. **D.** The National Association of School Psychologists (NASP) states, "Generally speaking no-suicide contracts have been shown to be ineffective and are no longer recommended." *Direct and Indirect Services for Children, Families, and Schools* and *Systems-Level Services*

Bibliography and Resources

Bibliography

Academic Success for All Learners. (2012). Utah students at risk: Online staff development academy. Retrieved from http://www.usu.edu/teachall/text/behavior/LRBIpdfs/Functional.pdf

American Psychiatric Association. (1994). *Diagnostic and statistical manual of mental disorders* (4th ed.). Washington, DC: Author.

American Psychiatric Association. (2000). *Diagnostic and statistical manual of mental disorders* (4th ed., text rev.). Washington, DC: Author.

American Psychiatric Association. (2013). *Diagnostic and statistical manual of mental disorders* (5th ed.). Arlington, VA: American Psychiatric Publishing.

Board of Education of the Hendrick Hudson Central School District v. Rowley, 458 U.S. 176 (1982).

Brain Injury Association of America. (2015). Living with brain injury. Retrieved from http://www.biausa.org/living-with-brain-injury.htm

Brain Injury Association of New York. (2016). About the brain. Retrieved from http://www.projectlearnet.org/about_the_brain.html

Brain Injury Networking Teams. (2016). TBI matrix guide. Traumatic Brain Injury Networking Team Resource Network. Retrieved from http://cokidswithbraininjury.com

Brock, S. E., Lazarus, P. J., & Jimerson, S. R. (2002). *Best practices in school crisis prevention and intervention*. Bethesda, MD: National Association of School Psychologists.

Brown v. Board of Education of Topeka, 347 U.S. 483 (1954).

Caplan, G., Caplan, R. B., & Erchul, W. P. (1994). Caplanian mental health consultation: Historical background and current status. *Consulting Psychology Journal: Practice and Research, 46*(4), 2–12.

Carter, R., Aldridge, S., Page, M., & Parker, S. (2009). *The human brain book*. New York, NY: DK Publishing.

Center on the Social and Emotional Foundations for Early Learning. (2012). Retrieved from http://csefel.vanderbilt.edu

Centers for Disease Control and Prevention. (2016). Retrieved from https://www.cdc.gov

Collaborative for Academic, Social, and Emotional Learning. (2016). Retrieved from http://www.casel.org

Diana v. State Board of Education, CA 70 RFT (N.D. Cal. 1970).

Educational Testing Service. (2016). Overview of the National Association of School Psychologists (NASP) Nationally Certified School Psychologist (NCSP) requirements. Retrieved from http://www.ets.org/praxis/nasp

Fagan, T. K., & Wise, P. S. (2007). *School psychology: Past, present, and future* (3rd ed.). Bethesda, MD: National Association of School Psychologists.

Finkelstein, J. (n.d.). Maslow's hierarchy of needs. Retrieved from https://commons.wikimedia.org/wiki/File:Maslow's_hierarchy_of_needs.png

Guadalupe Organization, Inc. v. Tempe Elementary School District No. 3, Cir. Act. No. 71-435 (D. Ariz. 1972).

Hale, J., & Fiorello, C. A. (2004). *School neuropsychology: A practitioner's handbook*. New York, NY: Guilford Press.

Hobson v. Hansen, 269 F. Supp. (D.C. 1967).

Honig v. Doe, 484 U.S. 305 (1988).

Hughes, J. N. (1989). The child interview. *Mini-Series on NASP at Twenty, 18*(2), 247–259.

Irving Independent School District v. Tatro, 468 U.S. 883 (1984).

Larry P. v. Riles, 495 F. Supp. 926, 987 (N.D. Cal. 1979).

Lau v. Nichols, 414 U.S. 563 (1974).

McAvoy, K. (2011). The REAP project. Retrieved from http://www.concussiontreatment.com/images/REAP_Program.pdf

Miller, D. (2013). *Essentials of school neuropsychological assessment*. Hoboken, NJ: John Wiley.

National Association of School Neuropsychologists. (2012). School neuropsychology training and resources. Retrieved from http://www.schoolneuropsych.com

National Association of School Psychologists. (2002). Times of tragedy: Preventing suicide in troubled children and youth, Part II. Retrieved from http://www.leanderisd.org/users/0001/docs/Crisis/SuicidePrevention.pdf

National Association of School Psychologists. (2012a). Professional ethics. Retrieved from http://www.nasponline.org/standards/ethics/ethical -conduct-professional-practices.aspx

National Association of School Psychologists. (2012b). NASP resources. Retrieved from http://www.nasponline.org/resources/index.aspx

National Center for Learning Disabilities. Retrieved from http://www.ncld.org

National Child Traumatic Stress Network. (2012). Retrieved from http://www .nctsn.org/about-us/national-center

National Institute of Child Health and Human Development. (2012). Helping children cope with crisis: Where can I get more information? Retrieved from https://www.nichd.nih.gov/publications/pubs/cope_with_crisis _book/sub12.cfm

Oberti v. Clementon, 995 F. 2d 1204 (3rd Cir. 1993).

Oritz, S. O. (2008). *Best practices in school psychology*. Bethesda, MD: National Association of School Psychologists.

PARC v. Pennsylvania, 334 F. Supp. 1257 (E.D. PA 1972).

PASE v. Hannon, 506 F. Supp. 831 (N.D. Ill. 1980).

Sweeney, M. (2009). *Brain: The complete mind*. Washington, DC: National Geographic Society.

Trochim, W. (2006). The research methods knowledge base (2nd ed.). Web Center for Social Research Methods. Retrieved from http://www .socialresearchmethods.net/kb/index.php

United States Secret Service and United States Department of Education. (2002). Threat assessment in schools: A guide to managing threatening situations and creating safe school climates. Retrieved from https://www .secretservice.gov/data/protection/ntac/ssi_guide.pdf

Resources

Academic Interventions and RTI Strategies: www.interventioncentral.org/ response-to-intervention

Center for Effective Collaboration and Practice: http://cecp.air.org/default.asp

Crisis Guidelines: Core Elements: http://store.samhsa.gov/shin/content/ SMA09-4427/SMA09-4427.pdf

Mental Health Problems and Interventions to Use With Children: www.school mentalhealth.org/Resources/Clin/QuickGuide.pdf

Resource for Foundations of Neuropsychology (Alexandria Luria): http://lchc .ucsd.edu/MCA/Mail/xmcamail.2010_02.dir/pdfhSRSAFKVs7.pdf

Resource for General Psychology: Extensive Review of Various Topics: www .bim.bilkent.edu.tr/~inanc/psy/92100_Lecturenotes.htm

Resource for Threat Assessment: Virginia Model by Dr. Cornell: http://curry
.virginia.edu/resource-library/the-virginia-model-for-student-threat
-assessment

School Neuropsychology Training and Resources: www.schoolneuropsych.com

School Psychology Key Topics and Resources: http://school-psychology.org

Traumatic Brain Injury in Children: http://cokidswithbraininjury.com

Abbreviations and Acronyms

AAS	American Association of Suicidology
ABA	Applied behavior analysis
ABAS	Adaptive Behavior Assessment System
ADA	Americans with Disabilities Act
ADHD	Attention deficit hyperactivity disorder
AEs	Age equivalents
ANCOVA	Analysis of covariance
ANOVA	Analysis of variance
APA	American Psychological Association
ASD	Autism spectrum disorders
BADS	Behavioral Assessment of Dysexecutive Syndrome
BASC	Behavior Assessment System for Children
BASIC-Ph	Belief, Affect, Social, Imagination, Cognitive, and Physiological
BIRT	Brain injury resource team
CAS	Cognitive Assessment System
CBA	Curriculum-based assessment
CBCL	Child Behavior Checklist
CBM	Curriculum-based measures
CBT	Cognitive behavioral therapy
CD	Conduct disorder
CEFI	Comprehensive Executive Function Inventory
CET	Cognitive-emotional therapy
CHC	Cattell–Horn–Carroll
CogAT	Cognitive assessment test
CTOPP	Comprehensive Test of Phonological Processing

CWPT	Classwide Peer Tutoring
DAS	Differential Ability Scales
DBM	Discrete behavioral modification
DBT	Dialectical behavior therapy
DIBELS	Dynamic indicators of basic early literacy skills
D-KEFS	Delis–Kaplan Executive Function System
DSM-IV-TR	*Diagnostic and Statistical Manual of Mental Disorders*, 4th ed., text rev.
DSM-5	*Diagnostic and Statistical Manual of Mental Disorders*, 5th ed.
DTI	Discrete trial instruction
EAHCA	Education for All Handicapped Children Act
ELL	English language learners
ESL	English as a second language
ESSA	Every Student Succeeds Act
ETS	Educational Testing Service
FAE	Fetal alcohol effects
FAPE	Free and appropriate public education
FAS	Fetal alcohol symptoms
FBA	Functional behavioral assessment
FCA	Federal Confidentiality Act
FERPA	Family Educational Rights and Privacy Act
GOM	General outcome measurement
ICEL	Instruction, curriculum, environment, and learner
ID	Intellectual disabilities
IDEA	Individuals with Disabilities Education Act
IDEIA	Individuals with Disabilities Education Improvement Act
IEP	Individual education plan
KABC-II	Kaufman Assessment Battery for Children, Second Edition
K-SEALS	Kaufman Survey of Early Academic and Language Skills
K-TEA	Kaufman Test of Educational Achievement
LAD	Language acquisition device
LDs	Learning disabilities
LRE	Least restrictive environment
MANOVA	Multivariate analysis of variance
mBD	Mild brain dysfunction
MLM	Multilevel modeling
mTBI	Mild traumatic brain injury
MTSS	Multi-Tiered System of Support

NAI	National Association of Interpreters
NASP	National Association of School Psychologists
NCLB	No Child Left Behind
NCLD	National Center for Learning Disabilities
NCSP	Nationally Certified School Psychologist
NIMH	National Institute of Mental Health
NOS	Not otherwise specified
NVLD	Nonverbal learning disorder
OCD	Obsessive-compulsive disorder
OCR	Office for Civil Rights
ODD	Oppositional defiant disorder
PASS	Planning, attention, and simultaneous and successive processing
PBIS	Positive behavioral interventions and supports
PBS	Positive behavior support
PCS	Postconcussion syndrome
PDD	Pervasive developmental disorder
PES	Psychoeducational support
PTPI	Peer-to-peer instruction
PTSD	Posttraumatic stress disorder
RBPC	Revised Behavior Problem Checklist
RCFT	Rey Complex Figure Test
REAP	Reduce, educate, accommodate, and pace
RET	Rational-emotive therapy
RTI	Response to intervention
SB	Stanford–Binet cognitive test
SDs	Standard deviations
SED	Significant emotional disability
SEM	Standard error of measurement
SES	Socioeconomic status
SIED	Significant identifiable emotional disability
SLD	Specific learning disability
SLIC	Significant limited intellectual capacity
SMM	Subskill mastery measurement
SS	Standard scores
STEEP	System to enhance educational performance
STM	Short-term memory
SQ3R	Survey, question, read, recite, and review

TBI	Traumatic brain injury
TEMA	Test of early math ability
TERA	Test of early reading ability
TOMAL	Test of memory and learning
TSDPG	Tell-Show-Do-Practice-Generalize
UNIT	Universal Nonverbal Intelligence Test
VABS-4	Vineland Adaptive Behavior Scales
WCST	Wisconsin Card Sort Test
WIAT	Wechsler Individual Achievement Test
WISC-V	Weschler Intelligence Test for Children, Fifth Edition
WRAML2	Wide Range Assessment of Memory and Learning, Second Edition
WRAT	Wide Range Achievement Test
ZPD	Zone of proximal development

Index